My family treads lightly on the lands of the Boon Wurrung
(Bunurong) people of the Kulin Nation.

We recognise their continuing connection to land,
waters and culture, and pay our respects to their
Elders – past, present and emerging.

Alice Zaslavsky

The Joy of
Better
Cooking

The Joy of
Better
Cooking

Life-changing skills & thrills
for enthusiastic eaters

alice zaslavsky

murdoch books

Sydney | London

Contents

Welcome aboard

What does it mean to be a 'good' cook? The flick of a wrist, a pinch of the fingers, the whiff of a waft. It's intuition and muscle memory. It's a way of life built on a foundation of flying hours.

From time spent at your grandmother's apron strings, podding broad beans and rolling pasta dough between chubby fingers. From home economics classes, rubbing butter into scone dough, committing the crack of golden caramel to canon and the reward of some kind of sweet slice to scoff on the school bus home. From student suppers, haphazardly flung together with bits rummaged from the vegie crisper, sploodged with whatever sauce is lurking in the fridge door until it makes some semblance of sense. From 'bring-a-plates', and 'grown-up' dinner parties where you learn to keep things simple ... eventually. It's first dates, and first sunken cakes hidden under cream.

But what happens if you missed a stage? Or three?

You're not alone. As we've become busier, the intergenerational family experience has become less common, and schools turn kitchens into science labs, when does the practice plane actually take off to get those flying hours under the belt? And when it *does* come time to start, how do we make the experience of cooking something to actually look forward to?

First of all, let's toss out the concept of being a 'good' cook, and replace it with the idea of becoming a *better* cook. Better Cooking is a lifelong journey. It's made up of single steps, with plenty of whoopsies and notes-for-next-time along the way. But every step gets you a bit closer to cracking the codes that unlock the confidence to feel freedom and joy in the kitchen.

I believe that 'foodie' is a word to be embraced rather than shirked, because it can also mean more conscientious consumption. But foodie culture does have a lot to answer for when it comes to making newbies feel out of their depth. Shaking off the imposter syndrome that can plague anyone who's watched a fancy food show or heard the loaded line 'It's just that easy' from a TV chef can feel impossible if we're stuck at the first hurdle. It can mean people give up and label themselves 'bad cooks' or say they 'don't cook' and never try.

Labels are powerful, for better or worse. I'm here to tell you that **you are already a better cook than you think you are.**

If you've ever found yourself thinking about dinner over breakfast, if bringing pleasure and nourishment to the people in your orbit gives you a glow, heck — if you already enjoy the *eating* part, you can find the fun in getting the food to the table, too.

Forget about cooking for someone else's tastes or expectations. I've tried doing that in the past, and would strongly not recommend. Why? Because fear lives here, and the paralysis of choice. Oh, and doubt, of course, about what it is you should be doing, and whether you're *good enough*.

The *joy* of better cooking is that you can stop second-guessing yourself. You can look into the fridge/freezer/pantry and instantly start to see ideas and inspiration before you,

rather than feeling overwhelmed or at a loss. Relax into the rhythm, release any expectations of perfection or outcome. Go with the flow, take a breath, and remind yourself: I've got this.

Oh, and you've got *this*. I've designed this book to act as an instruction manual, but you'd never know it. In fact, forget I ever said that. Instead, I've written a book with 70-ish recipes — plus loads of recipe riffs — that I know you'll want to cook, on a weekly basis, again and again, with heaps of extra tips and tricks so that, soon enough, cooking the recipes will feel like second nature. Like that scene in *The Matrix* where Trinity learns to fly a helicopter while she sleeps. You won't even know you're learning, until the learning has been done.

The recipes are stacked in sections from what I perceive to be easy to harder, as a gateway to lure you in, because I figure that anyone who loves to eat will get hooked on the slapping and dashing and not even notice when they start pulling out show-stopping sweeties on the reg. The techniques are transferable, and often come up multiple times to scaffold the skill and help it sink in permanently. If you're stuck on a skill or a fancy-looking cooking word, remember to check the index — it'll probably have some form of extrapolation in another part of the book.

You'll also find the kind of insider-intel it usually takes *years* to learn — the assumed knowledge that comes with better cooking — in the form of 'Bonus Bits' (on the pages that are ever-so-slightly tinged with a touch of lilac). These are the pages to turn to if you're keen to deep-dive while you cook, or want to ask 'why' — chances are, the answer's already there. They're also the pages you can choose to skip over if you're in a hurry to get dinner on the table ... you can always come back to them later when you're pottering about and up for a chinwag with me in written form.

Wherever I have found you on the spectrum of cooking confidence and success: if this is your first proper cookbook or if you're someone who reads cookbooks like novels; if you've just moved out of home or are using this with your kids or grandkids; or if you're simply ready to loosen those shoulders after decades of cooking recipes by rote, WELCOME! Removing the pressure of exactitude will make you a better cook instantly and release the pressure valve of getting it 'right'. Practising non-attachment, giving slightly less of a shiitake when the shiitake hits the fan, and faking it 'til you make it are all part and parcel of being a better cook.

Better Cooks are wily, wondrous creatures who can stride into the kitchen with carefree abandon, knowing that sometimes things won't turn out exactly as they're supposed to, and having a fix in mind just in case. (There's plenty of those in here, too.) Bloopers and burnt bits are just part of the process of getting better ... why do you think professional chefs don't moonlight as hand models?

The recipes in this book may look like a motley crew at first flick — nothing like your usual 'Home Sweet Home' beginners' collection. That's because I don't want to limit you, or bore you, and because I believe that everyone can benefit from going back to basics and understanding The Why every now and again. But the recipes do fit within a framework of my own design: namely, they encapsulate and enrich the qualities that define Better Cooks of the 21st century.

LIKE THE RECIPES IN THIS BOOK, 21st CENTURY BETTER COOKS ARE …

✦ **Adaptable.** Gone are the days of having to pop out for a cup of chestnut flour or some hard-to-source ingredient. In this book, substitutions and riffs abound.

✦ **Veg forward.** Many of the recipes are almost entirely vego, with plant-based solutions if you want to go the full veg. It wouldn't be a book of mine otherwise.

✦ **Low impact.** You can't learn to love food without realising the power that voting with your dollar has to ensure that the produce we love to eat is still around for our kids to enjoy. In this book you'll find plenty of 'Waste knot' tips for minimising food waste. I've also tried to ensure that any special stuff I've asked you to buy — often described in 'Ingredient spotlight' or 'Worth it' notes — gets used HEAPS in other recipes. Most of the dishes also make for great leftover makeovers (see 'Double duty' entries).

✦ **Low effort.** Certainly, there's a time and place for building a croquembouche. But to me, Better Cooking means finding shortcuts and loopholes to get you to flavour-town sooner, rather than forcing you into some cooking competition-style bake-off.

✦ **High return.** It's actually pretty easy to tell when you're onto a winner with a dish: how often do you want to make it again? Better cooks understand the value of ROI — how much bang will this recipe give me for buck, in terms of flavour, kudos and the silence that befalls a table when everyone is so content they can only make the odd audible intake of breath before going back in for more. (I'm pretty sure my own love language is my family, Nick and The Nut, asking for seconds.)

Every recipe in here will make you feel great — both physically (because, just quietly, they're nutritious by nature) AND because they're sure to make the happy recipients look at you like maybe you're a *magician*.

Better Cooks are always willing to try new things — and classic old things — and look at recipe photos and make the rest up. That's the place I want to take you. I hope this book gets positively trashed from use. (I have my friend Jamila's burnt copy of *In Praise of Veg* in pride of place on the bookshelf, because it was clearly *being used* — the biggest compliment to any cookbook creator.) But what I truly hope is that every now and then, you get to a place where you can leave this book on the shelf, along with any preconceived notions of The Kind of Cook You Are, and just *create*.

The best part about cooking, and about food in general, is the connection and sharing it encourages. Connecting people with ideas and concepts, with each other, with their community, their culture. The sharing we're privy to over a meal, and the sharing of recipes — old scrapbooks, laminated newspaper clippings, a link flicked over on the phone or in an email. Most of all, what brings me the deepest gratitude and joy in doing what I do, more than anything, is the opportunity to connect and share with *you*. Please do keep in touch.

Cheerio!

alice.

About the bonus bits

At the end of each recipe, you'll find golden nuggets of info to polish up your kitchen game exponentially. Think of these as answers to questions I'm assuming you'll ask, or handy riffs to help you build on the techniques and combos you've just banked. Here's what you can expect.

TIPS

Kitchen wisdom and wanderings. Whether it's advice on prep, how to store leftovers or pointing you in the general direction of where to find an ingredient, 'Tips' marks the spot.

SUBS

Gone are the days when a recipe would be hopelessly out of reach due to the fact that you were sans a pantry item or three. If you're looking at a recipe in this book and thinking 'I could sub that', then it is not only welcome, it is *encouraged*. It's one of the joys of the way in which I cook, and I can't recommend it enough. Sometimes I'll sub for the sake of subbing, just to see how it all pans out; you're welcome to do the same. Dietaries are accounted for here, too, with tips to turn the recipe fully plant-based or gluten-free.

SHORTCUTS

Whenever I make a dish, I'm already asking myself how I can make it faster next time. Whether it's microwave (nay, air-fryer!) instructions, or skipping steps that are terrific but time-consuming, here's the section where I encourage you to do less.

LONGCUTS

Look, I'm an equal-opportunity enabler, so if you would prefer to take your time, this is where to look for cooking-from-scratch success.

RECIPE RIFFS

Riffing is one step removed from subbing ingredients in or out. It's another reason to try a recipe again, with ideas of other key flavours you could include, or accounting for seasonal adjustments. Riffing means one recipe can become many. Bonus!

EXTRA EXTRAS

Most of the time, I rein in the recipe to keep it as simple and accessible as possible ... but sometimes, a little EXTRA-ness just can't help but rear its head. These might include bougie additions like shaved truffle, or some form of crumb or schmear, but extras are just that — not necessary, but important enough to mention, in case you're feeling like a little somethin' somethin'.

DOUBLE DUTY

If there's one thing I love more than cooking a great meal, it's knowing there's some left to flip into a totally new one. Double-duties mean leftover makeovers, and making the most of everything (actually, you'll find a whole chapter on that). Double-duty dishes work overtime, and make every skerrick work for you. It's the way our grandparents ate ... with extra cheese.

WASTE KNOT

A leftovers makeover is one thing, but whaddaya do with the scrappy bits that usually end up being binned? These tips will have you making use of every last bit of an ingredient, from the frizzles on a spring onion root to that has-been vanilla bean that's been steeped in a syrup. A better cook is a thrifty cook, and using ingredients to their full capacity is not just economical, it's also deeply satisfying.

WORTH IT

I've tried my best to double/triple/quadruple up on ingredients across the book, so that if you buy it, it's worth it. Here you'll find ideas for how to make the best of those less-familiar ingredients that might not be on your weekly basics list, but will really add the wow factor to your food.

INGREDIENT SPOTLIGHT

So much of cook-ing is in the shop-ping, which is why these spotlights will help you sort the wheat from the chaff when it comes to what to take off the grocery shelf and pop on your own. Questions of sustainability, provenance and bang-for-buck are answered — when to splash out, and when to save your pennies. You'll also find handy alternatives in the Subs/Recipe riffs, just in case.

SKILLS SPOTLIGHT

Here's where you can satisfy all your 'how-to' and 'why-tho' hankerings. These spotlights are a bit of a checklist that you can work through while the pot's simmering away — or before you begin, if you're a thorough recipe reader. Feel free to peruse these at your leisure, even if you're not planning on making a particular dish. They're like the cherry on top.

GADGET SPOTLIGHT

It's no secret that I am a gadget FIEND. I'll pore over every doohickey in every catalogue, marvelling at inventions and innovations. Open my kitchen drawers and it's like that scene out of *The Little Mermaid*: 'You want thingamabobs? I've got twenty!' Which is why I know which ones get pulled out and are actually used, versus those that linger in the drawers gathering lint and taking up space. There's usually a gadget-free solution for recipes in this book, but, very occasionally, I'll use this section to emphatically recommend you nab yourself a gadge to make your life easier. Feel free to ignore them all (except the one about salad spinners on page 28).

Slapdash

**Bits and bobs
tossed together**

Ready, set ... riff!

This chapter may seem an obvious starting point, bringing you dishes you can just whack together — more like arranging or assembling than really 'cooking' ... yet there's still a bit of an art to this kind of cooking, too.

Being able to understand how flavours go together, what tandem textures are terrific in the mouth, how a rainbow colours our enjoyment of a plate of food, even which aromas play well together as they make the short trip from saucepan to spoon to satisfaction zone ... all of that takes a little experience, too.

However, what I do love about a good slapdash, and why I think you'll be happy starting here, no matter whether you've been cooking since forever or only just beginning, is that it's infinitely adaptable, and a chance to take stock of what you've already got — in terms of both kitchen skills and pantry staples — and then build from there.

Take a note of the recipe riffs that abound in this section and throughout the book. They're like scatty stream-of-consciousness musings on recipe tweaks or serving ideas, plucked from a mental scrapbook of moments where I've tasted something memorable or seen it on a menu and thought, 'Oooh! Clever!', capturing those moments and committing them to these pages for another day.

Your personal 'slapdash scrapbook' will be different to mine. Use this as an opportunity to ask yourself: what combinations speak to me? Of course, there are classic combinations that will always go together: tomato and basil; parsley and garlic; avocado and lime.

It's okay to let others do most of the heavy lifting in the flavour stakes, by seeking out condiments, preserves, pickles, ferments, cheeses, smallgoods and other elements that have already been optimised for your indulgence. If your pantry and fridge are already loaded with these artisanal treasures, it's far easier and quicker to craft a delicious dish with little fuss.

I particularly love keeping Hugh Fearnley-Whittingstall's philosophy of 'three good things on a plate' in mind when slapdashing at home. It might be three elements, or simply three flavours: avocado, lime and cracked pepper; yoghurt, honey and walnuts. It always feels less overwhelming when you remember that you're only 1–2–3 steps away from making a memorable meal.

Tasting widely is so much a part of this kind of cooking: the more you can store up edible experiences, the faster you'll be able to cash in on your memory bank. If you see a combo on a menu that looks intriguing, order it. File away in your mind dishes you've enjoyed at dinner parties and barbecues. Ask their maker about them, because you'll learn something new and they'll be tickled to know that their recipe was worthy of remark. When you're flicking through a magazine or cookbook and you find an unusual pairing or technique, make a note of it. Chances are, these will all inform those 'eureka' moments that you'll find yourself leaning on as you develop your palate and hone your

The world is your oyster (mushroom)!

personal free-wheeling style. A bit like all those 'overnight success' stories you read about … they're almost always years in the making.

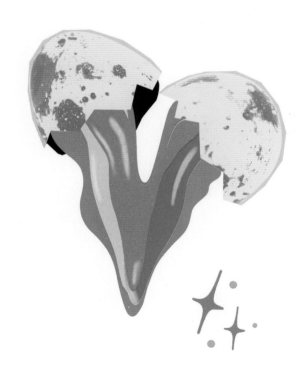

Smashed avo eggs with black garlic

8 eggs, at room temperature

50 ml (1½ fl oz) white vinegar
or lemon juice

2 black garlic cloves (see Ingredient
spotlight, page 23), or 1 teaspoon
black garlic paste or powder

1 tablespoon boiling water

2 ripe avocados

4 cubes marinated feta (see Tips and
Subs, page 22), plus a tablespoon
of the marinating oil

4–8 slices crusty bread, toasted

parsley or chervil sprigs, to garnish

Since this is likely the first recipe page you'll turn to, I thought I'd kick things off with a crowd-pleaser that's also a handy one to learn to cook (cos when you order this out, you're paying through the nose for the privilege of eating eggs that have been sitting around, often pre-poached). It's also a recipe that encapsulates what I hope to offer you throughout this book: stuff you'll love to eat again and again, plus riffs and ingredient inspiration for when you're ready to branch out — like black garlic!

To poach the eggs, bring a large, wide shallow pan half-filled with water to the boil (or you can poach in two batches in a smaller pan; see Tips on page 22). Meanwhile, crack the eggs into a bowl. Splash the vinegar or lemon juice into the bowl with the eggs (rather than into the poaching water), à la Nigella's method; you'll see the whites contract almost immediately.

Once the water is boiling, drop the heat down to a simmer, then plop the eggs and vinegar or lemon juice into the water from as close to the water's surface as possible, making sure all of the vinegar/lemon juice also makes it into the pan. The eggs will start to spin around and coagulate pretty quickly. If the whites start to foam up and threaten to inch towards the top of the pot, drop the heat a little lower until they calm down.

For runny poached eggs, 2–3 minutes cooking should do it. For firmer poached eggs, cook for 3–4 minutes.

Scoop the eggs out with a slotted spoon or spider skimmer (see Gadget spotlight, page 23) and drain on paper towel or a clean tea towel.

If using whole black garlic cloves, pour the boiling water over them in a small bowl, then mash with a fork to soften. (Skip this step if using garlic paste or powder.)

To make your smashed avo, scoop the avocado flesh into a bowl, then use your fork to mash it together with the black garlic paste, feta and oil. (If using garlic powder, this can go in now as well, or you can save it for sprinkling on top at the end.) Season to taste with salt and black pepper.

Portion the smashed avo over the toast. Top with the poached eggs and herbs and serve.

Smashed avo eggs Bonus bits

Tips

If you can't find marinated feta at the shops, use a creamy feta and add your own flavourings — chilli flakes, crushed garlic and herbs.

If you don't have a pan big enough, poach the eggs in two batches. After cooking the second batch, gently scoop the whole lot back into the still-warm water for one last plunge to briefly reheat them, then drain again before serving.

Subs

Go entirely plant-based by skipping the poached eggs and subbing in a plant-based marinated feta.

Avocado is already so creamy, so if you're cheese-poor but avocado-rich, you're welcome to use straight-up avo forked through with a squirt of lemon juice.

If you can't find black garlic, any kind of 'mite is a fantastic foil for creamy, sweet avocado — anything from traditional Vegemite to Marmite and Oomite.

Shortcuts

This is already fairly quick to whip together, but you could just swish your favourite paste or 'mite onto buttered toast and top with slices of avo, too. It's about the flavour combo here rather than finesse, so feel free to freestyle further as you make this a regular at your place.

Skills spotlight: Poaching

Poaching is a bit like blanching in that the liquid — be it water, milk (cow or plant), stock or sugar syrup — is boiling hot. Unlike blanching, there's no 'shock' component, and it usually takes more time. Poaching chicken or fish ensures a moist result (it's a wet-cook, after all), and is also much quicker than cooking with indirect wet heat, such as steaming.

Because it involves a longer languish in the water, poaching lends itself well to flavourings. Think whole spices such as star anise, cinnamon, cardamom pods and cloves for poaching fruit like pears and quince in winter, or stone fruit in summer, or infusing aromatics such as fresh ginger, lemongrass and citrus into tender tofu, fish or chicken.

If you're new to cooking, egg-poaching proficiency is a great kitchen skill to learn early on, because with it you can write your own cheques to café-style dishes, topping brunchy bowls, salads and soups with a glorious googy. Fresh, room-temperature eggs will always poach best. And it goes without saying that buying the best-quality free-range eggs will make all the difference — both to the flavour of your dish, and to the sustainability credentials of the industry.

THE JOY OF BETTER COOKING

Gadget spotlight: Holey scoop!

Skimmers, spiders and slotted spoons are all slightly different variations on a holey scoop. Which one to choose will depend on what you'll use it for.

Slotted spoons have the most spoon-to-hole ratio, so they retain some level of liquid when fishing stuff out of the pan. They're also the most gentle on delicate soft fruits and eggs.

Skimmers are like shallow little sieves with a long handle. They're great for skimming foams off stocks without taking too much juice along with them.

Spiders have a wider-weaved wire mesh, usually copper or stainless steel, and are excellent for scooping any deep-fried foods out of oil. Buy one with a metal handle if possible, as wooden ones wear out the fastest.

If you're investing in just the one item, a slotted spoon should do everything you need in the first instance (you can use tongs to fish out deep-frying items). If you can track down a rounded spider skimmer with softer coils, rather than weaves, this should work across all tasks, too.

Ingredient spotlight: Black garlic

Black garlic is becoming more widely available in specialty grocers, with good reason — it's probably the most exciting natural flavouring discovery since black truffle. The garlic is slow-fermented in special ovens for around 40 days, which concentrates the sugars and caramelises the colour to a broody black, as well as softening the texture to a liquorice-y consistency. It's a lot like black truffle in that it is best used like a seasoning on bland things like mashed potatoes, and creamy stuff like butter, and to up the umami factor in any dish from soups and stews to pasta sauces and aioli. I like to soften it with a sploosh of boiling water and spread it on toast.

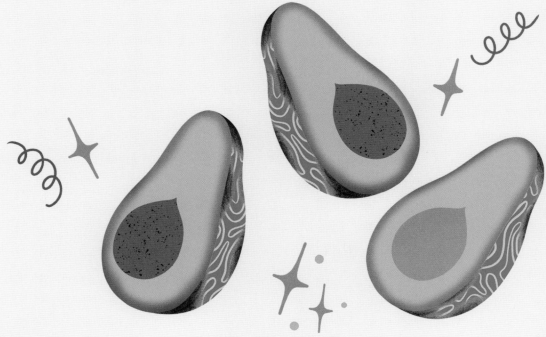

Folded crabby eggs

8 eggs

140 g (5 oz) picked spanner crabmeat, patted dry

¼ cup (60 g) thick (double) cream or crème fraîche

2 tablespoons butter (no need to be too precise)

a pinch of sea salt flakes

a small pinch of ground white pepper

2 tablespoons chopped chives

1 tablespoon picked chervil (optional)

This is essentially slow-and-steady silky scrambled eggs, but *way* bougier. You can totally change the crabmeat for goat's cheese, or just leave them both out and go heavier on butter. The gold standard for this recipe is a dish at the now sadly shut Lau's Family Kitchen in Melbourne. Lau's made theirs with just egg whites, which you're welcome to do, but I prefer to leave the yolks in for a richer flavour and colour. If you don't feel like clashing claws first thing of a morning, you can buy picked crabmeat in frozen packs and thaw overnight. The closer you can get the crab to room temperature before using, the less time it'll need to heat through, keeping it nice and tender, too.

In a bowl, lightly beat the eggs with a fork — there's no need to ensure the whites and yolks have combined. Pop the crabmeat in another bowl and mix 2 tablespoons of the cream through.

Heat a large non-stick frying pan. Add the butter and melt over medium–low heat. When the butter is foaming, pour in the beaten egg and stir gently with a flexible spatula, folding the mixture in on itself and gently tipping the pan around to allow the eggs to contact the heat as evenly as possible.

As soon as the egg mixture starts to turn opaque (about 2 minutes), fold in the crabmeat and remaining cream. Sprinkle with salt and pepper. Switch off the heat and allow the residual heat to finish cooking the eggs. Sprinkle with the herbs and serve straight away.

Bonus bits

Shortcuts

You can crack the eggs STRAIGHT INTO THE PAN! Just give them a vigorous swish with a spatula as soon as they land in the buttery foam, so the whites and yolks start to get friendly, then carry on as above.

Recipe riffs

Add these instead of the crab and cream in the final step:
• Corn kernels + parsley
• Goat's cheese + dill
• Smoked trout + chives
Or garnish with oyster sauce and spring onion.

Subs

Instead of crab, try shredding some lion's mane mushroom through the eggs. They're very 'crabby' texturally, and can increasingly be found at specialty grocers.

If you don't have white pepper, cracked black pepper will absolutely fit the bill. Some chefs prefer to use white pepper in light-coloured dishes because it's less visible, but I quite like a pepper fleck.

Skills spotlight: Scrambling eggs

Egg-scrambling isn't something to get hot 'n' heavy with. On the contrary, the best scrambles are done slowly, allowing the egg to set in ribbons rather than bitsy blobs.

A good non-stick frying pan will never go astray here, and will mean you're adding fat for flavour rather than trying to keep the mixture from sticking. If you'd prefer to scramble in a well-seasoned cast-iron pan, you can, but I find the heat gets way too intense, and its weight makes the pan harder to manipulate.

If making a scramble for one, two eggs is plenty. The cream component is optional, but excellent — and you can always just add extra butter towards the end of cooking to enrich the eggy mix.

Not just a side salad

the best-looking greens — a head of
    cos lettuce, iceberg, oak leaf, frisée
    (curly endive), radicchio, etc.
1–2 flat-leaf parsley sprigs,
    leaves only, cross-chopped
1 garlic clove, bruised
1–2 spring onions/scallions,
    finely chopped

Vinaigrette

1 tablespoon best-quality
    vinegar or citrus juice
a generous pinch of sea salt
a pinch of sugar
1 teaspoon mustard
3 tablespoons excellent-quality
    olive oil

What I've never understood about the expression 'You don't make friends with salad' is that there are few dishes as ubiquitous, reliable or versatile as a good leafy salad. Green leafies are no fair-weather friends. While other side dishes are wont to wane when times are tough and seasons change, you can bet your bottom dollar that there's leaf, allium and some form of herb available to you to dress sharply for lifting any table and filling out any flat-lay. If you're planning on transporting this salad, make the vinaigrette in a clean lidded jar, for ease of mobility and less washing up. Pop the bruised garlic into your jar to help emulsify onsite. If the salad's staying home, here's a handy habit I picked up from Stephanie Alexander, which she picked up from being an *au pair* in France. Make the dressing in the bowl you plan to toss the salad in, with the salad tongs or servers ready inside. When it's time to serve, grab the leaves you need from the fridge, pop them in the bowl and dress. Talk about a salad spin!

Prepare your salad greens and herbs as outlined on page 28 and set aside in the fridge until ready to serve. If your salad leaves have no time to chill, just soak, drain and rinse them, then use a salad spinner to dry them, or roll them in a clean tea towel to thoroughly dry off the excess water. Getting them really dry is crucial — the dressing will not adhere to wet salad leaves.

Rub your salad bowl with the cut side of the garlic. Prepare the vinaigrette by adding the vinegar, salt and sugar and giving a little whisk to dissolve. Add the mustard, olive oil and some freshly ground black pepper and leave to mingle.

Pop in your lovingly prepared greens, herbs and spring onion and gently toss them around in the bowl, being careful not to bruise the leaves.

Bonus bits

Tips

Buying mixed leaves may seem convenient, but remember that each leaf has a different water content and was likely picked at a different time, so these kinds of packs are the first to wilt. You're better off buying whole heads of lettuce — or, better yet, growing your own if you have space for a planter on a balcony or in a backyard.

To cross-chop herbs, place one hand on the handle of your knife, and the other on the spine of the blade. With the tip of the knife remaining on the board, lift the heel up and down and roll over the herbs in a criss-cross pattern.

Subs

Instead of using sugar in the vinaigrette, a dash of honey or maple syrup is also great.

Dill, tarragon, chervil and mint are all welcome in the salad, instead of parsley.

And instead of spring onions, you can happily use shallots, red onion or salad onion.

Waste knot

Parsley sprigs are more fibrous than the leaves, but no less useful. You can freeze them for stocks, or blitz them through juices, sauces and compound butters (page 197). I like to store mine in a jar of water in the fridge, even once the leaves are torn off, which extends their life infinitely.

Not just a side salad Bonus bits

Skills spotlight: Prepping and storing greens

Whether they're lettuce-y or herby, all leaves need TWO main moments in their story arc: to be hydrated to the very last minute, and to be spun dry before being dressed.

Proper storage can extend the life of your greens from only a few days to a good week. First, discard any brown stems off the head or leaves of a lettuce or other salad greens. Tear your leaves to the size you plan to serve them before soaking. Place in a bowl of cold or chilled water with a few ice chunks for 10–15 minutes; the cold helps to accelerate osmosis and revive crispness. (If you've not got a bowl big enough, but do have a sink to spare, clean it down, then fill with cold water and ice and pop your green stuff in there.) Drain the leaves in a colander, then place in a container lined with a few pieces of paper towel, pop a lid on top and chill in the fridge.

If you're a salad-spinner person (me!) with room in the fridge (sometimes me!), use your salad spinner (see right) as both your colander and your lidded vessel. What's best about this approach is that if you just want a little salad in your lunch or dinner, it's there ready to go. If you're washing and wearing right away, remember to spin the leaves well, as the dressing will slip right off otherwise. Leaves that have spent some time between the sheets in the fridge don't need to be spun again.

Herbs such as parsley, dill, chives, tarragon, mint, chervil, rosemary, sage and thyme can all be stored like this. Basil likes to be stored at room temperature in a jar of water, like a bunch of flowers.

The most important thing to know about leaves is that they need to be served ice-cold to optimise their crunch factor. Also, hot lettuce is just so wrong. If you've a penchant for popping leaves in a toasted sandwich or wrap, consider adding them after the toasting's done (along with any avocado, for similar reasons).

Refreshing is the answer for all green leafies — lettuce, stalk or herb. Anything with a propensity to wilt under warmth or refrigeration can be brought back to life with simple osmotic biology. Pop stalky veg such as asparagus in a jar of water in your fridge door.

Gadget spotlight: Salad spinner

If your head is spinning from all this salad spinner talk, you might be wondering, *Do I really need one?* YES, of course you do! Salad spinners are useful because they remove any niggling annoyance around making friends with leafy stuff, which often feels too-hard-basket to wash and dry without one. They make soaking gritty veg, such as leeks, and herbs like coriander much easier to loosen the sandy bits from, as the weight of the grit makes it drop to the bottom of the bowl, while the leaves refresh at the same time.

Invest in a good-quality spinner with grippy silicon at its base to stop it jumping around the benchtop, and made from sturdy material that'll last you for years.

If you're not yet ready to commit to one, you can create a makeshift spinner with your drained leaves in a tea towel, plonked into a shopping bag, spun around your head. Just be sure to do this outside, or away from any valuable family heirlooms!

Ingredient spotlight: Alliums

Salad is always better with a little allium action, whether it's some snipped chives, thinly sliced shallots, red onion or salad onion, or some spring onions (scallions), which can be pre-sliced and stored on damp paper towel in a sealed container in the fridge to keep them happy. (You can regrow the spring onion roots, too — see page 40.) I prefer using banana shallots to French ones, simply because their shape makes them easier to slice evenly, but both are lovely additions. Quick-pickling the onion or shallot adds an extra dimension, too. There's no need to be too precise — just steeping them in a little vinegar or lemon juice with a pinch of sugar and salt will do it (to speed this up, you can heat the seasoned vinegar first). For more detailed pickling instructions, skip over to the salad recipe on page 42.

THE JOY OF BETTER COOKING

Skills spotlight: Dressing for success

The best vinaigrette comes down to the quality of its ingredients — no surprises there. The better the oils and vinegars at your disposal are, the easier time you'll have balancing flavours and creating something delicious. Once your pantry is stocked with some easy wins, the actual vinaigrette concocting becomes playful and forgiving.

Different vinegars have varying acidity, colour, viscosity and sweetness levels. More often than not, you do get what you pay for, so at least one fancy dresser will do you good; think of it as your black-tie outfit. My favourites live in the bittersweet territory, like chardonnay vinegar or a really nice local apple cider vinegar. If you make a lot of salads, or find yourself cooking widely, you might need to expand your vinegar collection; otherwise, get your cost-per-wear on just the one at first.

For a light, bright, soprano flavour (I can't help but think of these vinegars as the high notes), go for white wine vinegars, verjuice or rice wine vinegars (which are very handy if you're cooking a lot of South-East Asian dishes). For classic French-style side leaves, chardonnay vinegar is my go-to ... bougie, but worth it. Lemon and lime juice live here too. If you or your neighbours have a citrus tree, life has handed you lemons in the very best way. And don't forget to use the zest.

For richer, slightly sweeter, alto flavours (deeper notes, darker colour), try red wine vinegar, apple cider vinegar or black vinegar (the one you use as a dipping sauce for dumplings — China's answer to balsamic ... yum!). Balsamic vinegar is great if you're making a lot of Mediterranean dishes, but if you don't want to fork out for something aged, you can fake this with a 'cheat's aged balsamic' by reducing budget balsamic vinegar with maple syrup or brown sugar over a medium heat until thickened and syrupy.

For a viscous, sweet tenor (perfect as an accent or harmoniser; just be careful it doesn't overpower), go to balsamic glazes and vincotto. The current most popular in this camp, thanks to The Ottolenghi Way, is pomegranate molasses, which can be used as both the sweetener and the acid in a dressing. Add a little at a time and taste as you go (which is a rule for all additions, actually). Orange juice and zest can live here, too.

Adding salt (I like pink sea salt flakes best) and any other flavourings to the vinegar allows them to dissolve before the oil is added. If your dressing tastes too salty or acidic, balance with more oil — but remember that a stronger dressing actually mellows once it's dispersed across all the green stuff.

Adding sweetness such as sugar, honey, maple syrup, citrus juice or syrup gives the salad dimension and helps with balance — especially when using more bitter, peppery leaves such as radicchio, red mustard, endive, frisée (curly endive), witlof (chicory), radish tops, dandelion greens and rocket (arugula).

Mustard is a great emulsifier in dressings and enables the vinegar to be suspended in the oil, even if just for a short time. You can use any mustard in your fridge, but dijon is the most neutral-flavoured, while wholegrain mustard gives texture and interest, for something a little different. Leave the hot English for your hotdogs.

Using the best-quality fresh local extra virgin olive oil is a must. Olive oil actually doesn't last longer than a year after pressing, and even then, only when it's kept in the right conditions — away from direct sunlight, with very little exposure to oxygen. Your best bet is to buy smaller bottles for dressings, so you can work through them faster, and have a larger quantity of less expensive olive oil for cooking with.

All-seasons avocado half

If you're regularly plagued by a mid-afternoon snack hankering, then you'll be pleased to know that not only are you not alone, but that what you're craving isn't sugar — it's fat! Your brain is crying out for something oily to lubricate the ol' gears after a day of staring at screens or screening spam calls. If this were one of Those Books, I'd tell you to have a handful of nuts or something, which is fine, I suppose. But I'm here to enable and empower your snackering ('snack hankering'). In our household, the best way to satisfy it is with a half-avo topped with a tablespoon's worth of whatever's in the fridge. The avocado is the edible receptacle for flavour, with a nutty butteriness that can carry its own. Please try some of the ideas that follow, but don't be afraid to slapdash your way to your own favourites. Just promise me one thing: don't ever ever EVER put that avo in the oven. I can abide almost any culinary creativity, but hot avocado is my line in the sand.

Ingredient spotlight: Avocado

It's one thing to tell you what to do with a good, ripe avo; it's another kettle of fish altogether to help you select one. Yes, this IS another thinly veiled ploy to continue my fight against foolhardy alligator-pear fondlers.

The key, really, is to pick your avo when it's nowhere near ripe. A truly ripe avo is actually not as soft as you think — it's still slightly firm on first press, softening towards the stem. Sometimes, if you're lucky, the nub is still attached, and you can tell when it's ripe as the stem comes away easily and the flesh underneath is vivid green.

Unfortunately, *some* people still feel the need to squeeze every single avo on the display like they're playing a selfish game of whack-a-mole, before deciding which to take home for their guac-a-mole. Coincidence? I think not. We can all be the change.

Pick the roundest avo — the more flesh in proximity to the seed (stone), the nuttier the flavour. And stop seeking soft. Hard as a rock is right on, and then let it ripen in the comfort and security of your home.

How can you tell it's still hard without squeezing? Find the ones furthest from the front of the display. Touch the very top around the nub, and if it's still firm, you're onto a winner.

If you *do* buy one that's beyond saving, you can always scoop around the bruises after giving these a ginger taste (some are merely surface bruises, while others taste like ... hot avocado blugh). Hide any funky flavour by turning it into the base for something stronger-flavoured, such as smashed avo (page 20), a smoothie or a choc-avocado mousse (which is as easy as melting a block of dark chocolate and blitzing with an avo or two, scooping into glasses or ramekins, then allowing to set in the fridge).

You can use a large metal spoon to scoop ripe avocado from its shell as a whole half, but first check to see if the skin peels off easily — sometimes it's easier to just pop the half flat on a board and peel the skin off, like a band-aid (this is especially useful if you want to slice the half thinly), then gently concertina the slices to place on toast. To pop avocado flesh out in quarters, slice a half in half again lengthways, flesh side up (but not down to the skin), then peel away the skin; the quarters should pop right out.

Speaking of popping out, you can loosen the stone by chipping into it with a sharp knife and giving it a twist. If you're worried about Avocado-Hand (a genuine affliction where people slice into their palm by going too deep with the knife — eek!), you'll be relieved to note that riper avos will release their stone by having a thumb pushed against the stone from the skin side while holding onto the flesh with index and ring finger as a counterpoint.

To store a cut avocado, keep as little of the flesh exposed to oxygen as possible. Leave the stone in if you can (or put it back in like a stopper) and cover with beeswax wrap or the like. Squirting some lemon juice onto the exposed flesh helps stop it browning, too. Some people store cut avocados submerged in acidulated (lemon-spiked) water, which is fine if you plan on using it quickly; water does leach out flavour, though, so I wouldn't leave it in there for more than a day.

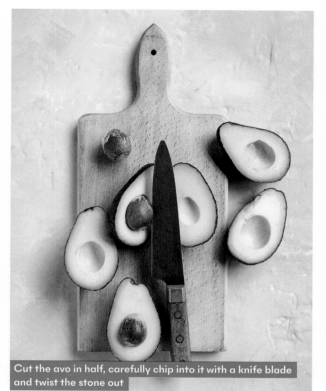

Cut the avo in half, carefully chip into it with a knife blade and twist the stone out

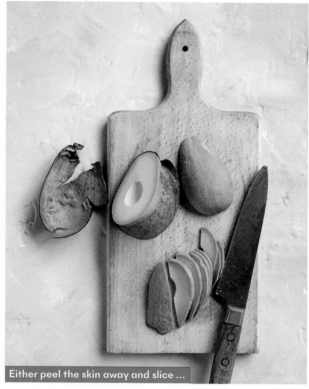

Either peel the skin away and slice ...

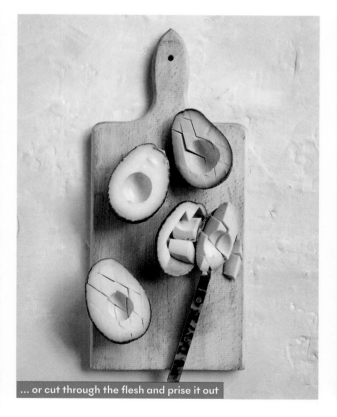

... or cut through the flesh and prise it out

Lemon juice or lemon-spiked water will prevent browning

All-seasons avocado half
page 30

Smashed
Goat's cheese/
marinated feta +
lemon juice + chilli

Funky
Kimchi + yoghurt

Curried avo
Warmed-up curry sauce
(use a jarred one or leftovers)
+ chives + peanuts + Thai basil

Sweet
Honey + yoghurt
(in South America, avo is
regularly served sweet,
so why not?)

Guac
Lime juice + chilli
+ chopped coriander
(cilantro) + yoghurt

Simples
Sliced spring onion
(scallion) + lemon juice
+ olive oil + sesame
seeds

Umami bomb
Miso paste + tahini
+ rice seasoning

Devilled tuna egg sandwiches

4 eggs, at room temperature

185 g (6½ oz) tinned tuna, drained

2 long celery stalks, finely chopped
(the closer to the heart, the sweeter)

1 French shallot, finely chopped

½ bunch of coriander (cilantro),
leaves and stems finely chopped,
plus extra to garnish

¾ cup (185 g) Kewpie mayonnaise,
or to taste — you do you

2 teaspoons curry powder

1 teaspoon ground coriander

1 teaspoon salt flakes

2 tablespoons butter, softened

8 slices soft white bread

1 cucumber, thinly sliced into ribbons

This combo is inspired by a Zaslavsky family classic, which almost always means 'things from tins, heavy on the spices'. I've *zhuzhed* it up by keeping the boiled eggs a little runnier, so that the yolks add richness to our mayonnaise base, but if your eggs boil hard, just consider it 'staying true to the original recipe'. The 'devilled' component here is in reference to de' spicing rather than de' stuffing, which I've unceremoniously usurped in favour of a chunky mix. I've made this more like a proper afternoon-tea sandwich with fluffy white bread, but you can use a dark rye, a gluten-free loaf, or even keep it as more of a salad by making the celery chunkier, chopping in cucumber slices and going heavier on fresh coriander.

To boil the eggs, use a skimmer or slotted spoon to drop the eggs into a saucepan of vigorously boiling water (the spoon means it's less 'drop', more 'place'). Dial down the boil to more of a simmer and leave the eggs in there for 5 minutes. Scoop the eggs out with your skimmer or spoon and immediately run them under cold water. Once cooled, peel the eggs.

Place the tuna, celery, shallot and coriander in a bowl, together with the mayonnaise, curry powder and ground coriander. Use a masher to combine, being careful not to break up the tuna flakes too much. Add the peeled eggs and mash these in, too. Add the salt and check the seasoning; a bit of freshly cracked black pepper is good, too, if you'd like a bit more 'devil' in your eggs.

Butter the bread on one side. Spread the devilled egg mixture over half the slices, then top with the cucumber ribbons. Enclose with the remaining bread slices, cut into thick fingers and serve garnished with extra coriander.

THE JOY OF BETTER COOKING

These take me right back to the tuna & beetroot rolls from my school canteen. You don't see value like that anymore.

Tips

Egg timings will differ if you cook your eggs from the fridge, rather than the pantry. I've intentionally calculated for a runny egg from room temperature. Add an extra minute if boiling from the fridge.

If you buy your eggs from a fridge, that's where they should be stored, whereas eggs bought at room temperature can be stored at room temperature. This makes them great for baking, because the closer they are to room temperature, the better the ingredients will behave together. Pull the eggs out of the fridge in the morning if you plan on baking in the afternoon.

Shortcuts

NAY! This is not a shortcut ... it's a stop sign. Don't be glamoured by the flavoured tuna tins. They are almost inevitably too sweet, or too salty, or just not how you would've done it. See the Ingredient spotlight (right) to fine-tune your tinned tuna game.

Double duty

Take this back to its roots by skipping the sandwiches and scooping the filling straight into some hard-boiled (10-minute) egg halves, for a retro throwback that's gluten-free and makes for fab finger food. Or pile it into vol-au-vent pastry shells.

Recipe riffs

Ever heard of tuna being described as Chicken of The Sea? Well, sub in some left-over poached/roasted chicken and you're in for the best chicken sandwich of your life. Use the same ratios of everything, omit the coriander (both ground and fresh) and swap in fresh chopped parsley or dill. YUM!

You can also swap the spicing for a bit of a twist — a teaspoon of harissa instead of the curry powder for a North African breakfast, or for a Mediterranean flavour, a teaspoon of mixed dried herbs (they're usually called 'Italian seasoning' or the like) and a squeeze of lemon juice.

Ingredient spotlight: Tinned tuna

Why is it that tinned tuna never seems to reek when you're the one eating it? Though I can't help you with such existential questions, I *can* point you in the direction of the best fish in tins. From a sustainability perspective, look for labels such as 'Marine Stewardship Council certified' (these logos will vary depending on what your local one is called). As far as fishing methods go, 'dolphin-friendly' is just the beginning, so scan for words like 'pole-and-line caught' or 'FAD-free purse seine'. Skipjack is the tuna type to look for, then albacore; try to avoid endangered species such as yellowfin, bluefin and big-eye.

Fish in springwater will retain more of its nutrient content and hold its shape better than fish in oil, though tuna steaks in olive oil are a stylist's choice if you're getting fancy with plating. Brine is basically salty water, and though you pour most of it off when you drain it, the salt still tends to dry out the flakes. Steaks or slices are best for flaking into salads like niçoise (page 216), while chunks are fine for sandwich fillings such as this one.

**Devilled tuna
egg sandwiches**

Page 34

Fennel & citrus salad with smoky spring onion dressing

Serves 4–6

juice of ½ lemon
2 fennel bulbs, fronds picked
    (see Subs, page 40)
½ bunch of dill fronds
    (keep the stems to use below)
1 chioggia (bull's-eye) beetroot (optional)
6 radishes (optional)
2 oranges
1 grapefruit or blood orange

Smoky spring onion oil

½ bunch of spring onions (scallions)
½ bunch of dill, stems and fronds
    separated
½ bunch of chives
100 ml (3½ fl oz) grapeseed oil
¼ teaspoon sea salt flakes
⅛ teaspoon caster (superfine)
    sugar (optional)

Chive vinaigrette

½ bunch of chives, finely chopped
1 garlic clove, bruised
¼ cup (60 ml) extra virgin olive oil
1 teaspoon dijon mustard
    (see Subs, page 40)
¼ teaspoon salt flakes
¼ teaspoon freshly ground black pepper

Whether you braise fennel with orange or preserved lemon in the colder months, or finely shave it and team it with the zip of fresh citrus juice and zest as we do here, fennel and citrus is one combo you should have on high rotation throughout the year. Conveniently, citrus is what helps fennel keep its snow-white sheen, so remember to squeeze some lemon into the cold water the fennel's bobbing around in, too. I must credit the supremely talented chef Jo Barrett with lending me her spring onion oil recipe — it takes this dish to the next level, and will make you feel way cheffy, too.

Pour some cold water into a bowl or salad spinner and add the lemon juice, ready for the fennel.

Trim the very bottom off each fennel bulb, and leave on enough of the top green stalks to use as handles. Using a mandoline or sharp knife, shave the fennel very thinly, in the same direction as the ribs run. Pop the fennel shavings into the bowl or salad spinner, along with the fennel and dill fronds. If using the beetroot and/or radish, shave these thinly and add to the bowl or spinner, too. Leave in the fridge to get super crunchy, crisp and cold while you get on with the rest of the salad.

To make the smoky spring onion oil, cut the green tops off the spring onions and reserve. Slice the spring onion whites into thin ribbons, about 3 cm (1¼ inches) long, then pop in the bowl in the fridge with the fennel to curl up. Toss the green spring onion tops in a heavy-based pan and heat over high heat for 3–4 minutes until they turn a brighter green, with flecks of gold and black. While still hot, use tongs to add them to a small blender with the dill stems, chives, grapeseed oil, salt and sugar, if using. Blitz for 2–3 minutes to a bright green mush; the heat generated by the blender blades will help to extract the green colour and the flavour of the herbs.

Drape a piece of muslin (cheesecloth) over a strainer and place over a bowl. Pour the spring onion mixture into the strainer. Leave the oil to drip through on its own, which should take about 20 minutes. Pour the strained oil into a squeeze bottle or small pouring jug and set aside for serving.

Meanwhile, zest the oranges and grapefruit, reserving the zest, then segment the fruit (see Skills spotlight, page 41). Squeeze the left-over citrus peels and membranes into a small jar to extract any remaining juice. Add all the chive vinaigrette ingredients and the reserved zest, seal the jar and shake vigorously to help them get friendly, to the point of emulsification.

Drain the chilled shaved fennel mixture and spring onion curls and spin until fully dry.

Toss the fennel mixture in the vinaigrette and place in a serving bowl. Garnish with the citrus segments and spring onion curls. Serve drizzled with the smoky spring onion oil.

Fennel & citrus salad Bonus bits

Tips

This salad makes a great bring-a-plate dish. You can prepare all the components the day before, then assemble closer to serving.

For a budget piece of muslin (cheesecloth), grab an unused light-weave kitchen cloth.

Shortcuts

The spring onion oil is phenomenal, but I'll let you dress this salad with just the vinaigrette if it means you'll give it a whirl. It'll be fab with a store-bought crispy fried shallot oil, too, or a drizzle of some MYO chilli oil from page 213. Just promise me you'll try making it with the spring onion oil once you've dipped a toe in.

Subs

No fennel? Try tearing or shredding radicchio leaves instead. The colours are just gorgeous.

No dijon mustard? Use wholegrain! Actually, any mustard will work ... just give it a taste to make sure it's not too hot once all of the ingredients come together.

Double duty

The smoky spring onion oil will keep for a week in the fridge, to flavour all sorts of salads, sauces and meat dishes. It also makes for a mean drizzle over mashed potatoes.

Recipe riffs

Turn this into a warm winter salad by roasting the shaved fennel for 30 minutes at 200°C (400°F), then tossing with citrus zest and juice, a little extra virgin olive oil, salt flakes and black pepper.

Extra extras

This salad would be WILD with some cheese — 100 g (3½ oz) feta, stracciatella, burrata or fresh buffalo mozzarella, at room temperature, would really take this to the next level. If you prefer a plant-based version, crumble on some almond feta or equivalent nutty cheese.

Some raisins, currants or sultanas wouldn't go astray, if you feel like adding a bit of extra sweetness.

Nuts like pistachio or hazelnut would give this salad some extra *je ne sais quoi,* especially if you're not going down the cheese route.

Frizzle the spring onion roots (washed and dried well) in a hot pan with a teaspoon or two of grapeseed oil until they crisp up, then drain on paper towel as an optional EXTRA garnish.

Waste knot

Don't discard the fennel tops or the mulched herbs from the spring onion oil. Stash them in the freezer and add to your pot next time you make a stock or soup.

If you don't feel like frizzling the spring onion roots as a garnish, pop them in a glass of water on your windowsill and they'll start regrowing within days.

Worth it

Grapeseed is a terrific neutral-flavoured oil, with a nice high smoke point. Buy a big bottle for deep-frying or shallow-frying, use it to make a mayo (like the one for the celeriac remoulade on page 46) and MYO chilli oil (page 213), and splice it into a vinaigrette or dressing where you don't want the olive oil flavour to be too shouty.

Combining citrus with fennel was one of the first flavour pairings I learned — a real penny-drop moment. It still makes me feel like a sophisticate whenever I whip it out.

Skills spotlight: Segmenting citrus

Place the peeled fruit on a chopping board and use a sharp knife to lop the top and the bottom off, so you have a flat surface to work from. The aim of the game is to keep as much flesh as you can on the fruit, while taking the bitter white pith off, by following the shape of the fruit. Start from the top, running the knife from top to bottom, and working all the way around the citrus until done. It might help to turn the citrus upside-down for some parts of this, especially for bigger fruit.

Holding the citrus in your hand, look to the skin membrane and slice in on a 45-degree angle, then turn the knife to follow on the opposite angle against the other membrane, to release each segment. Don't forget to squeeze the juice from the membranes into your dressing.

And remember to zest the fruit before you slice into it, even if the recipe doesn't ask you to. It's far easier to zest a whole citrus than to try to zest bits of skin!

Cucumber & watermelon ginaigrette salad

1 bunch of radishes, trimmed
and thinly sliced

½ medium-sized watermelon
(about 3 cups flesh), cubed
or scooped with a melon baller

1 lemon

1 small red onion, thinly sliced

2 Lebanese (short) cucumbers,
thinly sliced

100 g (3½ oz) kalamata olives,
pitted and sliced

a pinch of chilli flakes (optional)

100 g (3½ oz) mild creamy feta

good-quality olive oil, for drizzling

Ginaigrette

5 mint sprigs, leaves picked,
stalks reserved

3 dill sprigs, fronds picked,
stalks reserved

3 parsley sprigs, leaves picked,
stalks reserved

50 ml (1½ fl oz) white wine vinegar

50 ml (1½ fl oz) gin

⅓ cup (75 g) sugar

2 teaspoons salt

This recipe is a study in how to build a salad, using a variety of shapes to create texture (see Skills spotlight opposite), a tonal palette of complementary pinks, greens and deep purples to please the eye, and salty–sweet flavours that make every bite a blast. It's also easily doubled if feeding a crowd; the only thing you don't have to double is the pickling liquid quantity.

I love sidling this salad along as a bring-a-plate, because it's sure to get people chatting, and I'll pack the ginaigrette separately in a little jar for tossing through when we're all set to serve. If you get there and see a few Greek-ish-looking salads already, you can always leave the watermelon separate and serve it as a welcome treat before dessert. No-one ever says no to watermelon.

Plunge the radishes into a bowl of cold water, to refresh and crisp.

Scoop the watermelon with a melon baller (retro!), or cut into wedges, slicing the flesh off the rind, then chop into fork-sized chunks. Pop these in the fridge while you make the rest of your salad.

Zest the lemon, reserving the zest. Segment the flesh by slicing off the skin and pith, and cutting into each segment at a 45-degree angle to form wedges. Keep the remaining carcass of the citrus to squeeze over the salad. (You'll find more info on segmenting citrus on page 41.)

To make the ginaigrette, place the mint, dill and parsley stalks in a small saucepan with the vinegar, gin, sugar, salt and 50 ml (1½ fl oz) water. Bring to the boil, cooking for 4–5 minutes, until the booze stops stinging your eyeballs and the liquid reduces a little.

Pop the onion slices in a jar, strain the ginaigrette over them and leave to pickle for at least 15 minutes. There's no need to pop a lid on top, unless you're planning on taking this with you for drizzling at a party.

To serve, drain and thoroughly dry the radish wedges. Assemble the cucumber, watermelon and radish in a serving bowl. Add most of the reserved herb fronds from the ginaigrette, together with the olives, lemon segments and chilli flakes, if using. Crumble or cube the feta into fork-sized chunks and scatter over the top. Toss gently to combine, so the feta doesn't start collapsing.

Garnish with the remaining herbs and pickled onion. Drizzle with a few tablespoons of the pickling liquid and olive oil, then crack over some black pepper to finish.

Bonus bits

Tips

Keep the watermelon separate if making this ahead. Watermelon will turn all salads — whether leafy or fruity — to mush. To make this party last a little longer, try using honeydew melon instead, as it will keep its shape better, but won't be quite as sweet.

Subs

If you're not much of a drinker, buy a baby bottle of booze. Instead of gin, vodka will hit the spot, or even ouzo if you want to be true to the salad's Greek roots, adding a delightful anise note to the dressing. You can also just hold the booze and make the pickling liquid with an extra 50 ml (1½ fl oz) white wine vinegar instead.

Shortcuts

I love the combo of watermelon with something salty like cheese and/or olives; one mouthful and I'm on a Greek island! Strip back the rest of this salad and you're already there — crumble some salty feta and sliced black olives over cubes of watermelon and add a drizzle of olive oil and a squirt of lemon juice. The olives are optional, but excellent.

Double duty

You can keep the onion in the pickling liquid in a sealed jar for up to a week in the fridge. Its sharp sweetness will be a welcome addition anywhere you'd usually add pickles — burgers, shawarma, with falafels (oh hello page 208), and in place of straight-up onion in other types of salads.

Skills spotlight: Salad shapes

Deciding on the best salad combo is a lot like picking friends for a guestlist. You want to include enough complementary characters to ensure that everything goes smoothly, a few old faithfuls to hold the fort, then slip in a few newbies or known knockabouts to keep things interesting. In a salad, contrasting flavours are important to ensure that every bite is intriguing enough to prompt the next. Here it's salty stuff like the olives and feta, which might be replaced with anchovies, fried bacon or capers (brined or fried).

If including juicy vegetables and fruits such as tomato, cucumber or watermelon, think about what else you can add to build body and crunch, such as radish or sharp rocket (arugula), or other bitey bits such as capsicum (pepper) or crispy lettuce. Crunch can also be built up with toasted seeds and nuts, crispy fried shallots or baked croutons. Remember to add these just before serving, after the dressing has been poured.

Creaminess never goes astray, whether that's in the dressing, with ingredients such as avocado or mango, or with favourites like shaved parmesan or feta.

Sharpness or acid is the finishing touch that will make the salad really sing, whether that's in the form of some vinegar or citrus juice in the dressing, or pickled onion slices, à la this salad. And, as far as I'm concerned, a salad party isn't ready to start unless there's some form of allium family member invited, be it red onion, spring onion (scallion), chives or shallot.

Don't be afraid to experiment with sweet in savoury salads, too — maple syrup or honey in a dressing, stone fruit or mango in summer, melon to lift and cool, and apple or pear in the colder months.

Parties don't always go right, and neither do salads — but remember, all it takes is the right ingredient to walk through the door and change the whole dynamic, so never give up. When in doubt, treat the whole thing with a good pinch of salt (and/or humour). It'll all be over before you know it, and chances are that they'll just appreciate the invite.

**Cucumber &
watermelon
ginaigrette salad**

Page 42

The slaw with more

1 cup (140 g) walnuts

1 celeriac, peeled and julienned
(see Skills spotlight, page 49)

2 carrots, peeled and julienned
(see Skills spotlight, page 49)

2 granny smith apples, peeled
and julienned (see Skills spotlight,
page 49)

juice of ½ lemon

chilled water, for soaking the veg

½ cup finely chopped parsley

Remoulade

2–3 garlic cloves, peeled

1 teaspoon salt flakes

1 egg

1 teaspoon warm water

juice of ½ lemon

1 tablespoon apple cider vinegar

1 tablespoon wholegrain mustard

1 cup (250 ml) grapeseed oil

Up your slaw game by using celeriac, a robust veg that's a cousin to celery and surprisingly herbaceous. Celeriac is best friends with remoulade, a pimped-up mayo that cuts through any bitterness in the celeriac. These two are often just served together as a classic condiment, but are great extrapolated here into a classic, yet surprising, slaw. This recipe is a choose-your-own-adventure in two ways. For prepping the veg, you can go quick using gadgets, or slow down and go analogue with some slicing (see Skills spotlight, page 49). Same for the mayo. Read on!

Preheat the oven to 180°C (350°F). Spread the walnuts on a baking tray and roast for 6–8 minutes, or until just burnished. Set a timer ... walnuts burn! Remove from the oven and leave to cool.

Drop the julienned veg into a salad spinner with the lemon juice and enough cold water to cover, until ready to serve. No spinner? Plonk them in a bowl with the lemon juice and cold water.

To make the dressing, roughly chop the garlic, then sprinkle the salt flakes on top. Use the flat face of your knife blade on a 35-degree angle to press against the garlic, as though you're buttering bread, until it turns into a paste.

Choose one of the following three ways to make your mayo.

To make it by hand, crack the egg into a mixing bowl (see step-by-step pics on page 48). Add the crushed garlic paste, water, lemon juice, vinegar and mustard and whisk together. Then whisk in the grapeseed oil in a gentle, steady stream. Season to taste with salt and pepper if desired.

To make it using a stick blender, add the crushed garlic paste and remaining dressing ingredients to the cup attachment of your stick blender. Pop the stick blender in so that the blades are at the bottom of the cup, then blitz until an emulsion forms. Season to taste with salt and pepper if desired.

To make it in a food processor, add the crushed garlic paste to the food processor with the egg, water, lemon juice, vinegar and mustard. With the motor running, pour in the grapeseed oil in a gentle, steady stream. Season to taste with salt and pepper if desired.

Drain the julienned veg of all the water and give the salad spinner a few twirls until dry, pouring off any spun-out water as you go. If you don't have a spinner, drain well and dry thoroughly with a clean tea towel.

Tip the veg into a serving bowl. Add most of the parsley, and one-quarter of the mayo, stirring until combined. If you'd like your slaw to be creamier, keep adding the mayo a little at a time until the richness factor is to your liking.

Crumble the walnuts over and serve garnished with the remaining parsley. The salad and any left-over mayo will keep covered in the fridge for up to 1 week.

To make the dressing by hand, crack the egg into a bowl

Add the other ingredients and whisk

Then whisk in the oil in a gentle, steady stream

... until you have a smooth emulsion

THE JOY OF BETTER COOKING

The slaw with more Bonus bits

Tips

If the dressing looks grainy, it might have split. Whisk in 2 teaspoons boiling water to bring it back together again.

To give you extra stability while you're whisking, create a ring with a dampened tea towel to nestle the bowl into (see pic on page 14).

Shortcuts

Make an even quicker dressing by grating a garlic clove or two through some Japanese Kewpie mayo. Faster still, use garlic powder — add a little at a time to the mayo until you're happy with the heat.

Double duty

Toss any left-over mayo through salad leaves, or use as a dipping sauce for tempura veg or fish and chips. Fold in some chopped cornichons or pickles and finely chopped shallots, and you've just made yourself a tartare sauce!

Recipe riffs

I've added carrot to this recipe, because it's only one step removed from a family favourite — Dad's garlicky carrot salad, which contains, you guessed it ... carrot, garlic, mayo. If you can't find celeriac, make one with these three ingredients and be equally as happy.

Make a fully plant-based mayo by leaving the egg out of the dressing. If you want the dressing to be creamier, make a plant-based mayo using aquafaba (the drained liquid from a tin of chickpeas), or invest in a shop-bought vegan mayo.

For a nut-free version, toast some sunflower seeds instead of the walnuts.

Skills spotlight: Julienning

To julienne the celeriac, carrots and apples by hand, slice them into thin strips, stack them on top of each other on your chopping board, then slice again into long thin matchsticks. Why bother? Well, the more you slice, the better you get. Sure, that feels like a truism — but I've learned empirically that the difference between 'restaurant quality' and 'home cooking' often comes down to details as simple as the precision of the knife-work. Practice, practice, practice has seen me go from hacking at fresh ginger like a ... hack, to comfortably zipping through slaws with but a knife and a board. Just make sure that knife is sharp and the board is grippy (wet kitchen towel or silicon underneath please!), go slow and watch those fingertips.

If you want to inch towards julienning ingredients by hand, but aren't quite ready to take the plunge, you can get yourself a julienne peeler, which is especially useful if you're a fan of green mango salads and slaws like this one. Alternatively, you can use a mandoline, V-slicer or a food processor with the grating attachment.

Blistered grape & feta pasta

500 g (1 lb 2 oz) assorted seedless
    grapes, washed and taken off
    the vine (see Tips, page 52)
100 g (3½ oz) smaller grapes
    such as currants or muscatels,
    kept as small bunches
5 tarragon sprigs, leaves picked,
    reserving the stalks
¼ cup (60 ml) olive oil,
    plus extra for finishing
200 g (7 oz) block good-quality
    feta (see Subs, page 52), halved
1 garlic bulb, halved
500 g (1 lb 2 oz) orecchiette
½ bunch of chervil (optional,
    but excellent)
small nasturtium leaves,
    to garnish (optional)

Had I suggested that you bake a block of feta a decade ago, you might've thought it a typo. *Make* feta is what you mean, right, Alice? Yet since baked feta pasta went viral a few years back, the idea of coaxing flavours out of cheese and tomatoes by baking them together and serving them for dinner is now a thing. And the beauty of trends is that they can evolve and shape-shift into all manner of things — a bit of same-same-but-different-ness. As grapes bake, they transform into something surprisingly savoury, while baking the feta mellows its saltiness somewhat. The dish can be served hot, warm or cold — and I prefer it as more of a pasta salad than a pasta pasta. Mind you, if this gives you a hankering for having a go at the original, I've popped loose instructions for the tomato version in the riffs on page 52.

Preheat the oven to 200°C (400°F).

Cut some larger grapes in half and keep the rest whole. Toss them all in your largest baking dish with the tarragon stalks, half the olive oil and a pinch of salt flakes. Push the grapes to one side and add the feta and garlic, then drizzle the rest of the olive oil over. Roast for 30–40 minutes, until the feta is golden brown, and the grapes have wrinkled and started yielding their juices into the pan.

Bring a large saucepan of well-salted water to the boil. About 10 minutes before the feta has finished baking, cook the orecchiette for 1 minute less than recommended by the packet instructions. Drain, reserving a mugful of the pasta water, and toss a glug of olive oil through the pasta to stop it sticking.

When the grapes and feta are ready, pull out the tarragon stalks and garlic. Pour the pasta into the dish, squeeze the garlic cloves out of their skin and gently stir to combine, splashing in the reserved pasta water to loosen if needed. Season to taste, drizzle with more olive oil, and finish with snipped tarragon and chervil, and some small nasturtium leaves, if you have them.

This can be served hot like a pasta, or warm like a pasta salad.

Roasting vegies brings out their sweetness, while roasting fruit can transform them into meatier morsels — a complex cut-through for rich savoury dishes.

Tips

Grapes are seasonal, so check their origin; if they're being flung halfway around the world, look for ones from closer to home instead.

Subs

To make this plant-based, use a planty cheese that bakes well (it'll say so on the pack).

This pasta would also work quite well with greens such as chopped blanched green beans, broad beans, snow peas (mange tout), frozen peas ... anything you'd put in a pasta salad, tossed through the pasta along with the baked feta. To save on washing up, blanch the green stuff for 3–4 minutes in the pasta water towards the end of cooking.

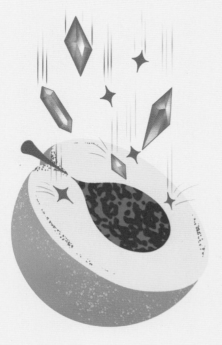

Shortcuts

No time to bake or boil? No biggie! Leave the grapes raw and crumble the feta through plenty of fresh herbs to make a zippy autumn salad. A splash of verjuice, vincotto or even caramelised balsamic vinegar will unite the lot. If you have a spare 5 minutes, make a cheat's caramelised balsamic by heating equal parts balsamic vinegar and maple syrup in a pan until it thickens. Toss the grapes into the pan once the heat's off to warm them through.

Recipe riffs

Instead of the pasta, add an interesting cooked grain or pulse (beluga lentils, freekeh, faro, millet) ... and voilà! You've got yourself another delicious dish in a jiff.

For extra colour and roughage, toss leafy stuff like rocket (arugula) or radicchio through the dish once it comes out of the oven. If you're serving it cold, feel free to incorporate fresh leafies just before serving.

To transform the dish into the baked feta pasta first brought to the world by Finnish food-blogger Jenni Häyrinen, just sub the grapes out for cherry tomatoes, the tarragon for thyme, pop in a few garlic cloves and bake in just the same way. Pour drained cooked spaghetti and a mugful of pasta water into the baking dish, along with some fresh basil leaves, and stir together until the feta breaks up, and the tomatoes yield into a rich, creamy sauce.

Skills spotlight: Roasting fruit for savouries

There's a finer line between fruit and veg than you may think, so while everyone's going gaga for vegetable desserts, I'm just over here trying to slip more fruit into every main. Think classic combos like roast pork and/or cabbage with apples, mushrooms with blackberries, game with quince, dried prunes and apricots in tagines and duck with oranges.

Consider building the sauce around your roasted fruit, as I have with the juice that the grapes yield. They'll often bring not only flavour, but gorgeous colour into the dressing, particularly those fruits high in anthocyanin, such as dark grapes, cherries and plums.

Keep chunks and shapes as uniform as possible to help them cook through evenly; I like to keep fruits resembling their original form, so consider leaving them halved and stoned, or even whole. Keep the skin on to retain the shape, or peel if you'd prefer a proper prolapse. Roast the fruits face side up in the dish, as this tends to help the moisture escape and concentrates the flavour; skin side down is a good option, however, if your aim is to burnish the bases (baking paper to line the dish + a sprinkle of sugar on each fruit face highly recommended!).

Some sort of acid, like lemon juice or vinegar, will help to lock in the vibrancy of colour for fruits such as plums and quinces. Roasting citrus brings out surprisingly bitter notes, courtesy of the pith, so keep this in mind and correct with extra seasoning and a little sugar to mitigate.

Accentuating the sweetness is never a bad idea, so whether it's a sprinkle of sugar, or a drizzle of maple syrup, honey or similar, it's a great insurance policy in case the fruit is not at its best. It's also a good way to guarantee the best bit about roasting anything sweet: caramelisation. That's those nigh-on-burnt bits that taste like bitter toffee, making something that could feel like pudding topping taste more sophisticated. I even sprinkle a little sugar into the pan when I'm roasting veg like butternut squash or sweet potato.

Frozen fruit also roasts up well — just remember to tack on some time to allow the extra moisture to evaporate.

Spicing will depend on where in the world you want to go. Easy wins will come from a cinnamon stick, a couple of cardamom pods, maybe a few cloves. Seeds such as caraway, cumin and fennel are also repeat rabble-rousers when roasting — though some would prefer to grind these to a powder rather than risk ruining the softness that roasted fruit brings to a dish texturally.

Roasting requires a dry heat, so try to avoid covering the fruit. (Unless they are on the drier side, like quince or the hard pears on page 258, since these can get parched if there isn't enough moisture circulating — and that ain't pretty. Instead, they enjoy a steam facial, getting a little sweaty under some foil; they'll also benefit from a little time uncovered at the end to blast their faces with a bit of bronzer.) A higher heat for a shorter time is my preference ... although those quinces I mentioned earlier will need ages to break down — which is lucky, because the whole kitchen will smell absolutely lush for an entire afternoon.

That word, lush, is probably the best reason to roast fruits for any dishes, savoury or sweet. Think of roasted fruit as an easy sauce — something between a purée and a jus that's seasonal, interesting and as daring as dipping into the fruit bowl.

Crispy sprouty leeky lentils

4 cups (1 litre) grapeseed or
   rice bran oil, for deep-frying
400 g (14 oz) brussels sprouts,
   trimmed and quartered if larger,
   or halved if small
400 g (14 oz) tinned lentils,
   drained and rinsed
1 leek, pale part only, cut into very
   fine discs (about 2 mm/¹⁄₁₆ inch)
coriander (cilantro) and/or Vietnamese
   mint sprigs (optional), to serve
¼ cup (25 g) finely grated parmesan
zest of 1 lime

Special sauce
juice of 1 lime
1 teaspoon sriracha sauce
1 tablespoon honey
1 tablespoon fish sauce

The inspiration for these sprouts came in an unlikely fashion. I was doing a radio segment with ABC Perth, waxing lyrical about brussels sprouts, and the presenter kept getting texts about a particular restaurant in Albany, Western Australia, that was turning sprout-deniers into sprout-evangelists. Lo and behold, the chef slid into my Direct Messages and shared the recipe for their special sauce with me, which I've bulked out here into a slapdash meal with the addition of a handy tin of lentils. Looking at the combo of classic South-East Asian flavours and decidedly Italian ones, you would assume this must taste absolutely bizzarro-world, but it's exactly what encapsulates modern Australian dining — a melting pot of cuisines, ideas and ingredients that offer untold possibilities.

Heat the oil in a medium saucepan to 190°C/375°F (see Skills spotlight, page 57). Thoroughly dry the brussels sprouts, ready for deep-frying.

Meanwhile, combine the special sauce ingredients in a small saucepan and simmer for a few minutes, until thickened and syrupy. Stir half through the lentils and set the rest aside for serving.

Once the oil is hot, add one-quarter of the brussels sprouts and deep-fry for 4–5 minutes, until light brown and crispy, then drain on paper towel. Deep-fry the remaining three batches of brussels sprouts, then deep-fry the leek until golden, which will take a similar time, surprisingly. Drain on paper towel.

Toss the sprouts and leek through the saucy lentils with half the herbs. Drizzle the remaining special sauce on top, finishing with a puff of parmesan. Sprinkle the lime zest and remaining herbs on top and serve.

Bonus bits

Tips
Zest the lime before you juice it — it's far easier in that order! If yours is organic, a quick rinse beforehand will do. Most commercially grown limes are coated with a thin layer of wax to help prolong their shelf life, so it might be worth giving these a more judicious wash under hot water and use a clean tea towel to scrub off any residual wax before zesting.

I've gone very light-on with the sriracha to make the dish toddler-friendly, although it'll still have a slight kick. I've tried it all the way up to 2 tablespoons, and it still works. It's a fiery mix, but will please any hotheads in attendance.

Subs
If you don't have a lime, a lemon will do, but do keep an eye on how much juice it yields — lemons are usually around twice as juicy.

When brussels sprouts aren't in season, you could just as easily fry cauliflower or broccoli florets.

To turn this dish fully plant-based, use fysh sauce or coco-aminos, maple syrup instead of honey, and vegan parmesan.

Shortcuts
Instead of the special sauce, toss the rinsed lentils with lemon juice and olive oil, and grate parmesan and lemon zest over the sprouts.

Not keen on deep-frying? Preheat the oven to 200°C (400°F) with a baking tray inside. Toss the halved sprouts and leek in 2 tablespoons grapeseed or olive oil and roast for 10–12 minutes, or until golden and crispy.

Crispy sprouty leeky lentils Bonus bits

Skills spotlight: Going deep on deep-frying

For a while there, it seemed the easiest way to win cooking shows was to deep-fry something and add a mayo. And with good reason, if I'm honest. The reason we're naturally drawn to deep-fried foods is the opposite of what you may think: crispiness and crunch is associated with *freshness* ... like a crisp lettuce leaf, but in varying shades of brown. Team this with salt and/or sugar, which our tastebuds register as flavour and energy, and you can see why people can get seriously hooked on the rhythm of the crunch.

Deep-frying's magic lies in its ability to lock in a crispy exterior, creating a moist heat inside that shell, essentially steaming the object's innards, rendering them soft and creamy. Cooks can harness that alluring wizardry to conjure deliciousness out of veg such as the brussels sprouts here, and the eggplant in the kharcho recipe on page 181. Both of these vegies are notoriously maligned, mostly for textural reasons — mushy overboiled sprouts and squeaky undercooked eggplants will put anyone off.

If you're worried about how 'fatty' deep-frying can be, remember that it's quicker to deep-fry than shallow-fry, which means the ingredient spends less time in said fat and absorbs less of it, especially if you scoop the fried goodies directly from deep-fryer to drainage device. I like to have a plate lined with a few sheets of paper towel to soak up the excess oil, while others prefer a rack over a tray; horses for courses, I say. Either way, don't overcrowd the draining station, lest everything starts to sweat and go soggy.

The best frying oil has a high smoke point — which literally means it takes more heat to make it smoke — and can be purchased by the litre. My favourite is grapeseed oil, but others back rice bran or sunflower oil. Some swear by deep-frying with olive oil, which is fine for Italian dishes like fritto misto, but the distinctive flavour isn't ideal for lighter dishes like tempura (page 213).

The best time to season something deep-fried is when it just comes out of the fryer, as it's most receptive to absorbing the salt and other flavourings most evenly.

If you're new to deep-frying, it helps to have a cooking thermometer handy, and to think of the temperature as quite similar to baking. 180°C (350°F) is a standard temperature at which to fry most batters to golden (like the fried green falafels on page 208). If you're frying ingredients where you'd prefer to colour them more quickly (like the sprouts here and the rice crisps on page 81), 190°C (375°F) or even 200°C (400°F) is a better bet.

If you don't have a thermometer, the common technique is to drop in a cube of bread and watch as it turns brown — 15 seconds is the gold standard for 180°C (350°F). I just wait until I *think* the oil is ready, and then drop in a single scrap of whatever I'm frying as a tester. If the temperature's too low, you'll know pretty quickly, because it'll sink to the bottom and turn soggy. Pull it out right away and wait another minute or so for the oil to heat up before trying again. (If you pop a clean wooden chopstick into the oil and bubbles rise up the side of the chopstick, your oil is hot enough to fry.)

Aside from ensuring your oil is hot enough, and that you have a draining station established, the most important rule is to ensure that whatever you're immersing into the oil is as dry as possible. Any moisture will cause the oil to spit, which is dramatic ... and DANGEROUS! Using a splatter guard is a good idea, even if you've spun the bejeebus out of watery items like brassicas.

Actually, I should bold this next bit. **If you don't have a splatter guard, stand at a safe distance and use long-handled tongs or a spider skimmer (see Gadget spotlight, page 23) to fish things out.** Do skim out any stragglers too, as they'll continue to cook and begin to impart your oil (and subsequent batches) with an increasingly burnt flavour.

Speaking of 'infused' oils, if you're regularly frying strongly flavoured ingredients such as fish or falafels, it might be an idea to have several clearly labelled frying oils going at once. You can reuse frying oils several times, as long as you pour them through a fine strainer before decanting. **Just make sure you wait until the oil has completely cooled before you do so.** I've made that mistake once, eagerly decanting my oil back into its glass bottle while it was still warm. Dear reader, I swiftly heard a whistle, an otherworldly rattle of warning. Thankfully it didn't explode, but it full well could have, and then you and I might not have been having this conversation!

If your oil has turned dark after several uses and you're ready to discard it, wait until it has cooled, then pour it into a disposable container and then into the bin, rather than straight into the bin or down the sink.

One-pan golden angel hair pasta

4 tablespoons olive oil,
   plus extra for dressing
100 g (3½ oz) butter
1 bunch of basil, leaves picked,
   stems finely chopped
4–5 garlic cloves, roughly chopped
500 g (1 lb 2 oz) cherry tomatoes
a pinch of saffron threads
   (see Ingredient spotlight, page 61)
a pinch of sugar
zest and juice of 1 lemon
5 cups (1.25 litres) chicken stock,
   vegetable stock and/or water
500 g (1 lb 2 oz) dried angel hair
   egg pasta (see Subs, page 61)
1 cup (100 g) finely grated parmesan
2 balls of burrata, torn
   (see Subs, page 61)
lemon cheeks, to serve

Imagine capturing the glowing golden hour of a summer's afternoon into a pan, and still having enough time to enjoy it while the pasta cooks. One-pot-pasta can be a little hit and miss — some people find the pasta over-cooking or under-cooking, others are put off by the starchiness, but I like to think of this as a risotto–paella–pasta situation, where the starch should be embraced, mitigated with cheesiness and acid. This makes an extremely generous amount for a lazy midweek dinner party, and is delicious cold for 'Ron (see page 300). But if you'd prefer to make a smaller amount, just halve the ingredients.

Heat the olive oil and butter in a heavy-based saucepan that's wide enough to fit the pasta lengths whole (see Tip, page 61). Add the basil stems and garlic and sauté for 3–4 minutes, or until the garlic is fragrant and turning golden.

Add the cherry tomatoes and sauté for 4–5 minutes, or until the tomatoes start to blister and burst.

Meanwhile, using a mortar and pestle, grind the saffron threads with the sugar to a rough bright powder. Add the lemon juice and allow the saffron to bloom (see Ingredient spotlight, page 61).

Pour your stock combo into a jug and give it a taste. Some shop-bought stocks can be quite salty, so keep this in mind before adding any further seasoning.

Deglaze the pan with the saffron lemon juice, by splashing it in and scraping the bottom of the pan with a wooden spoon or spatula. Pour in the stock and bring everything to the boil.

Add the angel hair pasta, using tongs to submerge the pasta as soon as it starts to soften, then pop on the lid and cook for 3–4 minutes, or until the pasta is *al dente* and the liquid has been (mostly!) absorbed. Stir in the parmesan and lemon zest. Season with salt and black pepper to taste.

Turn the heat off, plonk in the burrata and cover with the lid again for another 3–4 minutes while you set the table and get everyone organised.

Serve in the pan at the table, cascaded with basil, swirling into bowls with burrata blobs on top and lemon cheeks on the side.

Grinding saffron with sugar or salt helps unlock its flavour

A 28 cm (11 inch) casserole dish will fit standard-length spaghetti

The liquid will keep absorbing, even when the heat's off

Use the kinds of tomatoes you'll find growing in backyards and at greengrocers in summer

THE JOY OF BETTER COOKING

One-pan pasta Bonus bits

Tips

If you don't have a wide enough pan, hold the pasta with both hands, then twist it to break in two before adding. (This recipe might just sway you into buying a bigger pan!?)

Subs

For a gluten-free version, you can use gluten-free pasta. Sadly, it doesn't behave the same way in the pan, so it's better to cook the pasta separately, halve your stock allowance and toss the cooked pasta through the sauce at the end.

If burrata is eluding you, tear in some pieces of buffalo mozzarella or blob in some ricotta if you've any handy.

Extra extras

You can totally add frozen corn, or even peas, to this pasta for bonus veg. Just pour some boiling water over half a cup of them while the garlic's sautéing, and wait until they thaw before adding once the pasta's done.

If you've got any zucchini (courgette) or golden squash about, you could add these in, thinly sliced, with the burrata. If you're lucky enough to find yourself in the possession of some baby zucchini (courgetti), which often come attached to zucchini flowers, thinly slice them into discs or strips as per the less baby version, then tear the petals off the central stalk into individual long strips. Once the pan is off the heat, stir the petal strips through the pasta to warm through.

Got some spare CP butter from page 96? Smoosh this through instead of the burrata — this is, after all, one step away from risotto!

Ingredient spotlight: Saffron

There was a point in culinary history where saffron cost more per gram weight than gold, and with good reason: gold can be gaudy; saffron is always in vogue. If I had to explain what it brings to a recipe, beyond the exotic wispy stamen strands that adorn dishes along the spice trail, I'd say it adds a grounding element — an earthiness and aroma with the slightest floral note.

There is no substitute for the proper stuff, which has an even colour in a deep red or burnt orange, so if the saffron threads you're holding in your hands at the shops seem too cheap to be true, they probably aren't real. Be particularly judicious when buying powdered saffron, which you can easily make at home by grinding real stamens with a pinch of sugar for friction, to be added to dishes such as this one, tahdig (Persian rice) and sweets like the honey cake on page 278.

To unlock its subtle complexity, saffron either needs to be 'bloomed' or ground. To 'bloom' saffron, steep it in a few tablespoons of warm water (just below boiling point) for 10–15 minutes, then add the marigold-yellow liquid to your dish as it cooks, saving some of the stamens to stir through just before serving.

In brothy dishes like the sailors' sauce mussels on page 100, saffron would be a sublime addition, and it won't require any bloom time. Just add it fairly early in the cooking process so it has long enough to steep and reveal itself.

If you've read down to here and are still considering whether you should pop out to the shops and pick up some saffron, first make your chosen dish without it, then make it with saffron the next time and compare the pair! Both are good — but the saffron-y one just has that X-factor.

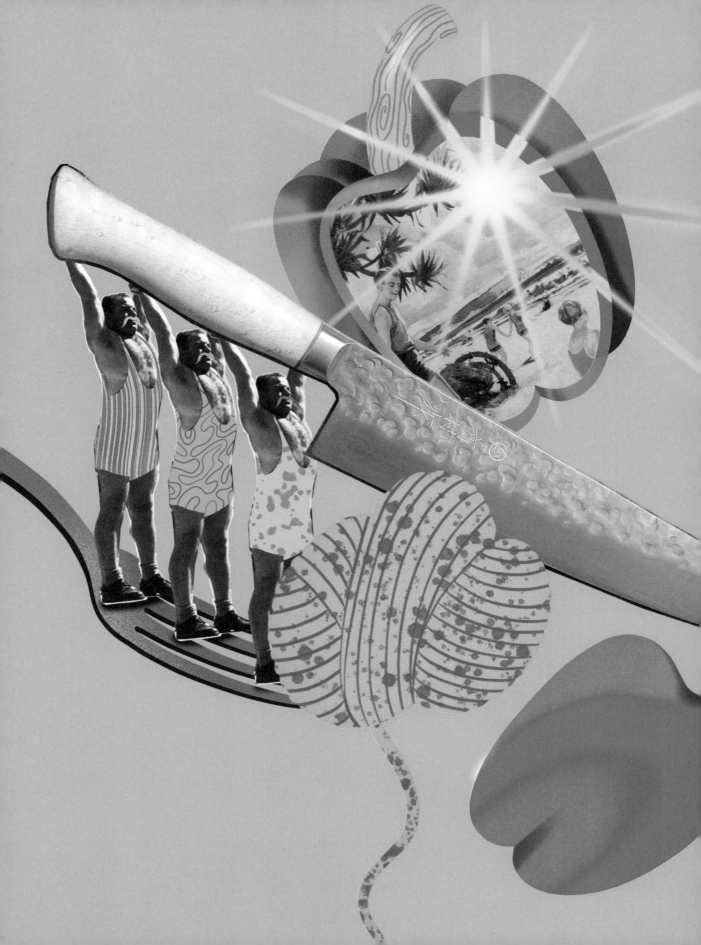

On autopilot

Great go-tos for weeknights on the fly

Dial up the flavour

Midweek meals are all about mind over matter. What matters is getting dinner on the table using as little mind-power and as few pots and pans as possible. Mostly, this is down to time management and muscle memory. What's the least energy-intensive pathway to dinner on the table, happy tummies and minimal clean-up?

Managing your time means not just identifying which dishes don't require too much in the way of fussing about or those that have low-slow cook times that only make themselves known halfway down the recipe (beware — read all the way down!), but also in thinking like a chef.

How *do* chefs manage to get so many plates out within minutes of an order being dropped? By forward planning and prepping ahead, or as the French would say, *mise en place*. Like an artist arranging their palette with paints and priming their canvas, all the work is done well before you lift the brush. In the home kitchen, that means lists on the fridge, shopping smart, batch cooking, meal-prep days and a pantry stocked with flavour shortcuts and staples.

Sometimes I like to stagger my dinner prep throughout the day, so when dinnertime rolls around there's little to do beyond heat, assemble, eat. That works for us because I'm loafing around the house, but if you're not working from home, investing in a slow-cooker or pressure cooker that takes the load off a little will make a big difference.

Some dishes actually taste *better* the next day. Soup, for example, only gets more flavoursome with time, and it's something we almost always have a big pot of in the fridge. Having plenty of veg means if you're home late with a hungry brood, it's easy to *zhuzh* together a glowing one-tray somethin' (page 68), or grate your veg box surprises into schi (page 66). Even if they're after an afternoon snack, a little bowl of soup will tide them over. At some stage in the day, that pot of soup comes in handy — whether it's magicked into a starter before the main event, or into a lighter option on days when lunch takes centre stage.

I harp on about 'starting with the veg', but midweek meals are where this is particularly useful — let the veg dictate what else goes with it. Roast a big tray of them, then distribute among leaves and shredded bits or crumbled cheese in a salad, toss through cooked pasta, or blitz into the aforementioned soup. Don't be afraid to use frozen veg, either. These used to get a bad rap, but they're actually a super simple and incredibly convenient way of slipping more colour, flavour and nutrition into all kinds of dishes. (To blanch and freeze your own vegies, check out the freezer section on pages 300–301.)

Jar sauce is not a dirty word in our household, either, it just depends on what's in the jar. Check the ingredients on the label, and if they're similar to what you'd make, and mean you're more likely to whip up dinner at home than phoning a friend (i.e. a home delivery service), then go for it! I've always got jars of curry paste ready to go for those times when I'm at my wit's end, yet the show — and dinner! — must go on.

Creating and sticking to good habits takes time, and the easier you can make it for yourself, the more wondrous your dinners will become … eventually. Most households have an average of 10 go-to meals on rotation, so if you can set yourself the task of acquiring at least one a month, then by the end of the year, you'll be

Grab great preserves, pickles and pastes as an express ticket to flavour-town.

operating these on autopilot. *Then* you can add to this bank the year after — or not … because there's always the weekend to get creative.

For now, you can simply marvel at what's just turned up on the table and wonder how it got there, because WHOOMPH … there it is!

Schi's all that

¼ cup (60 ml) olive oil

50 g (1½ oz) butter

2 onions, halved and finely sliced

4 garlic cloves, finely sliced

1 fennel bulb, trimmed,
    cut in half and thinly sliced

1 large carrot, shredded
    or cut into matchsticks

1 turnip or swede,
    peeled and cut into matchsticks

2–3 waxy potatoes, such as Dutch
    cream or nicola, (about 300 g/10½ oz),
    peeled and cut into 1 cm (½ inch) dice

2 bay leaves

½ cup (125 ml) dill pickle juice,
    plus 4 dill pickles, finely sliced

4 cups (1 litre) home-made
    chicken stock (page 174)

¼ white cabbage (or several wombok),
    finely sliced (about 4 cups)

1 cup (150 g) sauerkraut

1 bunch of dill, chopped, fronds reserved

200 g (7 oz) sour cream

Schi (pronounced 'she'!) is as canonical in our household as borsch, and about as omnipresent too. Think of schi as a white borsch, where the beetroot has been subbed out for nubby root veg like swede or turnip, and the flavour jacked up with kraut or pickle brine. It's like those scenes in movies such as *She's All That* or *My Fair Lady*, where with some coaxing, the roughness is buffed out of our unlikely hero and she emerges as a sparkling jewel ... or in this case, a gloriously steaming bowl. A savoury, sour, soul-renovation of a soup.

Heat a large heavy-based saucepan over medium heat. Add the olive oil and butter and sauté the onion, garlic, fennel and carrot over low heat for 10–15 minutes, without colouring the vegies, but cooking them until jammy.

Add the turnip, potato and bay leaves and sauté for another 5 minutes.

Deglaze the pan with the pickle juice. Pour in the stock, plus 1 cup (250 ml) water (or more if you'd like a more liquidy soup). Bring to the boil, then add the cabbage and the sauerkraut and cook at a simmer for 20–30 minutes, until the potato is fork-tender.

When ready to serve, throw in the sliced dill pickles, and the dill, keeping some of both to garnish the bowls once served, adding a generous dollop of sour cream to finish each bowl.

Bonus bits

Subs

If you're low on pickle brine, other acidy stuff — from apple cider vinegar to lemon juice to sauerkraut juice — will do. Even kimchi juice hits the spot, if you like a bit of heat.

You can totally keep this soup plant-based by subbing chicken stock out for vegie stock, and dolloping on a plant-based sour cream to finish.

Shortcuts

You can absolutely grate the carrot, turnip or swede using a food processor rather than mucking about with matchsticking. I like to take my time as a meditation, but midweek, using this 'schort' cut, schi can be on the table quick-smart.

Waste knot

Keep all the vegetable trimmings and peels (except the cabbage scraps) in a bag in the freezer, ready to make more stock for your next schi.

THE JOY OF BETTER COOKING

Orange veg one-tray soup

/ **Serves 4–6, plus generous leftovers**

1 kg (2 lb 4 oz) jap pumpkin,
   cut into wedges
½ butternut pumpkin (squash),
   halved, seeds removed
2 medium carrots, unpeeled
1 sweet potato, unpeeled, halved
1 swede, halved
1 onion, skin on, halved
4 garlic cloves, skin on
2 tablespoons olive oil
1 teaspoon sea salt
6 cups (1.5 litres) vegetable stock or water
1 good-quality stock cube
½ teaspoon ground white pepper
a rasp of nutmeg
juice of 1 orange
1 thumb-sized knob fresh ginger,
   peeled and finely grated

Accent #1
20 fresh curry leaves, fried with
   1 teaspoon brown mustard seeds,
   OR 40 dried curry leaves, gently
   warmed in 1 cup (250 ml) olive oil
   and left to infuse for 5 minutes
coconut cream

Accent #2
8–10 lime leaves, finely sliced
coconut cream
lime juice
Thai basil

Accent #3
pomegranate molasses
fresh pomegranate seeds
ground sumac
yoghurt

Accent #4
single (pure) cream
chopped chives

Accent #5
miso paste
yoghurt
rice seasoning (see page 70)

We've all been there. You see someone across the room and think, 'They look interesting — just my cup of tea', and then when you finally work up the courage to chat to them, it's like you've known each other forever. It's all so comfortable, and to top it all off, they also have an *accent!?* (*eyebrow waggle*). This is that, in a soup. Lovely sweet, creamy flavours, like a hug in a mug, plus a bonus accent of garnish to take the ménage to the next level (*emphatic eyebrow waggle*). And did I mention easy? Sit back my friend, because no heavy-duty chopping is required. Just pile in the veg for a warm, snug sit in the oven while you put the kettle on and slip into something a little more comfortable.

Preheat the oven to 180°C (350°F).

Arrange the pumpkins, carrots, sweet potato and swede on a baking tray lined with baking paper. Nestle in the onion halves and garlic cloves. Drizzle the olive oil over, sprinkle with the salt and toss to coat. Roast for 45 minutes, or until all the vegies are extremely relaxed and very susceptible to forking. Remove from the oven.

Once cooled, take the skin off the pumpkins and scoop out the flesh from the sweet potato and swede. Slip the skin off the onion, and pop the lush softened garlic cloves out of their skins with a squeeze. Be sure to scrape all the syrupy goodness from the bottom of the pan, too; this is vegie schmaltz (see Ingredient Spotlight, page 171).

Bring the stock or water to the boil and dissolve the stock cube in it.

Combine and blitz the roasted veg and stock together until super smooth, using a stick blender (see Gadget spotlight, page 151), or in batches in a blender.

Season to taste with salt, white pepper and nutmeg. Add the orange juice and stir the ginger through to give it some fresh bite.

Serve with your chosen accent. This one-tray soup is infinitely versatile, so feel free to riff to your heart's content.

THE JOY OF BETTER COOKING

Orange veg one-tray soup

You have carte blanche to roast any colour-coordinated veg combos and blitz to a soup. Tomatoes, capsicums, red onion. All sorts of greens and herbs. Let go, get a little loose.

Subs

If you've scanned the ingredients list and have most of the orange bits and bobs, but maybe only pumpkin or butternut squash, less carrots, or a turnip instead of a swede, worry not! This soup is accent-friendly, and the veg easily substituted. Just take a squiz at the photo of the tray and try to fill yours up with about the same amount of whatever veg you do have.

For a FODMAP-friendly option, sub out the onion and garlic for a teaspoon of asafoetida — a spice which mimics the flavour of alliums, but would really prefer not to be sniffed pre-cooking, thank you very much.

Waste knot

Whatever bits of skin you slip off the roasted veg can be popped into a freezer bag for the next time you make stock. Flavour! Colour! Waste Warrior!

Worth it

I've had several friends with romantic notions of writing down their bubba's chicken soup recipes, only to discover that the 'secret ingredient' isn't love: it's stock cubes. These canary-yellow cubes and powders, be they Massel, Vegeta or similar, are a brilliant way to add flavour and that special something to all sorts of dishes. Many of them are also accidentally vegan, even if they're called 'chicken flavour', so it's worth checking the ingredients on the label.

Keep your pantry stocked with stock, and even if a soup or braise recipe doesn't call for a cube, it couldn't hurt to pop one in. But be sure to taste your dish after adding the cube, as it will invariably mean you'll need to add less salt. This is especially true if you're using a shop-bought liquid stock, as these are usually jacked up with sodium, so be extra diligent.

To MYO stock, see the pressure cooker recipe on page 174.

Ingredient spotlight: Rice seasoning

Rice seasoning is more of a sprinkle — like a Japanese dukkah, full of seeds and spices. Asian grocers sell different varieties, from nori-rich savoury–sweet furikake, to spicy shichimi togarashi ('seven peppers' or 'seven spices'). It's handy as a salad sprinkle, to quickly *zhuzh* up steamed rice, and even to shake over tempura (see the caulini recipe on page 213). Once opened, I store my jar of rice seasoning in the fridge door for freshness.

My absolutely favourite way to use rice seasoning is sprinkled over deep-fried rice crisps (page 81) for an easy, delicious snack. It's something I'll whip up a batch of whenever I deep-fry anything and the oil's still hot.

That's a spiky meatball tomato soup

2 tablespoons olive oil

1 red onion, diced

1 red capsicum (pepper), diced

4 garlic cloves, roughly chopped

½ cup (125 ml) white wine

½ teaspoon sweet or smoked paprika
(whatever's in your pantry)

2 tablespoons tomato paste
(concentrated purée)

400 g (14 oz) tinned good-quality
whole peeled or chopped tomatoes
(see Ingredient spotlight, page 75)

2 cups (500 ml) chicken or vegetable
stock (no added salt, see Tips, page 75)

1 teaspoon sugar (any kind will do;
just add less if the crystals are finer)

1 bouquet garni, made with basil stalks,
a stem of dried Greek oregano and
2 bay leaves

½ teaspoon freshly cracked black pepper

Meatballs (makes about 35)

500 g (1 lb 2 oz) pork and fennel sausages
(see Subs, page 75)

½ cup (50 g) finely grated parmesan

½ cup (80 g) pine nuts (see Subs, page 75)

¼ cup (40 g) currants

¼ cup (50 g) long-grain white rice

¼ cup chopped parsley

To serve

finely grated parmesan

thinly sliced basil, to garnish

a drizzle of the very best olive oil

Many an Aussie kid who grew up in the 1970s and 1980s scored these meatballs cooked in tinned tomato soup, based on an old Dutch staple, on the regular. The meatballs were made to look like spiky little creatures with the addition of long-grain rice and, once added to the soup, they'd cook and flavour the broth, springing and puffing like magical hedgehogs — or echidnas, to keep the Australiana theme going. This tomato soup isn't quite out of a tin, but still uses the best processed tomatoes you can find, and the meatballs are made with store-bought sausages, spiked with extra fun bits like currants and pine nuts, making them practically a *polpette*. It's a great lesson in letting other people do the hard work for you flavour-wise, so it's still a super simple soup to prepare, and the taste is just *bonza* ('better than good' in Aussie slang) ... or *belissima* if you're that way inclined.

In a large heavy-based saucepan, heat the olive oil and sauté the onion, capsicum and garlic for a minute or two until the mixture starts to sizzle. Pop on the lid and leave to sweat over medium–low heat, stirring occasionally, for 5–8 minutes, until the onion has softened.

Pour the wine into the pan, scraping all the yummy flavoursome bits of caramelisation off the bottom to deglaze the pan. Stir in the paprika and tomato paste and sauté for another 2 minutes.

Add the tinned tomatoes, then pour some fresh water into the tin, slosh it around to clean out the dregs and add that to the pan, too, along with another tin's worth of water. Stir in the stock, sugar and another 4 cups (1 litre) water. Drop in the bouquet garni and bring to the boil, skimming off any froth that rises to the surface.

At this point, fish out the bouquet garni. Get your stick blender out (see Gadget spotlight, page 151) and give the soup a bit of a *zhuzh*. You can leave a few chunks in, or purée until smooth.

Meanwhile, make a start on the meatballs. Have a little bowl of water nearby. Slip the sausage meat out of the casings into a bowl, and combine with the remaining meatball ingredients. Wet your palms before shaping the mixture into balls the size of walnuts; they'll expand to golf-ball size as they cook. Some sausages can be fairly salty, so check the seasoning of one of the meatballs by poaching it in the soup for 5 minutes, then taste and add extra salt only if needed.

Pop all the meatballs into the soup and simmer for 35–40 minutes, or until the echidnas emerge out of their burrows and the oil rises to the top, adding more stock or water if needed.

Serve garnished with a grating of parmesan, some thinly sliced basil and a drizzle of your best olive oil.

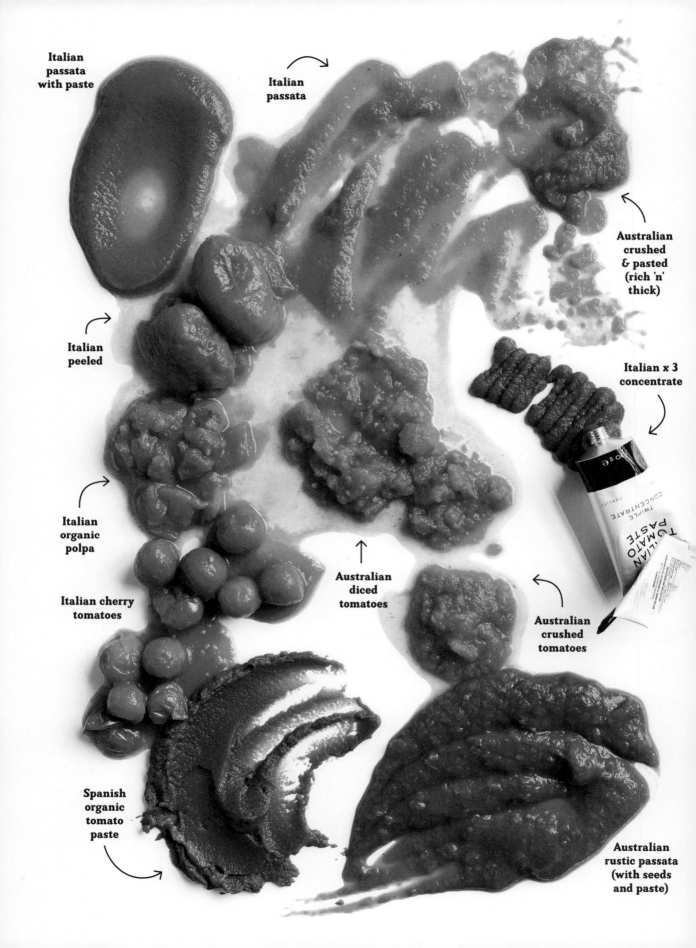

Italian passata with paste

Italian passata

Australian crushed & pasted (rich 'n' thick)

Italian peeled

Italian x 3 concentrate

Italian organic polpa

Italian cherry tomatoes

Australian diced tomatoes

Australian crushed tomatoes

Spanish organic tomato paste

Australian rustic passata (with seeds and paste)

Spiky meatball soup Bonus bits

Tips

Don't even think about adding salt to the soup — as the meatballs cook, they will naturally season the broth, in the same way that adding mussels to a bland broth brings brininess almost instantly. (There's a recipe for mussels on page 100, BTW).

Subs

You can absolutely make this with a bottle of tomato passata (puréed tomatoes) instead of tinned tomatoes. Just slosh less water in the bottom to extract the last dregs, as it'll already have a higher liquid-to-tomato ratio.

Go nut-free by replacing the pine nuts with another tablespoon of rice.

Turn this dish fully plant-based by making the meatballs out of barley. Nutritionist and author Dorota Trupp has a great recipe for these online, where the barley is ground and simmered in vegie stock, then mixed with onion and garlic and baked in the oven to set.

Double duty

The soup can be cooked right down to a sugo; after blending, keep cooking until it has reduced by half, and you'll have a rich sauce that you can toss through some cooked spaghetti with the meatballs, or pop inside a toasted Turkish pide with extra parmesan for a meatball sub.

Worth it

Herbaceous little bundles of bouquet garni can really take your dish next-level. They can vary in content, but they involve herbs (mostly dried) that have either been tied off in a bunch like a bouquet, or packed into some form of pouch for steeping. You can make up your own bouquet depending on what herbs you have. Thyme, parsley stalks and bay leaves are the traditional French Provençal version, but you can sub in herbs like rosemary or tarragon, tied off with twine or a heatproof rubber band. Because the herbs are bound or bundled, they can be easily lifted out at the end, to keep simple soups like this one free of bobbing bits of green stuff.

You can store pre-prepped bouquets in the freezer for expediency, or buy pre-prepared little pouches of the stuff in muslin (cheesecloth), which behave like little savoury teabags in the pot.

Ingredient spotlight: Tomatoes

Cooking with tomatoes — whether fresh, tinned, passed into passata or concentrated into paste — is one of the easiest ways to build body and add savoury-sweetness to dishes. No wonder they form the basis of so very many different meals across cuisines of the world.

These various tomato concentrations are a bit like the Golden Girls: it's great to meet just one, but when they all get together, they say 'Thank you for being a friend' to your tastebuds. If a recipe calls for just one form of tomato, feel free to layer in a few others regardless, or at least sub in and out depending on what you have. I've listed them above in ascending order of concentration (and hence increasing flavour intensity), so if a sauce is feeling a bit light-on, a teaspoon of tomato paste (concentrated purée) helps build this up, but also speeds up the cooking time, as you won't need to wait for lots of liquid to boil down.

Speaking of liquid, don't forget to give the insides of the tomato preservation vessel — whether jar or tin — a good glug with water or stock, to lift off any stubborn bits of produce that would otherwise end up down the sink or in the recycling bin. (Note: if you don't wash out these containers, they might be deemed 'contaminated' and unrecyclable — another reason to get glugging!) Just enough of a splash to slosh it all around will do, unless of course the recipe asks you for extra water like this one, where you can just use the tin as your measuring vessel pre-slosh.

If you look closely at the photo opposite of the various tomato textures, you'll notice that some are leaching out liquid, which is actually a good thing. It tells you they haven't been set with any emulsifiers or thickeners. On the ingredient label, less is always more; I'm especially on the lookout for salt and sweeteners, as I'd much rather add these to my own taste. On that, even if a recipe doesn't include sugar in a tomato-based sauce, I'll still add a pinch — it tricks your palate into thinking that the tomatoes are riper and more robust. I'll even do this with fresh tomato salads if the tomatoes are underwhelming.

Taco rice

Serves 4

1½ cups (350 g) sushi rice
2 teaspoons rice vinegar
2 teaspoons caster (superfine) sugar
2 tablespoons olive oil
500 g (1 lb 2 oz) minced
    (ground) beef
5–6 spring onions (scallions), white and
    green bits finely sliced separately
4 tomatoes, diced
4 coriander (cilantro) sprigs,
    roughly chopped
1 cup (100 g) shredded cheddar
100 g (3½ oz) corn chips (a good handful)
½ iceberg lettuce, sliced into thin wedges
lime wedges, to serve

Taco seasoning (makes enough
for a double batch — one for now,
one for 'Ron; see page 300)
2 teaspoons mild–medium
    chilli powder
4 teaspoons salt flakes (crush these a little
    between your fingers when adding)
4 teaspoons ground cumin
4 teaspoons cornflour (cornstarch)
2 teaspoons dried oregano
2 teaspoons ground coriander
2 teaspoons ground paprika
    (hot or sweet — whatever you've got)
2 teaspoons garlic powder
2 teaspoons onion powder
1 teaspoon caster (superfine) sugar

I was gifted this recipe by my mate chai mogul Johnny Aloha, who, as an army brat born in Hawaii, spent part of his childhood in Okinawa. Aptly, it was the American military bases set up in Japan after World War II that led both John's dad (an army doctor) and Taco Rice (a global sensation) to find their way there in the first place. The dish was originally created to feed hungry marines by an entrepreneurial Okinawan named Gibo, who founded the first King Tacos in Kin in the mid-1980s. He combined surplus army-rationed taco seasoning with minced beef and cut out the taco middle man. I love how the soft sushi rice is the perfect sponge for the spicy mix on top. The history of the dish's creation speaks to the way food borrows, adapts, enhances; a living language.

Pop the rice in a fine-meshed sieve and wash under cold running water until the water runs clear. Follow the packet instructions to cook the rice, either by absorption, or in a rice cooker (see Gadget spotlight, opposite). Meanwhile, combine the vinegar and sugar in a small bowl as your sushi seasoning.

For the taco seasoning, toss all the ingredients in a jar with a lid. Seal tightly and shake to combine. The spice mix will store well for a month in a cool, dark place (although you could easily get 6 months out of it, at a pinch).

Heat a large frying pan until you can feel the warmth radiating when you hold your palm at a sensible distance. Splash in the olive oil. While the beef is still in its container, squash it between your fingers to mash up any squiggles, then place as a whole piece into the pan. Cook over high heat for 5–7 minutes, or until caramelised underneath. Flip it over and cook for a further 2 minutes, then break it up with a wooden spoon. Sprinkle in the white spring onion bits, half the taco seasoning and ½ cup (125 ml) water and stir to combine. Simmer for another 3–5 minutes, until the water evaporates and the sauce thickens.

Toss the tomatoes, green spring onion bits and coriander together in a bowl to make a salsa.

Once the rice is cooked, transfer to a serving platter. Drizzle the vinegar seasoning over and stir to combine, using a wooden spoon or rubber spatula (not metal, as it is too rough on the rice). Top with the beef, then the cheese, then crush the corn chips on top. Arrange the tomato salsa on one side, and the lettuce wedges all about. Serve with lime wedges.

Bonus bits

Tips

For extra crunchy, crisp lettuce, pop it into a salad spinner full of cold water while you prepare the rest of the recipe. Drain and spin just before assembly begins.

If, upon tasting the simmered beef, you would prefer to mellow out the heat, add a few dollops of plain yoghurt to serve. Extremely inauthentic, but it works.

Shortcuts

I've offered you a seasoning mix to make up as a gift to your future self, to be whipped out the next time you want to MYO version from scratch, but you could *easily* just pick up a taco seasoning sachet from the shops, along with a jar of salsa. Both of these were very much a part of the original version — so you could argue that the shortie version is actually more authentic.

Subs

You can make this vego by swapping the beef out for beans and imbuing them with a chilli non-carne flavour. Add some tinned kidney beans to your sweated spring onion mixture, stir the taco spices through and allow everything to sizzle before serving as per the recipe.

If you don't have a mild chilli powder handy, use ½ teaspoon cayenne pepper instead. That is, unless yours is a chilli-loving household, in which case, go big!

Waste knot

You are extremely welcome to slice up the entire iceberg lettuce for this dish and snack on any leftovers as you might corn chips — it's so crunchy! You may also like to use the other half of your iceberg for a leafy salad (page 26).

Worth it

I know I'm asking a lot from you to commit to buying all these spices for the taco seasoning, but they're all used heaps throughout this book. Having a jar of garlic powder is, as far as I'm concerned, as useful on the table as salt and pepper — if something savoury tastes like it could 'use something', garlic powder will totally do it.

Gadget spotlight: Rice cooker

I'm a born-again rice cooker aficionado, as I came to it quite late and was very much of the 'what can that do that a pan with a lid can't?' camp. The answer, my friend, is FLUFFY RICE! If you ever wonder why your rice never gets as satisfactorily separated and lush like takeaway rice — let alone restaurant rice — then you need to get yourself a rice cooker. They're surprisingly inexpensive, especially if you choose a multi-cooker that also slow-cooks; some even air-fry!

Rice cookers create an optimal air-locked environment to ensure that each and every rice granule gets cooked to its full floof potential. I use mine way more than I expected, and love experimenting with what I add into its bowl — from pandan leaves and crispy fried shallots for jasmine rice, to curry powder and frozen veg for an easy basmati 'pilaf'.

Taco rice
Page 76

Broad bean, asparagus & soba noodle salad

500 g (1 lb 2 oz) broad beans
    (see Subs, page 82), podded
1 head of broccoli, chopped into small
    florets, stalk peeled and chopped
    into 8 mm (⅜ inch) discs
1 bunch of asparagus (see Subs, page 82),
    cut into 2 cm (¾ inch) lengths
3 bundles of buckwheat soba noodles
    (270 g/9½ oz)
100 g (3½ oz) baby English spinach
    leaves, washed and dried

Tahini ginger miso dressing

2 tablespoons tamari or soy sauce
2 tablespoons rice wine vinegar
2 tablespoons sesame oil
1 tablespoon tahini or smooth
    peanut butter
1 tablespoon honey or soft brown sugar
1 tablespoon rice seasoning (shichimi
    togarashi or furikake; see Ingredient
    spotlight, page 70)
2 teaspoons miso paste
½ teaspoon wasabi paste
a good pinch of freshly ground
    black pepper
1 cm (½ inch) knob fresh ginger,
    peeled and finely grated
1 garlic clove, peeled and finely grated

Rice crisps (optional)

4 cups (1 litre) frying oil (I like grapeseed)
6 rice paper rounds
rice seasoning, for sprinkling

To serve

1 ripe, creamy avocado,
    peeled and cut into cubes
¼ bunch of coriander (cilantro),
    washed and roughly chopped
2 spring onions (scallions), thinly sliced
rice seasoning, for sprinkling (optional)

Cold noodles, crispy rice paper wrappers – toss these textures on their heads with a bit of kitchen science. Shocking the noodles in boiling water keeps their texture toit, not slimy, while frying the rice paper wrappers sizzles the starch, curling and crisping them into puffy crackers. I usually fry a batch of these whenever I deep-fry, because they make such an easy accompaniment… that's if they ever make it to the table. The great thing about both these ingredients is that once you've bought a pack, they can sit in your pantry forever.

Bring a large saucepan of well-salted water to the boil.

Add the broad beans and blanch until bright green and soft: 2–3 minutes if they're small, 3–4 minutes if larger. Scoop them out and refresh under a cold tap until cool enough to touch. Double-pod the broad beans into a bowl by splitting the skin with your fingernail and popping out the bright green flesh.

Bring the water back to the boil and blanch the broccoli for 3–4 minutes, until vibrant green. Scoop out, refresh under a cold tap, add to the broad beans and set aside. Bring the water back to the boil and blanch the asparagus for 2–3 minutes, until bright green. Scoop out and set this aside with the broccoli.

Bring the blanching water to the boil again. Add the buckwheat noodles, wait until they soften enough to submerge, then cook for 1 minute less than suggested by the packet instructions. Drain the noodles and dunk into iced water to stop them cooking.

Combine the dressing ingredients in a medium-sized bowl. Plonk the noodles into the dressing and stir to coat. These can be further refrigerated if you want them cold-cold, but I quite like them at room temperature.

If you are making the rice crisps, heat the frying oil to 200°C (400°F) in a medium-sized pan; this should take around 5 minutes on medium–low heat. The oil should be shimmering, and if you drop a little of the paper into the oil, it should frizz up instantly. Meanwhile, stack three rice paper sheets together, cut them in half, then in half again, and then cut each one in half again, until you have what look like pizza slices of rice paper. Briefly deep-fry in batches of five or six, fishing them out with tongs or a slotted spoon once they puff up and turn white, which will happen almost instantly. Drain on paper towel and sprinkle liberally with rice seasoning. These are best eaten right away, as they start to soften if left out. (If the thought of deep-frying the rice crisps is overwhelming, try microwaving them. Cut the rice paper rounds into triangles, place six of them on a plate and microwave for 1–1½ minutes, until crisp.)

When ready to serve, add the blanched veg and baby spinach leaves to the dressed noodles, tossing everything together until well coated. Taste for seasoning — an extra splash of soy is worth it if the salad needs a salty kick.

Scatter the avocado, coriander and spring onion on top and sprinkle with extra rice seasoning. Serve with the rice crisps on the side, if using.

Broad bean salad Bonus bits

Subs

Use green beans when broad beans aren't in season; blanch for 4–5 minutes. Instead of asparagus, use broccolini cut into 2 cm (¾ inch) lengths and blanched for 2–3 minutes.

Recipe riffs

Give the salad a different spin by dressing the noodles and veg in a simple yoghurt and lemon dressing instead, and maybe a bit of tahini.

Turn this brothy! Cook the noodles in water and make a miso broth to slosh the noodles into, or pour a cupful of bone broth into the base of the bowls instead.

For extra protein, add fried slices of marinated tempeh.

Wet-fry some mushrooms (page 113) and toss through.

Flake smoked trout through with a squeeze of lemon.

Waste knot

You don't need to double-pod or even single-pod young broad beans. Just cut them on the bias and blanch a little longer.

DO use the broccoli stalks. They're actually my favourite bit. Just peel away the woody outer layer to reveal the sweet brassica heart within.

Skills spotlight: Cooking noodles & pasta

Who knew 'boiling noodles' was a skill — and yet, there *is* a certain art to it. For one thing, did you know it isn't always necessary to bring out your biggest pan and boil noodles in oodles of water? Indeed, for something like a cold noodle salad, where you actually *want* the starches to soften up and form a fluffy layer to absorb a dressing, boiling in a medium-sized pan is plenty. These noodles also benefit from a rinse if you're not using them right away or dressing them with something oily — that way the strands don't stick to each other and turn out clumpy. Just drain as you would pasta and run under cold water from the tap.

There's no reason to rinse pasta going into a hot sauce, as you want the starch to stay on each strand to help the sauce cling on, but if you're not using the pasta right away, tossing a bit of olive oil through it will help stop it sticking together.

With spaghetti or dried pasta shapes where you do want more of an *al dente* finish, a bigger pan does make a difference, as it gives the bits more room to bob about without bumping into each other and breaking up. Three-quarters fill the pan with cold water and season it well; 'as salty as the sea' is what the Italians say. This isn't to 'speed up the boil', but purely to help flavour the pasta itself. As the pasta cooks, the salt gets sucked in and seasons more evenly than if you just rely on seasoning the sauce.

Most recipes will say to 'follow packet instructions' for the cooking time. I'm not saying to ignore this, just don't stick too closely to it. If the pasta's headed straight for the pan with a hot sauce, deduct a few minutes from the suggested cooking time and transfer to the hot sauce (with the heat off) to let the residual heat cook it through.

Also, save a mugful of the pasta water before draining the pasta: the extra starch in the water is like gold. My foolproof finale is to plonk pasta straight from draining into the sauce, along with the reserved pasta water, which will incorporate into the sauce and help thicken it.

If I've made bonus sauce (which is always), I'll portion this out for 'Ron first (see page 300), to ensure the pasta:sauce ratio is just enough for the meal.

If all of this seems too-hard-basket, start with a one-pan pasta where, instead of draining any water, you actually use the pasta water to help build the sauce; see the golden angel hair pasta on page 58.

Cellophane noodles can be soaked rather than boiled

Place fresh rice noodles in lukewarm water to loosen

Reserve some starchy pasta water just before draining

If serving buckwheat noodles cold, cook them, then give them the ice-bath challenge

Pantry puttanesca

½ cup (80 g) salted capers,
   rinsed and drained
100 g (3½ oz) butter
150 g (5½ oz) pitted kalamata olives
a pinch of caster (superfine) sugar
3 cups (750 ml) tomato passata
   (puréed tomatoes)
1 teaspoon tomato paste
   (concentrated purée)
350 g (12 oz) dried casarecce,
   penne or tortelli, or any pasta
   that has ridges or twists
olive oil, for drizzling
2–3 garlic cloves, peeled
400 g (14 oz) tinned tuna in springwater,
   drained (optional)
finely grated Parmigiano Reggiano,
   to serve

This is not so much a recipe as a lifeline: in case of emergency, open pantry door. It'll require a little forward planning, since you'll need to have the goods on hand for whenever a puttanesca hankering strikes — but truly, this stuff should always be in there anyway, because they're shortcut flavour bombs! Splashing the tinned tuna in will pump up the protein, too.

Bring a large saucepan of well-salted water to the boil.

Meanwhile, fry the capers in the butter over medium–high heat for about 3–4 minutes, or until crispy and golden. The butter will foam — a sight to behold. Pour through a metal sieve into a small bowl, then pour the butter back into the pan, leaving the capers in the sieve over the bowl.

Add the olives to the pan, sprinkle in the sugar, crank the heat up high and toss about for 3–4 minutes, until the olives start to change colour and blister.

Pour in the passata. Splosh another cup's worth of water around the passata jar to clean out the dregs, then pour that in, too. Stir in the tomato paste and bring to the boil. Simmer vigorously for about 10 minutes, until reduced slightly; a splatter guard won't go astray here.

Meanwhile, cook the pasta according to the packet instructions. Drain, reserving a mugful of the cooking water. (If not using it right away, pop the pasta back in the empty pot and drizzle well with olive oil to stop it sticking.)

Crush the garlic into the pan. Flake the tuna in. Pour the pasta and a splosh of the reserved pasta water over the top and stir in with a spatula, so the pasta is well coated and the residual heat mellows the garlic out a little. The liquid will be reabsorbed by the pasta before you know it. Serve sprinkled with the crispy capers, parmesan, black pepper and a drizzle of olive oil if desired.

Bonus bits

Shortcuts

If you're in a hurry, just toss the olives and capers in together with the butter. Fry until the olives start gaining some colour, then splash in the passata and let it bubble away over high heat while you fuss with the pasta.

To speed things up even more, use a fresh pasta like gnocchi. It will cook in half the time of dried pasta, and even frozen fresh pasta can go straight from the freezer into boiling water.

Subs

To make this plant-based, leave the tuna out and use olive oil instead of butter.

You can use tinned tomatoes instead of passata, or even tomato paste (concentrated purée) and water, if that's all you have; more about this on page 75. If you happen to have some fresh cherry tomatoes handy, blister these along with the olives and capers for a fresh version, and add some chilli to make it fresh *and* feisty!

Ingredient spotlight: Capers

In this book you'll find plenty of capers; I like to think of them as vegan anchovies. You can buy them either brined or salted. They'll vary in size, from lilliput (teeny-tiny!) all the way through to caper berries, which are the natural conclusion to their growth. If brined, they just need to be drained, but salted ones need a rinse or two before use. Even though it's a bit of extra effort, I prefer the tighter buds of salted capers. Their brininess and bite on the tooth are perfect for adding acidity, texture and oceanic overtones to salads such as niçoise (page 216). Crispy capers are a gorgeous garnish, especially as the frying encourages these buds to 'bloom' in the hot oil. They're like a gluten-free crouton!

Loaded potato latkes

6 medium-sized starchy potatoes
(see Tips, page 89), about 1.2 kg
(2 lb 10 oz) in total, washed
and scrubbed
1 brown onion, peeled
1 teaspoon sea salt flakes,
plus extra to finish
160 ml (5¼ fl oz) olive oil
(see Tips, page 89)

To serve
Your choice of toppings or garnishes;
we've used sliced avocado, baby
red-vein sorrel leaves, sauerkraut,
plant-based cream cheese and
lemon cheeks

Can't choose between a latke and a rösti? A traditional Swiss rösti is larger than a traditional Jewish latke and contains nothing but potato. So I guess you could say that, true to form, this is a twist on both, making it a latke–rösti hybrid. The grated onion really sweetens the flavour and lightens the mix overall, and using the starch-harvesting trick that I usually deploy in latke season (Chanukah!) yields the crispiest crunch, without leaving the inside gluey. I also love to top it with the kinds of things latkes (and rösti) really love, then slice it like a potato-based pizza for serving. Incidentally, you can make these as individual latkes, too, if you've a need for speed.

Coarsely grate the potato and onion, using a box grater or food processor. Line a large mixing bowl with a clean tea towel, scoop the potato mixture into the tea towel and sprinkle with the salt flakes. Squeeze the salt into the mixture with your fingers.

Twist the towel up into a bundle, then squeeze with all your might to ooze the liquid into the mixing bowl. I use a wooden spoon as a tourniquet, but you could just use brute force. It's quite the workout! Don't throw out the liquid just yet.

Tip the potato mixture out of the tea towel into a fresh bowl, and leave to sit for 10 minutes. Carefully pour off the liquid in the other bowl, leaving just the gluey starch at the bottom, and reincorporate this into the potato mixture using your hands.

Heat a 28 cm (11 inch) heavy-based frying pan over medium heat. If your pan isn't non-stick, line the base with a round of baking paper. Add a quarter of your oil (roughly 2–3 tablespoons). Loosely sprinkle in half the potato mixture. Set the timer for 15 minutes, then walk away to live your life, get your toppings or garnishes together, maybe make a salad.

After 15 minutes, come back and scoop in the sides of the latke. Grab a large flat plate or round chopping board that fits just inside the pan. Shake the pan gently to loosen the latke, then pop the plate/board on top and flip the latke out with confidence (see Skills spotlight, page 89), being careful of leaky oil.

Pour another quarter of the oil into the pan. With a few choice words and the help of a spatula, carefully usher the latke back in, cooked side up. Set the timer for another 10 minutes. Go set the table, have a sip of water.

Slip the finished latke onto a serving platter or chopping board and load up with your chosen accoutrements, finishing with a good grind of black pepper. Serve immediately.

Before you head to the table, pop half the remaining oil into the pan, sprinkle in the rest of your potato mixture, set the timer for 15 minutes and away you go! By the time the first latke is well on its way to being devoured, your second should be coming up for a flip. Hit repeat.

The more liquid you squeeze out, the crispier your result

Save the starch from the bottom of the bowl

Turn a pan non-stick with baking paper as a go-between

Less lip on your plate means an easier return to the pan

THE JOY OF BETTER COOKING

Loaded potato latkes Bonus bits

Tips

Remember that the stickier the spud, the crispier the crust, which means it's a starchy potato you're after, so look for 'mashing' or 'roasting' potatoes. If you *must* use a waxy salad potato, consider adding a tablespoon of potato starch or instant powdered mashed potato to boost the sticking power. You can test the starch factor of a spud with The Sticky Spud Test: if the halved spud sticks to the flat of your knife, it's high starch and high stick!

If you've any schmaltz (see Ingredient spotlight, page 171) or duck fat in the fridge, try frying the latkes in that. It'll yield a richer flavour, and you'll likely need far fewer slices to feel satisfied — which is both a blessing and a curse.

Shortcuts

If you're low on time, make smaller latkes and cook them like fritters, heating plenty of oil in a non-stick pan and frying four or five at a time.

Recipe riffs

Unleash your inner Scando! Garnish with smoked fish or roe, crème fraîche or sour cream, dill, chives, red onion, a splash of lemon ... glorious.

Or, for plant-based, try avocado slices and plant-based cream cheese, a squirt of lemon and plenty of herbs.

Try a giant parsnip, potato and onion latke when they're in season, or any root veg. Just remember, the wetter the grated vegie mix, the longer it'll take to cook through.

Skills spotlight: Grating

A box grater is such a useful gadget, but can also be low-key injurious. Every one of those teeth is champing at the bit to chomp into a knuckle or nail. When grating, watch your fingers, not the grater or goods, and grate onto a flat surface, like a chopping board, rather than into a bowl. Box graters with grippy silicon feet and/or handles are handy for functionality, too.

If you have a food processor, using the grating attachment can help unlock recipes that may otherwise seem too-hard-basket. I promise the extra washing up is worth it, or maybe just delegate that to whoever's not cooking!

Skills spotlight: Flipping a lid

This is one manoeuvre that's sure to make you feel like a pro, every time you do it, no matter how far up the skills spectrum you are. Whether you're tossing ingredients in a wok, flipping a pancake, inverting a frittata, or even turning out a cake, there is absolutely a method to the madness of keeping it all together.

When it comes to the toss, it just takes practice. Some people will actually train themselves by tossing dry rice in a cold pan, flicking their wrist in a circular motion to encourage the rice to follow suit.

For pancakes and fritters, beginners might be best with the ol' Musashi two-sword approach. Use your widest spatula to lever the item out of the pan, and another to act as a counterpoint and keep the item suspended as you gently encourage it over. This is especially useful if you're shallow-frying, as a flubbed dismount can result in splashy hot oil, or an uneven landing that cooks itself into place faster than you can say, *Wait ... Musashi?*

If you're aiming to flip an omelette onto a plate, the real key is to do it decisively. Bring that bad boy to the bottom of the pan away from you, then angle the pan at the side of the plate closest to the eggy parcel ... and FLIP! This is another move you'll get better and better at, and, trust me, sometimes you'll still flub it, but no-one says no to an omelette, even if it's a bit skew-whiff.

For whole-pan items such as frittatas, rösti and latkes (and for schmaltzy matzo brei, a traditional Jewish Passover dish which looks a lot like this, but is made with unleavened cracker bread), because these are so big, your best bet is to use a plate or board as your 'second spatula', flipping the whole thing over, then encouraging it back into the pan on the uncooked side with a few fell swoops. Ergo, try to avoid plates with a high lip, as they'll catch the batter. Some people use a metal pizza tray, which works, but it might be worth having a tea towel underneath so you don't end up inadvertently cooking your supporting forearm.

For cake-flipping tips, check out the Skills spotlight on page 282.

Prawn, macadamia & asparagus stir-fry

250 g (9 oz) peeled
  raw prawn (shrimp) tails
  (see Subs, page 93)
¾ teaspoon bicarbonate of soda
  (baking soda)
1 generous thumb-sized knob
  fresh ginger, peeled
2–3 garlic cloves, peeled
2 tablespoons oyster sauce
  (see Subs, page 93)
1 tablespoon light soy sauce
1 tablespoon shaoxing rice wine
1 tablespoon sesame oil
1 tablespoon cornflour (cornstarch)
½ cup (125 ml) water, plus an extra
  ½ cup (125 ml) water on standby
2 tablespoons vegetable oil
2 bunches of asparagus, cut into 5 cm
  (2 inch) lengths (see Subs, page 93)
6 spring onions (scallions), white and
  green bits cut into 5 cm (2 inch)
  lengths, plus extra thinly sliced
  spring onion to serve
1 cup (150 g) roasted macadamias
  (see Subs, page 93)
steamed jasmine rice, to serve

What I love most about this stir-fry is how quickly everything comes together. By the time you've rinsed your jasmine rice and got it cooking away, the prawns will have 'velveted' (a technique that brings the bounce factor to everything from seafood to sizzling beef), and the rest of the ingredients will be ready to roll. If asparagus isn't in season, I've popped some suggestions in the Subs on the next page. The prawns can be replaced by other seafood, or even firm tofu. It's the kind of dish you'll have memorised and added to your repertoire in no time. A real winner.

To 'velvet' the prawns, slice the tails in half through the centre and massage the bicarbonate of soda into the flesh, then leave to rest for 15 minutes. Sounds weird, I know, but go with me here.

Finely grate half the ginger and all the garlic. Slice the other ginger half into rough chunks and reserve.

In a bowl, whisk together the grated ginger, garlic, oyster sauce, soy sauce, rice wine, sesame oil, cornflour and ½ cup (125 ml) water until combined. Set aside as your stir-fry sauce.

Rinse the prawns thoroughly in a colander and pat dry with paper towel.

Heat 1 tablespoon of the vegetable oil in a wok or large frying pan until very hot. Add the prawn meat and stir-fry for 30–60 seconds, or until it just changes colour; remove from the wok and set aside. Wipe out the wok with paper towel and reheat the remaining oil.

Boil a kettle. Pop the asparagus and spring onion into a colander and into the sink, then pour boiled water over them. Drain well, then add to the hot wok and stir-fry for 2 minutes.

Give your stir-fry sauce another whisk to reincorporate everything, then pour it into the hot wok and bring to the boil. Toss the prawns and nuts through. The sauce should be silky and glossy, which will happen almost instantly. If you find the liquid gets absorbed way too fast, splash in another ½ cup (125 ml) water and allow this to incorporate, too. Taste for seasoning.

Serve topped with extra spring onion, with bowls of steamed jasmine rice, and add this to the weekly rotation.

Heat your wok longer than you think: the oil should have 'legs' when you swish it in the pan

Cook things in batches to keep the heat in and stop them sweating

Some transluscence is good! Aim for #2, #3 is okay, #4 is overdone

Stir the stir-fry sauce again to mix in the cornflour, which always settles to the bottom

THE JOY OF BETTER COOKING

Prawn stir-fry Bonus bits

Tips

I've left the veg quite generous in length, to give them an elegant drape when cooked, and to help render them an easier pick-up with chopsticks. If you've toddlers in the hizzle, slice the veg into 2 cm (¾ inch) pieces instead.

For a juicier sauce, add an extra splash of water once the sauce starts to bubble, if you feel it could use it.

Subs

Asparagus is so seasonal, but this is the kind of stir-fry you're going to want to make all year round, so for any time that isn't spring, use baby broccoli (broccolini) or even broccoli florets chopped into fork-sized bits instead. Snow peas (mange tout) would be fantastic here, too.

No macadamias? Use cashews. If using raw nuts, toast them in a dry pan until golden and pull out before cooking the prawns.

For a nut-free alternative, you could try tinned water chestnuts, rinsed and chopped into chunks.

Go fully plant-based by subbing the oyster sauce out for mushroom sauce (Megachef is my favourite brand for this) and the prawns for firm or even extra-firm tofu. This doesn't need to be silkened, just boiled as a whole block (out of the pack) for 2 minutes or so, drained of liquid, chopped, pre-seasoned with plenty of soy sauce and other spices of choice, then tossed with cornflour (cornstarch) to coat each cube before searing as you would the prawns.

Waste knot

If you want to grow your spring onions (scallions), cut the white part off with the roots attached and pop into a glass of water. After a few days you will notice significant growth; these can then be planted in a pot, then transferred to the garden. Once they are established, just trim them as you need, and they'll keep you supplied with fresh spring onions all year round.

Ingredient spotlight: Frozen prawn meat

Prawns are such an easy protein option to have ready to go in the freezer — particularly if you can find the smaller-sized ones, often sold as 'prawn meat'. These are actually sweeter than the larger shell and tail-free ones, and are snap-frozen on the trawlers, so they're still super fresh once thawed, too. Indeed, almost all of the prawns you'll buy at the shops are thawed, so buying them frozen means you cut out the middle man, and you'll have them to hand when needed and at a more cost-effective price.

Since you're shelling out, do make an effort to find a local product, without too bright a colour when raw (this can often indicate that a bit of extra 'colour correction' dye is at play).

Sometimes if I'm in a massive hurry, I'll chip off a chunk, blitz them from frozen and add them to a simmering sauce, such as palak (page 109) or tomato sugo, for a quick prawn curry or pasta situation. This stuff is fab as a dumpling filling, too; keep some wonton wrappers in the freezer and add a tablespoon or two of curry paste for the easiest prawn dumplings ever!

Broccoli cassoulet

2 tablespoons olive oil,
    plus extra for drizzling
100 g (3½ oz) duck fat, schmaltz
    (see page 171) or butter
1 onion, finely sliced into rings
1 celery stalk, finely sliced
150 g (5½ oz) speck or
    streaky bacon, cubed
1 whole garlic bulb, peeled
    and roughly chopped
1–2 thyme sprigs
2 bay leaves
1 tablespoon tomato paste
    (concentrated purée)
1 teaspoon smoked paprika
    (hot or sweet, up to you)
¼ cup (60 ml) white wine
2 cups (500 ml) good-quality chicken
    stock (page 174) or vegetable stock
3 small heads broccoli, florets separated,
    stalks peeled and chopped
400 g (14 oz) tinned butterbeans,
    drained and rinsed

Cheesy crumb

100 g (3½ oz) fresh sourdough
    breadcrumbs or panko crumbs
50 g (1½ oz) hard cheese, such as
    parmesan, pecorino or Manchego,
    finely grated
1 handful of chopped parsley
¼ teaspoon smoked paprika,
    plus extra for sprinkling (optional)

With caramelised onion for sweetness, and bacon for smokiness, rounded out with creamy butterbeans, this is a hearty kishke-coater (kishke is Yiddish for 'your insides'). But it's the burnt brassicas on top that really bring it all together, resembling a furry forest of little broccoli 'trees'. I like to serve this in individual portions, like personalised cassoulet pots, but you're welcome to just keep it in the one pan and dish it out at the table. A cassoulet is traditionally loaded up as a rich, wintery, meaty casserole, but I've kept the meat to a minimum, and added meaty brocc instead, topping it all with a cheesy crumb. If you happen to have some schmaltz in the fridge, or duck fat in the freezer, now is the time to crack it out.

Preheat the oven to 200°C (400°F).

Heat half the olive oil and duck fat in a heavy-based saucepan or flameproof casserole dish over medium heat. Add the onion, celery and speck and sauté for 10–15 minutes, or until the onion is soft and the speck starts to turn golden and crinkly. There'll be a point where everything feels like a sweaty mess, but stay the course — once the liquid evaporates and the fat starts to render out, you're cooking with gas (even if you're not cooking with gas).

Add the garlic, thyme, bay leaves, tomato paste and paprika, and give everything a good stir (and a good whiff … ooooh yeah). Splash in the wine to deglaze, then add the stock, broccoli stalks and beans. Cook over medium heat for 5–8 minutes, or until the liquid has come to the boil and reduced by one-third; feel free to crank up the heat a little to speed up the process.

Meanwhile, combine all the cheesy crumb topping ingredients in a mixing bowl with the remaining duck fat.

In another bowl, toss the broccoli florets in the remaining olive oil until well coated, then arrange the broccoli florets over the top of the cassoulet mixture, sticking them in so they're standing up like little trees. Grind over some salt and black pepper, then scatter the cheesy breadcrumb topping over.

Bake towards the top of the oven for 35 minutes, or until the broccoli is tender and has browned a little more than is decent. Sprinkle with more paprika, if you'd like. Serve hot or warm.

Bonus bits

Subs

To go meat-free, use sliced shiitake mushrooms instead of the speck, and butter or oil instead of duck fat. If you're feeling like more fungi in your life regardless, add some wet-fried mushrooms (page 113) to this mixture.

Double duty

Any leftovers make great beans-on-toast the next morning, complete with bonus green stuff!

Cacio e pepe risotto

6 cups (1.5 litres) good-quality
    chicken stock (page 174)
    or vegetable stock
2 tablespoons extra virgin olive oil,
    plus extra to serve
1 small onion, or 2 French shallots,
    finely diced
2 cups (440 g) best-quality arborio
    or carnaroli rice you can find
½ cup (125 ml) white wine
½ cup (120 g) crème fraîche
100 g (3½ oz) aged parmesan
½ cup chopped parsley,
    plus extra leaves to garnish

CP butter
200 g (7 oz) butter, softened
1 cup (100 g) grated parmesan
    or pecorino
4 garlic cloves, finely chopped
1 tablespoon freshly cracked
    black pepper
1 teaspoon salt flakes
¼ cup chopped parsley

Cacio e pepe, that classic combination of cheese and freshly cracked black pepper, is here showcased in a risotto. This recipe takes me right back to the time I cooked risotto for the king of risotto milanese, Gualtiero Marchesi, in Parma, Italy. It was a *MasterChef* challenge, and there were nine others making their own versions, all of us in our own heads as to what was important to remember, and what we could afford to forget about. We were also cooking on camping stoves, on a blustery afternoon, the sun bearing down on us one minute, a gust of wind flapping gold leaf into the bushes the next. Even when cooking risotto at home, we can psych ourselves out with the steps, but I'm here to tell you that if the ingredients are good and you remember to add enough liquid, you'll be right. There's even a one-pan, hands-off version (opposite) if you're relishing risotto but haven't the time to stand around the stove … pretty sure Mr Marchesi would hate it.

Gently heat the stock in a large saucepan and keep at a simmer on low heat (not boiling). If you have any parmesan rinds in the freezer (see Ingredient spotlight, opposite), add these to the pan, too.

In a heavy-based pan that isn't necessarily too wide, gently heat the olive oil. Pop in the diced onion, wait for a sizzle, then close the lid and cook over medium heat for 5–10 minutes, or until the onion is transparent but not brown.

Add the rice and toast for 2 minutes, or until the rice is glossy, stirring the whole time to ensure every granule is coated.

Keep the pan over medium heat. Add the wine and deglaze the pan, stirring all the time. Once the alcohol has stopped stinging your eyes, start to add the stock, one ladleful at a time, occasionally stirring with a wooden spoon to stop the rice sticking to the bottom. When the stock has been absorbed and you start seeing the base of the pan, add more stock. Repeat this process for about 25–30 minutes. Once there is only about a cup of stock left, taste to see if the rice is cooked. Keep going if it needs longer, adding some hot water from the kettle if needed, but remember, risotto should be *al dente* (with a bit of chew), and silky, loose and creamy — not stiff and gluggy.

Meanwhile, make the CP butter. Put the butter in a bowl. Using a mortar and pestle, grind the parmesan, garlic, pepper and salt together into a rough paste, like you're making pesto. Mix the paste through the butter, folding the parsley through at the end.

Once the risotto is *al dente*, add the crème fraîche, parsley and 50 g (1½ oz) of the CP butter. Grate in half the parmesan and stir through. Take off the heat, put a lid on and leave for 5 minutes to rest.

Ladle the risotto into flat bowls, giving them a bit of a shake to settle the risotto. Add an extra dollop of the CP butter to the middle and microplane puffs of the remaining parmesan over the top. Serve sprinkled with the extra parsley, a final crack of pepper and a drizzle of olive oil.

Bonus bits

Tips

If you are using a store-bought stock, taste it for salt content before starting, and if you think it's too salty, dilute it! It's much easier to add seasoning than to take it out.

Shortcuts

A little bit of butter never goes astray when finishing a risotto, so if you don't have time to make the CP butter, just swirl in some dobs of butter at the end, along with lots and lots of freshly ground black pepper.

Double duty

You'll have more CP butter than you need for this recipe — which is good! Roll the left-over butter in baking paper and foil to form a sausage and keep it in the freezer. You can then cut off slices as you need them, to flavour-bomb everything from steaks to steamed greens.

Left-over risotto makes the best arancini balls. Roll the risotto into balls, stuff a little mozzarella in the middle for an added surprise, dredge in plain (all-purpose) flour, then egg wash, then breadcrumbs, then deep-fry or even air-fry.

If you'd prefer to bake rather than fry, pop the arancini on a lined baking tray and bake in a preheated 180°C (350°F) oven for 20–25 minutes, until golden and crispy. You can cook, cool and freeze your arancini for serving later, too. They'll last for up to 3 months in the freezer; simply reheat in a 180°C (350°F) oven until warmed through.

Recipe riffs

This great base recipe can be dressed to the nines to yield myriad risotto variations.

Risotto milanese: Make this classic by leaving out the CP butter and adding a good pinch of saffron threads to the wine. Or, instead of the CP butter, stir some saffron butter through.

Mushroom + thyme: Sauté mushrooms in olive oil with some thyme sprigs, salt and pepper and add at the end.

Pumpkin + sage: Sauté small cubes of pumpkin (squash) with olive oil until golden, then add butter and sage leaves and sauté until the sage is crisp. Stir through at the end.

Roasted beetroot + dill: Pop left-over roasted beetroot cubes through the cooked risotto, along with dill fronds.

Lemon + crab: At the end, stir in the juice and zest from 1 lemon and 100 g (3½ oz) picked crabmeat.

And all of the above — perhaps even the risotto milanese — would be even better with some of the CP butter stirred through.

Ingredient spotlight: Parmesan

It's always the dishes with the fewest ingredients that leave the least margin for error. That's why it's always best to shell out for a good-quality Parmigiano Reggiano for risottos (and don't forget to ask for any spare rinds).

Parmesan is one cheese we always have in the fridge, ready to be rasped over pasta, or chipped off and eaten as a snack. Parmesan can also be frozen, as can the rinds, which should be saved for using in home-made stocks, or to plop into ready-made stocks when making dishes like this.

Aged parmesan is always best, as it gives the amino acids in the cheese time to develop bonus umami flavour. The older parmesan gets, the crumblier it is, and in good-quality Parmigiano Reggiano you'll be able to taste salt crystals.

Resist the urge to buy the powdered stuff, as it is filled with anti-caking agent, and is often not even real cheese. (Yikes!)

Cacio e pepe risotto

Page 96

Sailors' sauce mussels with picada crumb

¼ cup (60 ml) extra virgin olive oil
1 leek, trimmed of the darkest
   green tops, julienned
   (see Subs, page 102)
2 pale inner celery stalks, finely diced
4 garlic cloves, finely sliced
1 cup (250 ml) white wine
½ teaspoon sugar (see Tips, page 102)
1 tablespoon tomato paste
   (concentrated purée)
1 cup (250 ml) good-quality tomato
   passata (puréed tomatoes)
1.5–2 kg (3 lb 5 oz–4 lb 8 oz) mussels,
   scrubbed, beards removed
   (see Tips, page 102)
½ cup roughly chopped parsley
½ cup roughly chopped coriander
   (cilantro)
zest and juice of 1 lemon,
   plus extra lemon cheeks to serve

Herby picada crumb
⅓ cup (50 g) blanched almonds
   (see Tips, page 102)
4 garlic cloves, peeled
2 thick slices fresh or stale sourdough
   bread (100 g/3½ oz), crust and all
a pinch of sea salt flakes and
   freshly cracked black pepper
½ cup finely chopped parsley
½ cup finely chopped coriander (cilantro)
⅓ cup (80 ml) extra virgin olive oil

Mussels' strength (ha!) is in the broth they form as they steam open, providing an easy mariners' sauce/sailors' sauce/marinara/marinera — which, depending on who you ask, refers to either the day's catch, or to the quickfire tomato sauce whipped up by southern Italian sailors (or most likely their wives), to be sopped up with crusty bread. The herby picada crumb, a totally addictive addition, means that as you dig in, the crumbs cascade into the broth and get caught in every crevice, so that you get a lovely interplay between swollen spongy sauciness and crunch, with no extra bread necessary. Mind you, some crusty ends to mop up the last of this slurpy sauce wouldn't go astray either.

To make the herby picada crumb, pulse the almonds in a small food processor with the garlic, bread, salt, pepper and herbs until a rough crumb forms. Heat the olive oil in a large heavy-based frying pan and toast the crumbs over medium heat until golden. Set aside.

Heat a large heavy-based lidded saucepan over medium heat until you can feel the warmth radiating when you hold your palm at a sensible distance. Splash in the olive oil and sauté the leek, celery and garlic over medium heat for 5–10 minutes, or until the leek is super soft and smells heavenly; if it's starting to brown, splash in a tablespoon of water and drop the heat a little.

Once the leek is sufficiently softened, splash in the wine and sugar and crank the heat up to cook off the alcohol and reduce the liquid by half. Spoon in the tomato paste and cook for a minute before adding the passata. Cook down the liquid over medium–high heat for about 10 minutes, until it starts to get thick and jammy.

Drain the mussels of any excess liquid, then tip the whole lot into the screaming-hot pan. They will instantly release more juice to make a deliciously deep-flavoured and briny broth.

Place the lid on and shake the pan occasionally for 4–5 minutes, or until all of the mussels open. Scatter in the herbs and lemon zest and juice.

Serve in deep bowls, scattered with the herby picada crumb, with lemon cheeks for squeezing over.

Where there's a port, there's a sailors' sauce — hence the origin of the name, 'marinara' sauce.

Shortcuts

Think of the herby picada crumb as an optional but excellent extra. Instead, you can cut out the middle man and serve with crusty bread.

Tips

Mussels don't need to be purged prior to cooking, unlike clams (vongole). To clean them, grab on to the overhanging beard and pull it around the shell towards the hinge. The beard should snap right off. Most commercially grown mussels are kept relatively tidy for on-sale, so you shouldn't need to rinse them too heavily in preparation for the pot.

Some people say to never eat a mussel that doesn't open, but I'd use my senses before ditching it — if it smells A-OK and looks right, I'd give it a whirl.

You can use any type of sugar — caster (superfine), raw, granulated. You can also leave it out. I just like how it brings out the sweetness of the mussels, the wine and the tomatoes.

You can buy blanched almonds, but it's super easy to make your own. Just soak raw almonds in some boiling water from the kettle and leave for 10 minutes, then plonk into cold water until cool enough to peel. For more on blanching, check out the Skills spotlight on page 164.

Subs

If you've no leek, any ol' allium will do — from brown onion to French shallot. Just finely dice these instead.

Recipe riffs

Mussels are (to borrow from singer/songwriter Deborah Conway) *only the beginning*! Mariners would come home with all manner of catch, so feel free to sploosh this sauce with any sort of mollusc, from clam to vongole. It only stands to reason that a marinara mix from the fishmonger's would lap this sauce right up.

Throw in some prawn (shrimp) meat, scallops and/or delicate white-fleshed fish and you're only some diced

potatoes and a chilli pepper away from a bouillabaisse of sorts.

Turn this sauce from *rosso* to *blanco* (red to white), and Spanish to French — controversial! — by making a mussel dish that's popular in Calais on the French side of the English Channel. Sub out the tomato paste and passata for dijon mustard and crème fraîche in the same ratios, and use cider instead of white wine.

Extra extra

You know what else would benefit from this here saucy sauce? Spaghetti. Cook any strandy pasta alongside this dish and combine in the bowls for a terrifically textural treat that is also (confusingly/conveniently) referred to as spaghetti marinara.

Double duty

If you've any herby crumbs left over, they'd make a really great topping for cauliflower ajo blanco (page 164), or as an ace topping on something like a broad bean and noodle salad (page 81).

Waste knot

Don't chuck out the green leek tops. Wash them and keep them in the freezer for making stock.

Skills spotlight: Cooking out wine

Lots of recipes call for splashes of booze, and you might have questions about it. Like, 'How dodgy can my wine be?' and 'What does "cooked out" even mean?' and 'Why am I doing this anyway?'. Well, let's work our way backwards.

Wine and spirits are used in recipes in a similar way to lemon juice and vinegar — they cut through richness, intensify flavour and enhance aroma. A splash of sake is particularly proficient at pumping up the umami flavour in a dish — I regularly reflect on a divine prawn (shrimp) pasta sauce spiked with sake which I tasted at a pop-up from Japanese–American chef Niki Nakayama; it was *chef's kiss*. Vodka is another common cool-kid addition to pasta sauces, and of course both red and white wine make regular appearances in dishes across the Mediterranean.

Booze is also used in marinades, though I wouldn't recommend splashing it in raw (even if the recipe calls for it), as this hardly ever cooks out and instead cures the surface of your meat, rendering it tougher. The best way to use wine in marinades is to mull it with the hard herbs and spices to cook out the alcohol, allow it to cool, then cover your protein with it, at least overnight.

For both of these methods, you can tell when the alcohol's cooked out by using your senses. A simmering sauce is hot enough to evaporate the alcohol out, so splashing it in when there are bubbles on the surface is best. Keep it bubbling away, sniffing regularly until you can no longer feel the sting of the alcohol hitting your nostrils. Diligence is less important for slow braises like a beef bourguignon or similar, but for quick-fire recipes, and lower-temp cooks like risotto, it's better to err on the side of more cook-out time than less.

Don't be tempted to splosh in last month's wine, either. If it's been in the fridge door for long enough to start transmogrifying into vinegar, it's going to throw your whole dish out. The general rule is that if you wouldn't drink it, you shouldn't cook with it. No need to splash out though — a bog-standard table wine should do it.

Gadget spotlight: Heavy-based pan

A heap of recipes start with the instruction to use a heavy-based pan. Why? Because the heavier your pan base, the more evenly it warms through, and the more protection your ingredients have between them and a direct heat source.

If you need to invest in just one, I'd suggest a shallow 28 cm (11 inch) cast-iron casserole dish with a lid. These are easily taken from stovetop to oven to table, they're wide enough for one-pan dishes such as the golden angel hair pasta on page 58 — and they look fantastic coming to the table. The lid means you can sweat your onions without fear of fiery retribution, and the heavy insulation is perfect for absorption-style cooking in dishes such as pilaf. To stop stuff sticking, you can even slide some baking paper on the bottom before popping your ingredients in.

To clean those baked-on bits, sprinkle bicarbonate of soda (baking soda) and vinegar into the bottom until foamy, leave to soak, then swish away without the need for harsh abrasives or elbow grease!

Cauli tom yum

2 tablespoons coconut oil

500 g (1 lb 2 oz) raw king prawns
    (jumbo shrimp), deveined, heads
    and shells reserved

150 g (5½ oz) baby king brown
    mushrooms, larger mushrooms sliced

1 large head cauliflower, cut into florets,
    stem peeled and sliced, small outer
    leaves reserved

200 g (7 oz) dried vermicelli rice noodles

Soup broth

½ bunch of coriander (cilantro),
    stems and roots washed and chopped

5 cm (2 inch) piece fresh galangal,
    peeled and sliced

1 lemongrass stem, bruised with the back
    of a heavy knife and tied in a knot

10 kaffir lime leaves, finely sliced

2 large garlic cloves, crushed

2–4 red bird's eye chillies, finely sliced

2 cups (500 ml) good-quality
    chicken stock (page 174)
    or vegetable stock

¼ cup (60 ml) lime juice

¼ cup (60 ml) fish sauce

1 tablespoon grated
    palm sugar (jaggery)

To serve

250 g (9 oz) cherry tomatoes, halved

2 boiled eggs (see Skills spotlight,
    page 219), peeled and cut in half

100 g (3½ oz) roasted peanuts, chopped

coriander (cilantro) leaves

Thai basil sprigs

mint sprigs

finely sliced lime leaves

crispy fried shallots
    (see page 172; optional)

finely sliced red chilli (optional)

chilli oil, to taste (optional)

lime cheeks

Just as I was entering my most petulant late tweendom, Mum scored a residency at a university in Bangkok, which meant that my summer holidays would have to be spent there, rather than at the Sydney youth camp most of the other kids in my class were looking forward to. AND I'd miss out on singing a solo from *The Prince of Egypt* at speech night. Can you imagine!? How I wept and wept. Thankfully, my parents did not capitulate to those tweenie tears, and instead I spent the month drowning my sorrows in the Pathumwan Princess Hotel pool, eating my weight in pomelo and ordering every tom yum soup I saw on a menu. They were sweet, sour, bitter and just the right side of salty ... just like 12-year-old me.

In a large heavy-based saucepan, heat half the coconut oil until smoking hot. Add the peeled prawns and mushrooms and stir-fry for a minute, or until the prawns change colour. Remove from the pan and set aside.

To make the broth, add the reserved prawn heads and shells to the pan and stir-fry for another few minutes. Stir in 6 cups (1.5 litres) water. Toss in the coriander stems and roots, galangal, knotted lemongrass, lime leaves, garlic and chilli. Bring to the boil and simmer for 20 minutes.

Strain all of that delicious broth into a clean saucepan, squeezing all the goodness out of the solids with the back of a wooden spoon. Bring back to a simmer and stir in the stock, lime juice, fish sauce and palm sugar. Taste for a pleasing balance of salty, sweet and sour.

Add the cauliflower to the broth and cook for 2–5 minutes, depending on the size of your florets, until they are fork-tender and translucent, but not mushy. For the last minute of cooking, add the reserved cauli leaves.

Pop the dried noodles in a heatproof bowl, cover with warm water and leave to rehydrate for 2 minutes.

Drain the noodles and divide among serving bowls, along with the cherry tomatoes, boiled egg halves, peanuts, prawns and mushrooms.

Arrange the cooked cauli in the bowls. Ladle the broth over and scatter each bowl with coriander, Thai basil, mint and lime leaves. Add some crispy fried shallots, chilli slices and a drizzle of chilli oil, if you're up for it, and serve with lime cheeks for squeezing over.

Bonus bits

Skills spotlight: Building brothy flavour

Although this recipe pertains specifically to building a Thai-style broth, the principles of unlocking the flavours of aromatics such as herbs and spices, as well as proteiny bits and bobs, can be applied to any cuisine.

Take master stock, for example, which is often simply thrown together and simmered for ages. Self-professed 'broth guy' Dan Hong prefers to pound shallots, garlic and star anise into a paste before frying until fragrant, deglazing with shaoxing rice wine, and only then adding the liquid and simmering for ages (he's got a great recipe in his eponymous cookbook).

Chicken soup is the same. Some people just chuck everything in raw, while others (myself included) swear by sweating the onion down first with garlic and bay leaves, preferably with schmaltz (page 171) as the fat component. (Incidentally, I'll occasionally throw a star anise or two into my chicken soup because it helps onions taste ... onionier!)

Bone broth is never as good if the bones aren't roasted first until dark, to release both the Maillard sweetness in the flavour (see page 232), but also the nutritious minerals that people are likely making the broth for in the first place.

And see how you fried off the heads and shells of prawns to give this broth its colour and flavour? You are officially halfway to a prawn bisque! Simply switch out the aromatics listed for ones that are more *à la française*, such as bay leaves, garlic, lemon zest and white pepper (with optional cayenne pepper and tarragon, if you're working with Julia Child's version), deglazing with plenty of wine and/or Cognac, and finishing with cream or butter.

Tips

Galangal is much woodier than ginger, so it can be tricky to cut. Try to find younger galangal, which will be more tender. Do your best; there's no need to cut it too fine.

Shortcuts

There are some good tom yum pastes out there. Just check the back label and make sure the ingredients are as close as possible to the ones you were planning on using.

Recipe riffs

Add a can of coconut cream to the broth before serving and the soup becomes a *tom kha goong*.

Subs

Turn the soup plant-based by subbing the prawns out for tofu. For extra sponginess, you can freeze a block of soft tofu, thaw it with a weight on top, then flake it. Feel free to slice the block into cubes or slices first, to help it freeze and thaw faster; it'll last in the freezer like this for up to 3 months. This process helps to push out any waterlogged pockets and refill the bubbles with broth. Delish!

Palm sugar (jaggery) is fab for its sappiness, but if you don't have any, some brown sugar to taste will give you all the sweetness you need.

Cauli tom yum

Page 104

Palak & potato curry

6–8 new potatoes, washed and
    scrubbed, halved or quartered to
    fork-sized (see Subs, page 110)
1 brown onion, roughly chopped
1 thumb-sized knob fresh ginger,
    roughly chopped (no need to peel)
2–3 garlic cloves, roughly chopped
2 long green chillies (or to taste),
    finely chopped
2 teaspoons salt flakes
1 teaspoon garam masala
1 teaspoon ground cumin
1 teaspoon ground coriander
2 bunches of English spinach, washed
    and spun (see Shortcuts, page 110)
1 tomato, roughly chopped
¼ cup (60 ml) neutral-flavoured oil
    (see Subs, page 110)

Tadka topping
2 tablespoons neutral-flavoured
    oil (I like grapeseed)
24 fresh curry leaves (roughly 2–3 stems)
2–3 small whole dried red chillies
2 teaspoons brown mustard seeds
2 teaspoons cumin seeds

To serve
cooked white or brown basmati rice
lemon wedges
½ cup (125 ml) single (pure) cream,
    or plain or coconut yoghurt

A commonly held belief of curry connoisseurs is that a murgh makhani, or butter chicken, is the benchmark dish to judge a cook by. But for me, it's all about a benchmark palak, or spinach sauce. I love tasting how far different cooks take their spices, what paneer or other protein they use, and how creamy they're willing to go with the ghee. This palak is decidedly decadent, applying the principles of emulsification you'd normally associate with a hollandaise sauce, along with the traditional tempering of spices, which brings out their richness and warmth. Adelaide chef Ragini Dey is the spice queen who taught me to wilt, rather than blanch, the spinach, locking in an impossibly verdant shade of green. I've made this version with potatoes, but have added some subs in, too, because you'll want to make this again and again. And, as with all curries, it tastes even better the next day.

Place the potato pieces in a saucepan of well-salted cold water. Bring to the boil, then drop the heat to a simmer and cook until fork-tender (about 15–20 minutes). Drain and set aside.

Meanwhile, get cracking on the topping. In a large, heavy-based saucepan, heat the oil to shimmering. Fry the curry leaves until crispy and vibrant green, then remove and drain on paper towel. Keeping the heat low, temper the whole spices, largest to smallest, making sure not to burn them (for more on tempering, see Ingredient spotlight, page 110). Add the whole chillies and mustard seeds in the first minute; once the mustard seeds start to pop, add the cumin seeds. Once aromatic, skim the spices out of the oil and set aside with the curry leaves for garnishing.

Add the onion and ginger to the left-over spice oil in the pan and listen for a sizzle. Stir about, cover with the lid, and turn the heat down low. Allow the onion mixture to sweat away for 8–10 minutes. Once the onion has softened but not coloured, add the garlic, green chilli, salt, garam masala and ground cumin and coriander and stir until fragrant.

Pop the spinach leaves into the pan, stirring to coat. Cover with the lid for 4–5 minutes over low heat, preparing for The Ultimate Disappearing Spinach Trick that takes what seems to be an inordinate amount of spinach and makes it … practically disappear, like magic.

Once the spinach has wilted, transfer the mixture to a blender, add the tomato and blitz until finely chopped. With the motor going, slowly pour in the oil to emulsify to a fine, creamy gravy.

Pour the palak back into the pan, add the cooked potato and gently warm everything through.

Serve the palak over the rice, scattered with the tempered spices and curry leaves, with lemon wedges and cream or yoghurt.

Palak & potato curry Bonus bits

Shortcuts

Use baby English spinach instead of the grown-up variety to speed up the washing/cooking time. You can also totally use an Indian curry paste, stirring through baby spinach and blitzing together before adding in any left-over roasted/steamed veg or protein.

Subs

Go traditional: instead of potatoes, use paneer, which is a kind of Indian cottage cheese that can be found at specialty shops, Indian grocers and some larger supermarkets.

If you've any frozen prawn (shrimp) meat, chop this up finely and add it to the blitzed palak gravy when you put it back on the stovetop. Leave to heat through for a few minutes until the prawn meat turns translucent.

For a richer result, use ghee in the palak rather than a neutral-flavoured oil. You might even like to temper your spice topping in ghee instead of oil, too. You can easily make your own ghee — read all about it on page 233.

Skills spotlight: Spice up your life

Spice racks are a bit like star signs ... you can tell a lot about a person by taking a squiz at their pantry shelves. Are you a 'neatly arranged, labelled and dated, with perfectly spaced amber jars' type? Or are your spices more of the 'still in their little baggies from 2014' variety, names all but rubbed off, crumbled to dust and smelling about the same? Everyone's on a spice spectrum, so wherever you are, we can work with it.

Older spices, especially if they're ground, need to be used up before you go ahead and buy new ones — and if you know you're an infrequent spice user, you're better off buying whole ones and grinding as you go, because they'll last longer.

Now might be a good time for a spice audit. Give them a sniff to make sure they still smell of anything, and if they don't, into the compost bin they go. Or, to reinvigorate at least some character to the aroma and flavour of dried spices, you can lightly toast them in a dry pan (you can do the same with nuts that are tasting a little blugh). If you're worried about overcooking the spices, preheat your pan, then add the spices, give them a few tosses, then turn off the heat. The residual heat of the pan will toast them through just enough, without burning.

When working with whole spices, you can dry-roast them to help dry them out and make them easier to grind before whizzing to a powder. A spice grinder is worth investing in if you're whizzing whole spices regularly. Alternatively, you can use a coffee grinder, then grind a teaspoon of dried rice through to clean the spices off before your next brew. Otherwise, a mortar and pestle is perfectly fine if you have the time, and don't mind a rougher grind.

Dry-frying is often used for dried whole chillies in Mexican cuisine to caramelise the flavour and bring out more smokiness.

Heat doesn't necessarily have to be applied to all spices, so if the recipe doesn't call for toasting, don't do it! For example, in Georgian cooking, we don't toast our coriander seeds (a staple of most of our spice mixes), because we want the lemony fruitiness of the raw seeds, rather than the toasted nuttiness you'd normally get in Indian cookery, where they're toasted or tempered. Spice master Ian Hemphill describes the difference as fresh bread versus a slice of toast.

Frying spices in fat, also known as tadka, or tempering, helps to release a different kind of characteristic from the aromatic compounds in whole seeds such as coriander, cumin, mustard and fennel seeds directly into the fat — usually oil or ghee, which are both great flavour carriers. However, if you're in a hurry, sprinkling your ground spices into sweated onions and stirring about a bit until you can smell them before adding the rest of the ingredients is a great shortcut.

For more luxuriating, you might like to temper the spices separately (as we do in the curry on the previous page), to really unlock the spices' full potential.

Fork-tender means you can literally stick a fork in it

Let the onion sweat it out before adding the aromatics

Spinach magically disappears in a pan, so you need a lot!

Spices, dried chillies and curry leaves come alive under heat

Wet-fry mushroom noodles

400 g (14 oz) Swiss brown mushrooms,
thinly sliced

6 fresh shiitake mushrooms, thinly sliced
(see Ingredient spotlight, page 114)

200 g (7 oz) shimeji or oyster mushrooms,
pulled apart into smaller clusters
(see Ingredient spotlight, page 114)

1 cup (250 ml) water

3 tablespoons neutral-flavoured oil
(I like grapeseed)

¼ cup (60 ml) oyster sauce
(see Subs, page 114)

2 tablespoons dark soy sauce

2 red Asian shallots, finely sliced

1 thumb-sized knob fresh ginger,
peeled and grated

2–3 garlic cloves, grated

250 g (9 oz) fresh rice noodles
(see Tips and Subs, page 114)

2 tablespoons light soy sauce

1 teaspoon sesame oil

3 spring onions (scallions), finely sliced

MYO chilli oil (page 213),
for a bit of extra kick (optional)

I learned to wet-fry mushrooms on a mushroom foraging tour with Jim, a tall Texan, and Chris, a mycologist-slash-Hobbit. Chris showed us how to find even the most magic of mushrooms, while Jim explained that as mushrooms aren't technically vegetables, they behave differently when boiled; magic happens! Rather than their cell structure breaking down or toughening up, they pretty much stay the same, absorbing whatever flavour you throw at them — or into them. That's why I wash mushrooms with abandon now and just crank the heat up to full blast to help the extra water to *Exit, pan left*. For maximum flavour infusion, it pays to keep the heat high until all of the liquid in the pan evaporates, holding off adding any fat until after the mushrooms have started turning browner. You may not go the full noodle every time, but I guarantee that frying mushrooms this way will revolutionise your breakfast 'shrooms forever.

Plonk all of the mushrooms into your wok, or your widest pan with high sides. Add ½ cup (125 ml) water and crank the heat up to high. Bubbles are good. The amount of mushrooms will appear to reduce by half (don't worry — they're still there). Allow at least 10–15 minutes over high heat for the water to completely evaporate and the mushrooms to start to brown. (I know, I know ... they were already brown to begin with.)

Splash in a tablespoon of the oil to help the caramelisation along. The mushrooms will quickly start to colour, but be patient and let them caramelise for about 10 minutes over medium–high heat, stirring now and then, so all the mushrooms have a sweet little burnished edge to them.

Splash in the oyster sauce and dark soy sauce, stirring to deglaze the pan. Pull out the mushrooms and set aside in a bowl.

Add the shallot to the wok with another tablespoon of the oil. Fry for a minute or two, until golden, then add the ginger and garlic and sauté for a few more minutes. Tip the mixture over the mushrooms.

Crank the heat back up under your wok. Splash in the rest of your oil, add your noodles and leave them alone for at least a minute or two, or as long as it takes to get a little char on them (try not to move them too much, as this can cause breakage).

Splash in another ½ cup (125 ml) water and let it evaporate; the steam will break up your noodles if you think they are stuck together. Add the mushrooms and ginger mix back in and toss everything about.

Splash in the light soy sauce and the sesame oil and let it sizzle for a minute. Turn the whole thing off, top with the spring onion and serve with the chilli oil, if you like it spicy.

Wet-fry mushroom noodles Bonus bits

Tips

Depending on how fresh your noodles are, they might need a little love to soften them enough so that they stay pliable. If they start crumbling into many, many sad pieces as you pull them out of the packet, try popping them into the microwave, with a splash of water in the bottom of the bowl or plate, and zapping them for 20–30 seconds to bring them back to life. Or, place the noodles in a heatproof bowl, pour a kettle of boiling water over them and stand for 3 minutes, then drain and add to the stir-fry.

If your pan refuses to char the noodles without them sticking to its surface, use some baking paper as a go-between. Once the pan is hot enough, slip in the paper, pop the oiled noodles on top and let them colour without moving them about too much.

You'll find more about cooking noodles on page 82.

Subs

Try hor fun rice noodles, which you'll find in the fridge at specialty Asian grocers. You could also use fresh cheung fun noodle pastry, which can be cut to thick noodle size.

Alternatively, you can use dried flat rice noodles, which will need to be softened in boiling water according to the packet instructions first. Go for a minute or so less than they suggest, as the noodles will get a quick cook-up in the pan.

Oyster sauce is one of my go-to splashes when stir-frying veg as it adds such a sweet, savoury boost. It's also fab for marinades, especially if you're a chicken-wing roaster. If you don't have oyster sauce, use extra soy sauce and an extra sprinkling of sugar and/or honey.

Double duty

The wet-fry mushroom mixture is brilliant as an omelette or crepe filling, too. Or just keep them nude and serve on toast or as a side with dinner.

This mushroom filling is also perfect for making cheung fun noodle rolls; you'll find the pastry in the fridge at specialty Asian grocers. Wrap the pastry sheets around the filling, into log-shaped rolls, and steam them, then drizzle with light soy sauce and a pinch of sugar. Food writer Camellia Ling Aebischer has an incredibly clever recipe where she makes microwave cheung fun pastry, which is worth taking a squiz at online.

This mixture is glorious repurposed into a soup on day two. Benjamin Cooper from the Melbourne restaurant Chin Chin once showed me a great mushroom broth using a shiitake-load of coconut water, and I love whipping it out when people with dietaries are coming for dinner on hot summer nights, because you can do all of the prep the day before, and just reheat it with about 4 cups (1 litre) coconut water as your stock and classic South-East Asian aromatics such as lemongrass, lime leaves, chilli and ginger just before serving. Finish with plenty of fresh herbs like Thai basil, coriander (cilantro) and Vietnamese mint.

Recipe riffs

To keep this completely plant-based, instead of the oyster sauce, use 1 tablespoon mushroom sauce, or even mushroom soy and a pinch of sugar.

Once you have the hang of the wet-fry, the sauce shelf is your oyster! Go Southern BBQ with barbecue sauce and smoked salt, or classic French with stock, thyme and butter.

You can totally bulk this dish out with some firm tofu, beef or chicken, if you're so inclined, searing once the 'shrooms are out of the pan. Feel free to 'velvet' the protein first (à la the prawn stir-fry on page 90), for extra bounce.

Go for a different spot on the globe once the 'shrooms are wet-fried — add cream, then serve over pasta.

Ingredient spotlight: Exotic mushrooms

When it comes to building that elusive 'umami' flavour, the 'shrooms have it. More exotic types such as fresh shimeji or shiitake are thankfully becoming easier to find, but if you're stumped, fear not. Just use whatever exotic mushrooms you can access — the slipperier the texture, the better. You can also use dried 'shrooms like shiitake instead, rehydrating them in warm water first. Be sure to pop the rehydration water into your pan for the wet-frying component instead of straight-up water.

I love shiitakes bobbing around in broths for taste and texture, while slippery 'shrooms such as shimeji, enoki and oyster are wonderful in stir-fries like this one.

THE JOY OF BETTER COOKING

Hunan steamed fish with black bean & stringy leek

/ Serves 4

1 heaped tablespoon fermented salted
black beans (see Worth it, page 118)
800 g–1 kg (1 lb 12 oz–2 lb 4 oz) skinless
firm white fish fillet (see Tips and Subs,
page 118, and Ingredient spotlight,
page 119)

Saucy ginger marinade

4 tablespoons oyster sauce
2 tablespoons shaoxing rice wine
2 teaspoons rice wine vinegar
2 thumb-sized knobs fresh ginger,
peeled and grated
4–6 garlic cloves, grated
2 teaspoons sesame oil

Stringy leek

1 leek, pale part only, washed well
(see Subs, page 118)
4 tablespoons grapeseed oil

Bok choy stir-fry

2–3 bunches of bok choy or pak choy
1 tablespoon grapeseed oil
1 thumb-sized knob fresh ginger,
peeled and roughly chopped
a pinch of sugar
a pinch of salt flakes
2 tablespoons water or stock

To serve

coriander (cilantro) sprigs
steamed jasmine rice

When I was reviewing restaurants, I found myself craving nothing more than 'steamed fish and vegetables' on my nights off. Eating rich restaurant meals may seem like a non-stop party, but it can be exhausting on the digestive system, and not everybody is cut out for it … myself included. This offering, though, is still on the menu on market days, and when the fish is super fresh it doesn't even make it into my fridge, because the closer it is to room temperature, the quicker and more evenly it'll cook through. Traditionally, this dish is usually loaded with fermented chillies, but I've left these out to make the dish friendlier for non-hot-heads. Serving with chilli oil means heat-seekers can still get their fill, but you're welcome to go right ahead and add fermented chilli into the mix, or even use finely chopped fresh chilli instead.

Pop the black beans into a little bowl, then pour in enough cold water to comfortably cover them. Set aside.

If the fish is in one whole section, slash into the thicker bits with a sharp knife, as you might a leg of lamb, to ensure even cooking.

Combine the saucy ginger marinade ingredients together in a bowl. Place the fish on a tray or plate with a slight lip to catch the sauce, then pour half the sauce over the fish and leave to soak in for 10–15 minutes.

Preheat your steaming device, be it a wide bamboo steamer or an electric one. (If you don't have said contraption, see Gadget spotlight on page 119 for a makeshift version.)

Drain the black beans, rinse and dry. Sprinkle these over the fish.

Place the fish (still on the plate, to catch the delicious cooking juices) in your steamer and steam for 10–12 minutes, or until the flesh is opaque and starting to flake a little. Remove from the steamer and allow to cook through completely in its own residual heat.

Meanwhile, prepare the stringy leek. Cut the leek into 3 cm (1¼ inch) batons, then slice into thin julienne strips along the grain. Rinse off any grit, then dry thoroughly and place in a heatproof bowl. Heat the grapeseed oil in a large pan or wok until shimmering, then pour the oil over the leek to soften it.

For the bok choy stir-fry, reserve the leaves and cut the bok choy into quarters if they're on the smaller side, or into sixths if large. Rinse well under the tap, rubbing between the layers to remove any grit.

Heat the grapeseed oil in your large pan or wok and stir-fry the bok choy bases for 2 minutes, or until their colour changes. Chuck in the bok choy leaves and ginger and toss together for another minute. Sprinkle in the sugar and salt and splash in the water or stock.

Pour the fried leek strips and leeky oil over the fish and garnish with coriander. Serve with the bok choy, jasmine rice and remaining saucy marinade, with some chilli oil on the side for hot-heads.

Hunan steamed fish Bonus bits

Tips

I like to use hapuka or trevalla (cod) here, but any firm-fleshed, skinless and boneless white fish will do. If your fishmonger asks if you want it boned, nod emphatically, otherwise run your finger over the fish to pull out any spiky bones before you cook it.

If you're not able to grab a whole piece, just buy 200–250 g (7–9 oz) fillets per person. If you do score a whole big side of fish, slashing into the thickest parts with a knife helps the flesh cook through evenly. You can totally still cook the fish with the skin still on, if that is how it is sold — just slide the flesh off the skin to serve.

Subs

Go fully plant-based by swapping the fish for silken tofu, and the oyster sauce for mushroom sauce.

Finely sliced spring onions (scallions) can easily sub in for the leek. Scatter the paler bits over the fish to steam, and pour the hot oil over the green bits to adorn the fish before serving.

The MYO chilli oil on page 213 is fantastic, and easy to make, but you can also use store-bought chilli oil at a pinch.

Recipe riffs

Switch up the flavours: lose the saucy marinade and, while the fish is steaming, reduce ½ cup (125 ml) white wine with lemon juice and tarragon (or thyme) in a saucepan, then toss in a few dobs of butter. Pour over the fish just before serving. Or go Provencale by topping the steamed fish with a punnet of cherry tomatoes blistered in a frying pan with plenty of olive oil, olives, capers, orange zest and parsley.

If you want to try something entirely more authentic, look up chef and cookery teacher Tony Tan's fermented chilli version of Hunan steamed fish; it's exquisite.

Waste knot

Don't chuck out the green leek tops. Wash them and keep them in the freezer for making stock.

Worth it

Not to be confused with the dried or tinned black beans used in Central or South American cooking, you'll find salted black beans – a.k.a. douchi – sold in a bag or canister at Asian grocers and some supermarkets.

These black, shrivelled soy beans have been imparting salty-savouriness to Chinese cooking — particularly Cantonese dishes and those from Sichuan and Hunan provinces — for more than 2000 years. Needless to say, since they're salted and fermented, salted black beans will last for ages in the pantry.

If you're a fan of funk, and big flavour, add a teaspoon or so of black beans to stir-fries and steamed dishes like mapo tofu, along with other usual suspects like garlic and ginger.

Their saltiness is mellowed with soaking and through cooking, but remember to hold back on adding seasoning until you taste the final result.

Teach yourself to steam a fish and you'll never go hungry.

Gadget spotlight: Steamer

There are so many ways to harness the power of steam in the kitchen — a cooking method that helps retain moisture and gives you more control through indirect, wet heat. You might have a steamer insert stuffed down the back of the cupboard, or a fancy steam oven, or even a multi-cooker with a steaming attachment. A bamboo steamer can be purchased from specialty stores and Asian grocers, and will come in handy for steaming all manner of vegetables, not to mention dumplings.

If you don't have a steaming device, you can create a makeshift one using a wide-based saucepan or casserole dish with high-ish sides, a heatproof plate, and some foil (or several small empty tuna tins). Scrunch three or four pieces of foil into balls the size of squash balls. Arrange the foil balls (or tuna tins) in the bottom of a wide-based pan in an even way to support the weight of the fish. Find a wide heatproof plate that fits inside the pan, and also fits your fish. Cover with a lid if the sides of the pan are high enough, or create a lid by covering the pan snugly with foil. Add enough water to reach a third of the way up the foil balls or tins and bring to the boil before topping with the plated fish.

Ingredient spotlight: Fresh fish

Wading into the waters of fresh fish buying can be tricky at first, but finding a fishmonger you know and trust is step numero uno. A good-quality fish shop should never smell 'fishy'; this is one time you shouldn't be able to 'follow your nose'.

The sustainability of catching and eating fresh fish — and of aquaculture practices for farmed fish — has become increasingly top of mind for many in the food space, particularly those who've turned pescatarian only to realise they've opened a whole other can of worms.

Look for signs like 'line-caught' and 'local' where you can, and if you aren't sure if the fish varieties are sustainable, download your local marine stewardship council app, which will offer region-specific advice.

You can tell how fresh whole fish is by looking at the eyes, which should be raised, glossy and clear, rather than collapsed and murky; shiny skin with a wet-look sheen is another good sign (unless you're visiting a specialist fish dry-ageing joint, such as Josh Niland's Fish Butchery in Sydney). Judging the freshness of fillets is a little trickier, so just ask your fishmonger which fish they'd be taking home for dinner tonight — it's less offensive than asking what's fresh, and you're far more likely to get a friendly answer and genuine recommendation.

Making the most of it

Gluts, windfalls and leftover makeovers

Zero waste hero

There are few things more glorious to our family than a glut. Give a box price for any fruit or vegetable, and you can guarantee it's being loaded up onto Dad's shoulder. Text me that your tree is laden with produce and I'm there with a bag at my side and bells on. Surely some of that is a symptom of that 'empty-shelf' sensibility, where you're not quite sure if you'll catch a particular item again so best to stock up, but it's compounded by the joy of knowing that there's something to look forward to when that produce is no longer around.

It's no accident the name for such things is 'preserve'. It's preserving the feeling of the sun on your face in a jar of golden peaches, or the crunch of crisp winter cabbages in a crock of kraut.

Think of this as an Aesop's fable — the grasshopper and the ant — except you don't have to choose between singing through summer or stocking your reserves, because you can do both! These kinds of big-batch cook-ups are FUN, and really great to get others involved in. Tomato passata days (or in our case, Satsibeli Sundays) rope in the whole family, and turn into a real Thing.

Much of Making The Most Of It is motivation. You've gotta be in the mood to process the produce, to squirrel away the proceeds, and to then remember what you squirrelled. It can be highly meditative, so if you have a busy head and a loaded fridge, an afternoon at the kitchen bench might be just what you need to steady your thoughts out of fight-or-flight beta brainwave mode and back onto the creative alpha channel.

Whether you've grown it in your garden, inherited it from a neighbour, or scored big at a farmers' market, this is the chapter where you can potter about and find inspiration to load up your pantry, fridge and freezer for 'Ron (turn to page 300 to meet 'Ron).

It's also the section that encourages you to love your leftovers (something I cannot recommend

This is the kind of cooking that saves stuff from the bin, saves you time at the other end, and saves your head when it's too busy. Make the time for it.

highly enough) in the form of 'double duty' tips throughout the book. These leftover makeovers are designed to help you see the dregs differently. Whether it's last night's roast chook, some dodgy-looking dairy in the back of your fridge, or some steamed rice that's just waiting to be reinvented, you've come to the right place, pal. Let's make the most of it!

Nature strip cordial

1 kg (2 lb 4 oz) sugar
8 cups (2 litres) water
6 medium-sized unwaxed lemons
10 sprays of elderflower flowers

How do you make elderflower cordial? Make small talk to build rapport, and maybe complement its sprigs. Oh, you mean the *other* cordial? Well, that's as easy as steeping a big pot of tea. Elderflowers are simple to spot once you know what you're looking for and, come spring, you'll see them on nature strips everywhere. Indeed, any fruit or edible flower glut can be cordial-ed — lavender, rhubarb, rosehip. If you can tea it, you can cordial it. Just use this proportion of sugar to water, and remember to add something sour for a bit of zip. If no florals are forthcoming, this can be made as a straight citrus cordial, and you can shake things up with some lemon verbena or lemon myrtle leaves, or a few stems of freshly bruised lemongrass.

Place the sugar and water in a large saucepan, stirring to help the sugar dissolve. Bring to the boil.

Meanwhile, use a speed peeler to peel the zest of the lemons into strips, retaining maximum zest and minimum pith (that's the creamy-coloured bit under the skin, which can be quite bitter). Juice the lemons, yielding about 2 cups (500 ml) of juice, pulp and pips.

Once the sugar syrup is up to the boil, add the lemon zest, pulpy juice and the elderflower sprays and bring back to the boil. Turn off the heat, pop on a tight-fitting lid and leave to steep overnight.

The next day, have some sterilised bottles and a sterilised sieve, bowl, jug and funnel at the ready (for sterilising tips, see page 127).

Pour the cordial through the fine-meshed sieve into the bowl, then transfer to the jug. Use the funnel to pour the liquid gold into your bottles, then seal with the clean lids. The cordial will keep in the fridge for up to 1 month.

To serve as a summer refresher, add ice to a glass, pour in your desired amount of cordial, then top with sparkling water.

Bonus bits

Tips

Decant the cordial into smaller sterilised bottles and tie with tizzy ribbon for great gifts. Include a little label to remind the lucky recipient to store the cordial in the fridge.

If you can't find unwaxed lemons, run regular waxed ones under hot water and use a clean tea towel to scrub off any residual wax.

Double duty

Splash a dash of the cordial into cocktails and mocktails, tasting as you go.

Make elderflower jelly! Add plenty of water and set with gelatine (see coffee jelly, page 244), plonking in some berries such as raspberries or blueberries to set in the jelly as jewels.

Recipe riffs

To turn into a fruit shrub, muddle the florals (or fruit) in a large jar with the sugar, then cover and macerate in the fridge for 2 days. Swap one-third of the water for apple cider vinegar, bring to the boil and pour over the mixture. Cool slightly, then strain through a muslin-lined sieve into a clean jar. Chill overnight, then decant into sterilised bottles or jars.

Serve the shrub as you would the cordial — with added digestive health benefits from the vinegar.

Elderflower may be growing in a garden near you!

Capture the yellow zest without much of the bitter pith

You can infuse all sorts of botanicals in here

Serve over ice and dilute with a little fizzy liquid to taste

Space jam

500 g (1 lb 2 oz) berries (fresh ones
    are best, but frozen will totally work)
2 tablespoons lemon juice
1½ cups (330 g) granulated white sugar
hot sterilised jars and lids
    (see Tips opposite)

There's one main reason people buy jam instead of making it: because they think it takes ages! What if I told you that you could make jam in about the same amount of time it'll take you to get to the shops and buy a jar, with far less sugar, and for way less dosh? It's no accident that microwaves came about during the space age. This recipe is one small step for you (well, maybe a few more), and one giant leap for our kind.

Pop a small plate in the freezer (all will be revealed soon).

Place the berries and lemon juice in a large microwave-safe bowl and microwave on high for 5 minutes, stirring halfway through. Stir in the sugar and microwave for another 10 minutes, again stirring halfway through.

Give it a good stir and microwave again for another 10 minutes.

At this point, the jam will be searing hot, like molten lava. Gingerly take your cold plate from the freezer and use a teaspoon to drop a little hot jam onto the plate. Leave for a minute to cool, then swipe your finger through it. If the surface wrinkles, the jam is done (this is known as the 'setting point'). If not, cook it a little longer, but remember, like lava, the jam will thicken when cooled.

Pour the hot jam into hot sterilised jars and seal with the clean lids. Leave to cool, then store in the fridge and use within 6 months.

Bonus bits

Tips

You can cook this jam in a heavy-based saucepan on the stovetop. Stir frequently until the sugar dissolves, then cook over medium heat for about 15 minutes, or until setting point is reached.

To sterilise jars in the microwave, give them a rinse in hot, soapy water, then rinse and pop the wet jars (not the lids!) in the microwave and blast on high for 30–45 seconds. In the meantime, pour boiling hot water over the lids and any other equipment you're using, like sieves, bowls and funnels. Another way to sterilise jars and lids is to wash them in warm soapy water and rinse well. Turn the jars upside-down on a lined baking tray and dry them for 15 minutes in a 120°C (235°F) oven. To sterilise the lids, boil them in a saucepan of simmering water for 5 minutes, fish them out with tongs and leave to air-dry on a cooling rack. Or, you could run the jars and lids through the dishwasher and leave them to dry naturally.

Subs

Why ARE store-bought jams so sweet to begin with? Jamming is a fine balance: you want enough sugar to help preserve the fruit and set the jelly, but not so much that you can no longer taste the actual fruit itself. Traditional recipes in older books almost always use about a 1:1 ratio of sugar to fruit by weight, but you can definitely reduce this to 2:3 — or even slightly less sugar if using sweeter, riper fruit with high pectin levels. Just be sure to store the jam in the fridge and consume within a couple of weeks.

Recipe riffs

This jam will work with any ripe, softer fruit. When using bigger fruit such as plums, figs or peaches, cut the fruit to the size of a marble first.

Add aromatics such as cinnamon, cardamom, a scrape of nutmeg or even vanilla bean paste or Chinese five-spice. Since it's a quick cook, ground spices are better here.

Waste knot

This is a great jam to make in summer when berries are cheap and in abundance, but try to avoid using fruit that's on the turn, as the pectin levels will have diminished and the jam won't set properly. I usually scoop off any really mushy bits and simmer those separately, where they melt into a pseudo compote or coulis. Or freeze squashy berries for scattering over breakfast.

Gadget spotlight: Microwaves

Microwaves fell out of favour with the foodie set for a few decades, but with the advent of improved technology and fandangled additions like convection cooking, grill functions and even air-frying included, the ZAP is back. Don't be surprised when you start seeing microwave cookbooks on shelves again, particularly now that they've had the blessing from the cheffiest of chefs like David Chang (whose own microwave cookbook is worth a squiz), and even queen Nigella, who's irrever-reference to it as a 'microwavé' sent social media into meltdown.

Before you go off and buy the fanciest one you can find, decide what you plan on using it for, and what your other kitchen gadgets can already do. Remember, the more tech involved, the more that can go awry, so sometimes the simpler machines are best.

If the idea of those invisible 'microwaves' worries you, it may be reassuring to know that studies have shown that the microwave 'photons' in commercial ovens are nowhere near small enough to change the chemical structure of food, or somehow escape and turn you into MicroMan from the radiation.

Just remember the three golden rules: cover your food to help prevent any food explosions; cook food in increments of time rather than in one big go to monitor for done-ness; and stir about to help distribute heat evenly before tucking in.

Finally, there's nothing worse than a grimy microwave, so to clean up any spills, I love this nifty tip from thrifty cook Jack Monroe: blast a lemon half for 30 seconds on high, then rub the lemon on any baked-on grit to loosen and wipe it clean.

Oladiki pancakes with sour cherries

yoghurt or sour cream, to serve

Oladiki batter

50 g (1½ oz) butter
1 cup (150 g) plain (all-purpose) flour
 (gluten-free works fine here)
¼ teaspoon bicarbonate of soda
 (baking soda)
1 teaspoon salt flakes (optional)
1 cup (250 ml) room-temperature
 milk kefir/buttermilk/yoghurt/
 any 'dodgy' dairy (see Subs, page 130)
1 egg, beaten with a fork

Sour cherry compote

400 g (14 oz) fresh pitted sour/morello
 cherries, or drained jarred pitted sour
 cherries (see Shortcuts, page 130)
1 tablespoon caster (superfine) sugar
juice of 1 lemon
¼ cup (60 ml) water (or sour cherry
 juice from the jar)
½ tablespoon cornflour (cornstarch)

Oladiki (oh-lah-dzi-ki) are Eastern Europe's answer to buttermilk pancakes. They're puffy, fluffy and everything you'd hope for from a hotcake stack, as well as a really great way of using up any 'dodgy' dairy in the fridge. Growing up, Mum would chuck everything from sour cream to yoghurt, ricotta, quark and cottage cheese in these. The batter should have the consistency of Clag paste or thick (double) cream, and will be lumpy, so have faith — it all comes together in the pan. Once you've made these a bunch of times, you'll get to know the consistency you're after by eye, rather than any precise measuring. This recipe makes enough for a two-person household, so if there's more of you, go double, or triple … do what you've gotta do!

First, make the compote. If using fresh cherries, place them in a bowl, sprinkle with the sugar and leave to macerate (soften) for 10 minutes.

Meanwhile, using a whisk, mix the lemon juice, water and cornflour into a slurry in a small saucepan, then whisk over medium–low heat for 4–5 minutes until it starts to thicken.

Tip the macerated cherries and juice, or the drained jarred cherries, into the saucepan, switch over to a spatula or wooden spoon and stir to combine. Let the mixture bubble away and continue to thicken for another 5 minutes, without the cherries breaking up. If you used jarred cherries, taste and add sugar if needed, then remove from the heat and set aside.

For the batter, melt the butter in the frying pan you plan to cook your pancakes in.

Use a whisk to incorporate the flour, bicarbonate of soda and salt flakes together in a bowl. In a pouring jug, mix together your chosen milk product and egg. Make a well in the middle of your dry ingredients and slowly pour in your dairy mixture, stirring as you go; use a flexible spatula to help get every bit of dry friendly with the wet, without overmixing. Stir the melted butter through. The batter will be lumpy, with the consistency of craft glue … be cool … it'll relax on its own. Allow the mixture to stand for 10 minutes.

Meanwhile, wipe out your buttery frying pan with a paper towel, reserving the buttery paper for greasing purposes.

Heat the frying pan over medium heat, then scoop in a large spoonful of the batter. The optimum amount of pancakes in a large pan should be three — any more, and you risk overcrowding; any less, and you're expending excess energy by the stove.

When the surface of the pancakes forms bubbles and a slight skin, which should take 3–4 minutes, flip! Repeat!

Serve warm, topped with the compote and yoghurt or sour cream.

Pancakes with sour cherries Bonus bits

Tips

For an optimum batter, work with room-temperature ingredients.

The batter will keep in the fridge overnight, and actually benefits from a little time to get fizzy. Add the melted butter as your final stage before frying.

If you're making a large batch of oladiki, preheat the oven to 120°C (235°F), to keep your first lot of pancakes warm while you're cooking the rest.

Subs

If you're after a buttermilk version, but don't have any buttermilk on your personage or in the fridge, make your own by adding 1 tablespoon lemon juice or vinegar to 1 cup (250 ml) milk.

To make this recipe plant-based, swap any milk for oat milk or similar, any yoghurt for coconut yoghurt or the like, and the egg for banana (1 mashed banana = 1 beaten egg!).

Shortcuts

Sour cherries are very seasonal, and a bit fiddly to pit (satisfying as this may be when you're in the mood). If you've a hankering but no supply, you'll find pitted sour cherries in juice at most continental delis, and often on the higher shelves in the tinned fruit section at the shops. Their liquid content is obviously far greater, but it also means you can do a quicker version of the topping by just mixing the lemon juice and cornflour into a few

tablespoons of the cherry juice, then warming it all together in a pan over low heat to thicken and relax.

Double duty

Any left-over sour cherry compote makes an excellent stuffing or topping for the French toast on page 193. Oooooft.

Recipe riffs

To make blinchiki (Eastern Europe's answer to crepes), leave out the bicarb and add an extra egg and an extra 1 cup (250 ml) milk. The batter should have the viscosity of pouring cream.

Whatever you like to top your pancakes with is welcome here. I'm particularly fond of the classic combos of

lemon juice and sugar, or crème fraîche and maple syrup. A flavoured butter, like the one on page 196, will work a treat too.

My mate Sandro Demaio likes to add oats to his pancakes. If you do too, get ½ cup (40 g) soaked oats into your batter. He adds a tub of ricotta, too.

Waste knot

When I say any dairy will work, I'm talkin' ANY DAIRY! Anything from cottage cheese to yoghurt, mascarpone and crème fraîche will do. Even if it's past the suggested 'best before' date, as long as it doesn't smell too funky, just scoop any mouldy bits or film off, and in many cases the stuff underneath will be as good as new.

Make a well in the dry ingredients to pour the wet into

Depending on the type of dairy, adjust the liquid amount for a batter this thick

Wait until bubbles and a skin form on top before flipping

You could make thinner crepes instead; see Recipe Riffs

Every-morning-ever oats

If your pantry is overflowing with oats, you're in luck, because no matter what the weather, there are so many quick and simple ways to put those oats to good work, as you'll see on the following pages. Oats are like novelty-sized grains of flour: the more liquid you add (milk, water, juice), the creamier they'll get; and the more fat you add (butter, oil), the crispier they'll be. You can eat oats raw, as in the overnight bircher muesli below, but applying heat really helps to activate the aforementioned creaminess or crunch. These recipes all use classic rolled oats, rather than instant or steel-cut ones.

Plain ol' podge

Serves 4

1 cup (100 g) rolled oats
⅛ teaspoon sea salt (or a pinch; you'll get the hang of it, but don't leave it out)
2 cups (500 ml) water or milk of choice

Add the oats, salt and water to a saucepan and bring to the boil. Reduce the heat to medium–low and simmer for 5–6 minutes, stirring occasionally. Your porridge will start to look creamy and bubble up like lava.

Depending on how you like your oats, add another splash of water, milk or yoghurt to serve.

NOT-SO-PLAIN OL' PODGE: *ZHUZH* IT UP WITH A FEW FAVOURITES

- Grated fresh pear + yoghurt + almonds + honey
- Left-over roasted pears (page 258)
- Stewed fruit + maple syrup + pecans
- A square of cold butter + brown sugar for a classic butterscotch
- Single (pure) cream + brown sugar (try crunchy brown coffee sugar crystals)
- Blueberry compote (frozen blueberries, heated through in a pan) + oat milk (see opposite page) + LSA (linseed, sunflower seed, almond mix)
- Banana slices + tahini + torn dates + walnuts
- Tinned apricots or apricot jam + almond butter
- Toasted coconut + golden syrup, honey or maple syrup
- Grated apple + frozen berries + yoghurt
- Straight-up milk + honey!

Overnight bircher muesli

Serves 2–4

Wonderful warmer weather fare, particularly if you want to pre-prep in jars and yoink from the fridge. Bircher was one of the OG muesli recipes, created by Mr Bircher-Benner in Switzerland and prescribed to patients. Thankfully it doesn't taste 'medicinal' in the slightest.

1 cup (100 g) rolled oats
1 tablespoon chia seeds (optional)
⅛ teaspoon ground cinnamon
a pinch of sea salt flakes
1 apple, grated
1 cup (250 ml) milk, apple juice, kefir, yoghurt or water
juice of ½ lemon
¼ cup (60 g) plain or coconut yoghurt
fresh raspberries, to serve
1 tablespoon maple syrup (optional; no need if using apple juice)

Combine the oats, chia seeds (if using), cinnamon, salt and half the grated apple with your liquid of choice and leave overnight in the fridge — either in a bowl, or in individual jars if you're planning on rushing out the door the following morning.

In a separate container, stir the lemon juice through the remaining apple and pop in the fridge, too.

Next morning, top with the yoghurt, raspberries, remaining grated apple, and maple syrup if using.

Golden granola clusters

Makes a 500 g (1 lb 2 oz) jar

This granola is the BEST. A useful and delicious snack straight from the jar, it also doubles as a topping for sweet poached fruits for breakfast, or warm roasted pears and custard (page 258) for a supreme dessert.

½ cup (125 ml) coconut oil
½ cup (125 ml) maple syrup, or ½ cup (175 g) honey
1 cup (100 g) pecans
1 cup (150 g) raw almonds
1 cup (55 g) flaked coconut
1 cup (155 g) pepitas (pumpkin seeds)
1 cup (145 g) sesame seeds
1 cup (100 g) rolled oats, and/or 1 cup (200 g) buckwheat groats
1 teaspoon ground cinnamon
⅛ teaspoon sea salt flakes

Preheat the oven to 150°C (300°F). Line a deep baking tray with baking paper.

Warm the coconut oil and maple syrup or honey together in a small saucepan.

Combine the remaining ingredients in a large bowl. Pour the warm coconut oil mixture over and toss together until well coated, then spread on the baking tray.

Bake for 30 minutes, until the coconut flakes are golden, stirring halfway through. Leave to cool in the tray, then break up into clusters.

Serve with milk of your choice (try the home-made oat milk, see right!), or straight out of the jar as a snack. Keeps for up to 1 month in the fridge in an airtight container.

MYO oat milk

Makes 4 cups (1 litre)

Oat milk is froth-able, so whether it's for smoothies or coffee, this one's a keeper!

1 cup (100 g) rolled oats
1 tablespoon maple syrup
¼ teaspoon sea salt
4 cups (1 litre) cold water

Blitz all the ingredients in a blender on high for 1 minute. Pour through a strainer lined with muslin (cheesecloth) into a bowl, then through a funnel into a clean glass milk bottle. Seal and keep in the fridge for 3–4 days. Shake the oat milk before using.

Bonus bits

Waste knot

You can keep the oat pulp from making the oat milk and add it to your porridge, or use as an exfoliant or face mask, mixed with a bit of honey, avocado or yoghurt.

Recipe riffs

When you're on the run, make a quick banana smoothie by blitzing 1 cup (250 ml) oat milk and 1 ripe banana in a blender. For extra oomph, sprinkle in some ground cinnamon or cocoa powder, a drizzle of honey, or even a tablespoon of nut butter. Whack into a clean jar or glass; straw optional.

Clockwise from right: Apricot jam and almond butter; Blueberry compote, oat milk and LSA; Grated apple, frozen berries and yoghurt; Cream and brown sugar

Page 132

OTT bars

2 cups (200 g) rolled oats
1 cup chopped nuts and/or nut meal
 (hazelnuts are fab, but pecans or
 even roasted peanuts would work)
1 cup mixed seeds, such as pepitas
 (pumpkin seeds), sesame seeds,
 sunflower seeds, linseeds, hemp
 and/or chia seeds
1 cup (60 g) flaked or shredded coconut
1 cup chopped dried fruit
 and/or choc chips
1 teaspoon salt flakes
½ cup (110 g) raw sugar
½ cup (175 g) honey
125 g (4½ oz) butter
1 teaspoon vanilla bean paste

These oaty tea bars (see what I did there?) are great for school lunchboxes and afternoon snack slumps with a cuppa, using up the last of those packets or jar ingredients floating around your pantry taking up space. They are simply divine as is, but better still, dipped in chocolate (what isn't?) to make them even more OTT (see Tips). Maybe leave the dippy bit out if it's headed for a lunchbox in the middle of summer, though.

Preheat the oven to 160°C (315°F). Dig out a high-sided 15 x 25 cm (6 x 10 inch) tray. (This isn't a non-negotiable size — just note that the bigger the tray, the thinner and snappier your oaty bars will be.) Grease the tray with cooking spray, or brush oil or a little butter up the sides and then a smidge in the base. Press a sheet of baking paper over the base; the oil will help stick the baking paper neatly in place, so your bars don't get random waves in the bottom.

In a large mixing bowl, combine the oats, nuts, seeds, coconut and dried fruit (and/or choc chips). Sprinkle in the salt flakes and sugar and mix well.

In a small saucepan, combine the honey, butter, vanilla paste and ½ cup (125 ml) water, bringing this delicious concoction to the boil. As soon as it starts to bubble and smell like honeycomb, add it to the dry mixture and stir well.

Pour the mixture into the tray and press down. You might even like to place a sheet of baking paper over the top and really press down with the flats of your hands to get a lovely smooth finish. Pull this piece of baking paper off before transferring to the oven, but keep it handy for wrapping bars or keeping layers separate.

Bake for 30 minutes, or until golden brown. The slab will be a bit puffy and HOT, so it needs to cool in the tray a little, before you can again place your baking paper over and press down with the flats of your hands to compress the mixture a little to get an even, pro-looking result. Feel free to leave the surface puffy and rustic, if you'd prefer.

Chill in the fridge before cutting into squares or bars. Store in the fridge in an airtight container, with baking paper separating the layers. The bars will keep in the fridge for up to 10 days. They may go a little bendy, but will still taste great.

Bonus bits

Tips

Spray your measuring cup with cooking oil before measuring out the honey; it will slip straight out like it's Teflon-coated. This trick works with any pesky, sticky syrup.

If you want to *zhuzh* up the bars, drizzle melted chocolate over them — or dip the corners in — and add a sprinkle of nature's glitter: sea salt flakes.

Subs

To go vegan, you can exchange the honey for rice malt syrup or maple syrup, and use a plant-based butter spread in place of the butter.

THE JOY OF BETTER COOKING

Anzac bikkies

1 cup (100 g) rolled oats
1 cup (220 g) raw sugar
1 cup (150 g) plain
   (all-purpose) flour
¾ cup (65 g) desiccated coconut
   (that's the fine one)
125 g (4½ oz) butter, melted
2 tablespoons golden syrup
½ teaspoon bicarbonate of soda
   (baking soda)
3 tablespoons boiling water
1 teaspoon sea salt flakes (optional)

My pal Monique Bowley's Anzac bikkies are a viral sensation Down Under every April, and I'm so pleased to have been given her blessing to share these oaty wonders far and wide. I've added a sprinkle of salt flakes on each biscuit, because I couldn't help myself. Feel free to ignore this addition, which is decidedly un-true to the recipe. (You can read more about salt in desserts on page 277.)

Preheat the oven to 160°C (315°F). Line two baking trays with baking paper. (Light-coloured trays are preferable here. Dark ones are okay, but they absorb more heat, so you'll need to keep an eye on the biscuit bases, to make sure they don't get too dark.)

Pop the oats, sugar, flour and coconut in a bowl and stir together with a wooden spoon.

Melt the butter and golden syrup together in a small saucepan over low heat. Meanwhile, pour boiling water over the bicarbonate of soda in a small bowl and stir until it dissolves. Add the 'soda' water to the butter mixture in the pan and let it foam up. Pour the foamy mixture into your dry ingredients and stir to combine.

With a small bowl of water by your side, wet your palms and roll the biscuits into golf balls — 35 g (1 oz) per ball, if you're using scales. Space them out on the baking trays with 4–5 cm (1½–2 inches) between each to allow for spreading. Sprinkle a little salt flake action on each ball, if you like.

Bake for 15–18 minutes, or until golden brown, watching for uneven hot spots (where the biscuits on one part of the tray start colouring faster than the rest) and rotating the trays 180 degrees if need be.

Allow to cool on a wire rack, then store in an airtight container in a cool, dry place (not the fridge, or they'll go soggy!).

Bonus bits

Tips

For chewier biscuits, add another tablespoon of water. For crunchier ones, bake for 20 minutes at 150°C (300°F).

If you're the type who craves a perfect circle, place a round heatproof jar slightly bigger than the biscuit over the top while the biccies are still warm on the tray, and shake the biscuit to shape.

Check out more biscuit-related tips on page 265.

Subs

Gluten-free flour will work here. It gives a crumblier finish, so adding an extra tablespoon of water will help. Some people who are gluten intolerant will be okay with rolled oats, but do check first and replace with something like quinoa flakes instead.

If you don't have golden syrup, you can use treacle, honey or molasses instead.

Double duty

Turn these into the ultimate ice-cream sandwich by scooping some vanilla ice cream between two bikkies, squashing them together and getting stuck in. You can even refreeze them as sangas for special occasions. Or, you can grab them while still warm for a taste sensation (as long as your teeth can handle it).

Easy crumble topping

½ cup (50 g) rolled oats
½ cup (75 g) self-raising flour
¼ cup (55 g) sugar
100 g (3½ oz) cold butter

A crumble is such a hearty, hearthy finish to a meal, and a satisfying way to use up the last of your rolled oats. You can scale up this basic crumble mix and make it in advance, ready to have on hand. Quadruple the quantity of oats, flour and sugar, mix well and keep in a big jar in the pantry. Then, when needed, scoop out one-quarter of the mixture, rub in 100 g (3½ oz) cold grated butter and *voilà*, you're done. Sprinkle over chopped sweetened raw fruits, or any poached pieces, compote or frozen berries fossicked from your pantry, fridge or freezer. This simple crumble mix works brilliantly with whatever's in season — be it apples, pears, quince, stone fruit, berries, Gruffalo … that sort of thing.

In a bowl, mix together the oats, flour and sugar. A good way to incorporate the butter is to grate it on the large holes of a box grater and then just toss it through, using the very tips of your fingers to rub the floury buttery brilliance together until your mixture looks gravelly. Hey presto, your crumble is done!

This amount of crumble will cover a 15–20 cm (6–8 inch) baking dish to a depth of about 1 cm (½ inch), to conservatively serve four.

Spread your choice of fruit in the baking dish. Crown your crumble topping over the fruit (we've used stewed rhubarb and apple with frozen raspberries in the pic). Bake in a preheated 180°C (350°F) oven for 20–25 minutes, until golden on top and bubbly at the sides.

Serve warm, with a generous dollop of cream, vanilla ice cream or yoghurt (coconut or otherwise).

Bonus bits

Recipe riffs

One of the best things about a crumble topping is that you can keep it simple, or trick it up a bit with pantry stars such as coconut flakes and crushed nuts, or even nut meals for extra richness. A little spice goes a long way, too — a pinch of cinnamon or ground cardamom here, a scrape of nutmeg there. It's even a fab way of using up Chinese five-spice, with ½ teaspoon making for a great eyebrow-raising, same-same-but-different factor.

Subs

For a vegan crumble, use coconut oil or plant-based butter instead of butter.

Oats are technically gluten-free, so do check with any intolerant folk in your vicinity before subbing them out, but you can use quinoa flakes or rice flakes instead of oats, and a gluten-free self-raising flour too.

Potato fritters that glitter

⅓ cup (50 g) gluten-free plain
    (all-purpose) flour (see Subs, page 145)
½ cup (125 ml) frying oil (I like grapeseed)
60 g (2 oz) butter
sea salt flakes, for sprinkling
25 g (1 oz) baby rocket (arugula)
    leaves, to serve
¼ cup (60 g) crème fraîche
finely chopped chives, to garnish
lemon cheeks, to serve

Fritters

1 leek, pale part only, washed
    and very finely chopped
1 tablespoon butter
2 cups (460 g) left-over cold mashed
    potato (see Longcuts, page 145)
100 g (3½ oz) gruyère cheese, grated
1 egg, beaten
¼ cup finely chopped flat-leaf parsley
1 tablespoon finely chopped chives
1 tablespoon gluten-free plain
    (all-purpose) flour (see Subs, page 145)
½ teaspoon sea salt flakes
¼ teaspoon freshly cracked black pepper

There is one particular left-over dinner item that is as good as gold to me, and that's mashed potato. In fact, I'll always make double what I need for a meal, just so I can look forward to some gorgeous new mash-up on day two or three. Whether magicked into a kedgeree, hash browns, croquettes or potato gems, or even a filling for potato pasties, squashed spuds as a flavour boat is the epitome of making seconds sparkle.

To make the fritters, sauté the leek in the butter in a large heavy-based frying pan over medium heat for 10 minutes, or until the leek is soft and silky and starting to turn golden. Leave to cool.

In a large bowl, mix the softened leek with the mashed potato, cheese, egg, herbs, flour and seasoning until combined.

Place the ⅓ cup (50 g) flour in a flat dish for dusting. Using a ⅓ cup (80 ml) measure, scoop out some mash mixture, flip onto the dusting flour and shape into a fritter; you should be able to make eight family meal-sized fritters. If you prefer, you could use a 1 tablespoon measure to make 16 gems (see Tips, page 145) or a ¼ cup (60 ml) measure to make 10 croquettes (see Extra extras, also page 145). Place on a tray until all the fritters are shaped, adding more flour if needed.

Leave in the fridge to set for 15–20 minutes — or overnight, if you're planning a bougie breakfast.

When you're ready to get frying, add the oil and butter to your frying pan and heat until shimmering.

Working in batches, gently add the fritters to the pan; the oil needs to come halfway up the sides of the fritters. Cook for 5 minutes on each side until golden brown, flipping carefully a couple of times once the sides are set. (Gems and croquettes won't need as long to cook: 3–4 minutes should do it.)

Once done, drain each batch on a tray lined with paper towel, seasoning with a little salt flake action on top.

Serve 2 fritters per person on a bed of rocket, dolloped with crème fraîche and sprinkled with chives, with lemon cheeks on the side.

Potato fritters Bonus bits

Spuds are simply alchemical, encapsulating the transformation of states of matter from solid to liquid to semi-solid all over again.

Tips

These fritters are delicious cold, but reheat really well in the oven or back in the pan (no extra oil necessary, but I won't stop you if you want to reinvigorate an extra crispy coating).

For nibbles with drinks, you can cook gem-sized ones in advance; they'll keep for up to 1 week in the fridge, or you could freeze them flat on a tray, then bag up and keep for up to 3 months.

Subs

You can use either regular plain (all-purpose) flour or gluten-free plain flour here. I like using gluten-free here, as it actually gives a lighter result, and can be enjoyed by more people.

Longcuts

If you want to make the fritters without waiting for mash leftovers, boil 700 g (1 lb 9 oz) scrubbed, chopped roasting potatoes (sebago, Dutch cream or similar) in just enough well-salted water to cover, until they're fork-tender. Squash them through a ricer, or mash with 50 g (1½ oz) cold butter and a splash of cold milk. It's better to have a mash on the stiff side for these fritters, so you can mould them into whatever shape and size you like.

Double duty

Whack any left-over fritter mixture into puff pastry to make pasties. Throw in ½ cup (75 g) frozen peas/corn and cook according to the pastry packet instructions.

Pop a fritter into a greased ramekin, squash a hole in the middle, crack an egg in and bake for 10–12 minutes at 190°C (375°F) until the egg just sets. If you're in a hurry, crank the oven to the grill (broil) setting after 5 minutes or so to help set the egg faster — but watch it like a hawk!

Extra extras

Turn these fritters into croquettes by using panko breadcrumbs to coat instead of flour. Shape the mixture into oblongs or cylinders instead of patties, then leave to set in the fridge as per the recipe. Dust with flour, dip into egg wash (1 beaten egg plus a half-eggshell's extra water in the bowl), then dip into panko crumbs and shallow-fry. Some people prefer to deep-fry their croquettes, which you're more than welcome to do. Just be sure the mixture is well-crumbed. A double-crumbing never hurts, either.

Recipe riffs

You could include the below as well as the existing ingredients with some extra mash and egg to bind, or sub out the leek, gruyere and herbs and replace with ...

- Feta, peas, spring onion + mint: Add ⅓ cup (50 g) grated feta, ¾ cup (110 g) frozen peas, 1 finely chopped spring onion (scallion) and 1 tablespoon chopped mint.
- Tuna, caper, anchovy + lemon: Add a drained 120 g (4 oz) tin tuna in oil, 1 tablespoon brined capers, 4 finely chopped anchovies, and the zest and juice of 1 small lemon.

Spana in the works

1 medium–large onion, finely diced

3 tablespoons olive oil

300 g (10½ oz) rainbow chard, leaves and stems roughly chopped (about 4 cups)

2 cups (100 g) finely chopped Tuscan kale (cavolo nero) leaves

zest and juice of 1 lemon

1 bunch of dill or parsley, roughly chopped

2–3 large eggs (depending on the size of your pan ... the less egg, the better!)

1 teaspoon salt flakes

¼ cup (40 g) pine nuts

60 g (2 oz) crumbly feta

250 g (9 oz) truss cherry tomatoes

a pinch of caster (superfine) sugar

toasted sourdough, to serve

Think of this as a spanakopita cop-out (kop-out?). Instead of wrapping with filo pastry, we're simply glueing with egg into a loose-leaf binder situation, and serving it on a crunchy sourdough toast boat. I love using this recipe to chew up the bitter greens in our veg box (kale, chard, chicory), because the wide surface area and higher oven temp means you essentially get a crispy, burnished kale chip crust on top — and all that lemon really helps bring the zing.

Preheat the oven to 190°C (375°F).

In a shallow, flameproof casserole dish, cook the onion in 2 tablespoons of the olive oil over medium heat for a minute or so. Put the lid on, reduce the heat to low and let the onion sweat for 5 minutes. Finish with the lid off until the onion is well and truly translucent and softened.

Add the chard and kale. Cover and cook for 5 minutes, or until softened and wilted. Remove from the heat and stir in the lemon zest, juice and herbs.

Crack the eggs into a bowl and beat with a fork. Add the salt, stirring well to incorporate. Pour the egg mixture over the sautéed greens and stir to combine. Crumble the pine nuts and feta on top. Drizzle with the remaining olive oil.

Bake for 30–35 minutes, or until firm to touch and slightly golden. Toss the cherry tomatoes in a glug of olive oil and a pinch of sugar and salt flakes and place on top of the slice.

Enjoy straight out of the oven on toast, or as a fab cold lunchbox option.

Bonus bits

Tips

Add an extra egg and bake in a 20 x 30 cm (10 x 12 inch) baking dish lined with baking paper. You can turn it out and cut into lunchbox squares, which can also be frozen.

Shortcuts

Sauté the veg in a pan. In a separate non-stick pan, crumble the feta into the beaten egg, giving it a few stirs until the egg has firmed up, then serve atop the sautéed greens as an accidental feta scramble.

Ingredient spotlight: Bitter greens

If you're subscribing to a weekly veg box (if not, do it now!), you'll often find green leafies poking out of the top. These should be one of the first things you cook for the week, as they deteriorate far quicker than woodier, rootier veg. If chopping through the leaf against the grain proves difficult, it's probably a sign that the stem is too tough to chew, so just pull the leaves off the stems, against the grain, then finely chop just the leaves. Chard and silverbeet (Swiss chard) stalks are perfectly edible, though, and Tuscan kale can be left whole, but they need a little extra cooking to break down the fibres.

If you're not sure what you feel like doing with your bitter greens, my advice is to finely chop the stalks and shred the leaves, then sauté in oil or butter when you have a spare moment; some sweated onion or leek in there never goes astray. You can then serve it up as 'wilted greens' for breakfast with a squirt of lemon juice, add into tray bakes, savoury pastries, pasta sauces, soups and stews as needed for bulk and bonus nutrition, or it can be egged-up and baked in something like this. Or, freeze and thaw as needed later on.

To mitigate the bitterness, add something salty, such as cheese (feta or parmesan), and something acidic, like vinegar or lemon juice. This routine of sweating the green stuff will mean you'll stop sweating the small stuff about your food waste contribution.

Pkhali

Serves 4–6

Base paste

1 cup (140 g) walnuts (see Tips, page 151)
½ teaspoon ground coriander
½ teaspoon curry powder (a basic one
   is always good to have in the pantry)
½ bunch of coriander (cilantro), stems
   roughly chopped, leaves picked
   and reserved
1 tablespoon red wine vinegar
   (see Subs, page 151)
1 tablespoon olive oil,
   plus a little extra if needed
1 tablespoon pomegranate molasses
1 teaspoon salt flakes
¼ teaspoon garlic powder,
   or 1 young garlic clove
   for added freshness and punch

To garnish

seeds from 1 pomegranate
   (see Tips, page 151)
coriander (cilantro) leaves, picked

This chunky Georgian dip, pronounced 'P-KCHA! (like you're clearing a fur ball)-LEE', features walnuts as a thickener like so many Georgian dishes, as they grow so prolifically there. This is more of a technique than a recipe, infinitely adaptable to the veg in your crisper — even if they're looking a little lank. It's a wonderful way of utilising any soft green leafies like spinach and rainbow chard, and will finally see you beat your beets into submission from root to leaf, which is why it's a perfect weapon to add to your use-it-up arsenal. I like to include a couple of these versions on the same platter, as they add such lovely vibrancy to the table and can be made in advance; perfect for festivities and bring-a-plates. The base recipe is enough to make two of the veg portions, so if you'd like to make one of each of the four, just double the base ingredients. Maths!

Heat a heavy-based frying pan until smoking. Switch the heat off and add the walnuts, ground coriander and curry powder and give everything the odd toss until they start to become even more aromatic and turn slightly golden brown.

Tip the mixture into a food processor. Add the remaining base ingredients and blitz to a rough paste. You can make this paste ahead and store in the fridge for a day or so. Use in any of the following dips, depending on what vegetal stuff you have at your disposal.

When you've blitzed your chosen vegies into the base paste, oil your hands with a little olive or grapeseed oil. Shape the mixture into balls the size of squash balls. Press a dimple into the middle of each and fill with pomegranate seeds and a walnut. Finish with a little coriander leaf action and serve at room temperature alongside other small dishes and soft bread.

SPINACH/SILVERBEET/CHARD/BEET LEAVES

Pull the leaves off 4 silverbeet (Swiss chard) stalks. Wash well, ensuring there's no grit left in any nooks and crannies. This may require a few soaks and a judicious rub of each leaf, especially if there's been recent heavy rain.

Alternatively, you can use the same amount of beetroot leaves, or a bunch of regular English spinach leaves, or 50 g (1½ oz) baby spinach leaves.

Bring a large saucepan of well-salted water to the boil. Add the leaves to the water and submerge. For baby spinach leaves, 30–40 seconds is plenty. For regular spinach, a minute will do. Chard, beet leaves and silverbeet will need 2 minutes — you can tell these are cooked when they turn a more vibrant shade, and they soften enough to tear by hand.

(You can also wilt the rinsed leaves in a lidded saucepan rather than blanch, if you prefer. There's no need to add oil or extra water — just shut the lid tight and check every now and then until they're sweated and softened.)

Cool slightly, then squeeze out, reserving any expressed liquid in a little bowl for loosening. »

Pkhali continued

Chop the leaves roughly, then blitz together with the base paste, adding a splash of the reserved liquid or olive oil if the mixture needs to be loosened slightly (but don't get too loose with the loosening, as you want a firm enough mixture to form balls).

Note: You can use the stalks of these vegies, too; they're just going to need more time to blanch until soft, and will need to be chopped finely first to break down the fibres before blitzing.

BEETROOT

Mum has always used pre-packed cooked baby beets for this dish (3–4 little ones); even tinned ones will do it, just add half the vinegar and taste before adding the rest. If you want to boil your own baby beets, scrub them of dirt, but leave them unpeeled. Squeeze a little lemon juice or vinegar into a saucepan of well-salted boiling water, to help set the deepest beetroot colour shade. Add the beets and boil until fork-tender, 30–40 minutes, depending on their size. Drain, leave to cool slightly, and *then* peel away the skins, which will slip right off; oil your hands or use paper towel to avoid stainage.

Roasted beets have more intensity of flavour, so you're welcome to give that a whirl too, if you've got the time. Scrub them clean, leave the skins on, oil them and wrap in foil. Place on a baking tray and roast at 200°C (400°F) for at least an hour, or until fork-tender. Leave to cool slightly, then peel.

Roughly chop the beets, then blitz together with the base paste until puréed.

CABBAGE/CAULIFLOWER LEAVES

Pull the leaves off a cabbage quarter and remove the stalks. Slice the woodiest parts off the stalk and chop the stalks finely to put through the mix as well. Wash the leaves well, ensuring there's no grit left in any nooks and crannies.

Alternatively, pull off the outer leaves and stalks of 1 whole cauliflower and rinse them clean of any dirt.

Bring a large saucepan of well-salted water to the boil. Add the leaves to the water and submerge. For cabbage leaves, 5–6 minutes should do it. For cauliflower leaves and stalks, particularly if they're more fibrous, it might take a little longer. Pull them out when they turn a more vibrant shade and have softened enough to tear by hand. In case you're wondering, you can totally blanch the cauliflower florets for this as well — 4–5 minutes, until they just turn translucent, is plenty. Save a little of the blanching water.

Blitz together with the base paste, adding a splash of the reserved blanching water if the mixture needs to be loosened slightly (but don't get too loose with the loosening, as you want a firm enough mixture to form balls).

LEEK/JARRED CARAMELISED ONION

Chop 1 leek into 1 cm (½ inch) slices, all the way up the greens. You can probably lose about 2 cm (¾ inch) from the top and the very bottom of the root end, but for this dish the rest will be useable. Soak and spin the slices a few times in your salad spinner to eliminate any grit. Give it all one last shake about.

Bring a large saucepan of well-salted water to the boil. Add the leek and simmer for 8–10 minutes, or until softened. Drain, reserving a little of the blanching water.

Alternatively, you could use about 250 g (9 oz) ready-made caramelised onion.

Blitz the leek or caramelised onion with the base paste, adding a splash of reserved blanching water or olive oil if the mixture needs to be loosened slightly (but don't get too loose with the loosening, as you want a firm enough mixture to form balls).

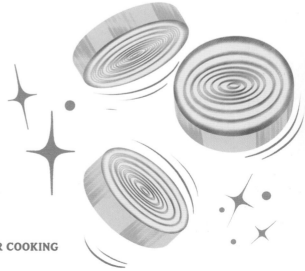

THE JOY OF BETTER COOKING

Pkhali Bonus bits

Tips

Freshly cracked walnuts are always the sweetest, but if whole walnuts are not around, or you're not in a cracking mood, find the freshest ones you can — robust without being crumbly.

You can sometimes buy pre-picked pomegranate seeds from greengrocers, but you can also try your hand at picking your own. Try the 'whack a wooden spoon from the back end' method to release the seeds from a halved pomegranate, lop off the top and cut an incision at each segment to tear open the whole thing, or do as I do and take your time to pop each seed out individually, treating every twisting motion as a meditation. Any left-over seeds can be eaten as is, or used to garnish salads.

Subs

If you don't have red wine vinegar, you can use apple cider vinegar, or the most delicate vinegar in your arsenal. Add a little at a time, and taste, as the amount you need will depend on the natural sweetness of the vegetables you're using. I like this description from my favourite Georgian cookbook, *The Georgian Feast*: 'the purée should taste slightly sharp, but never vinegary'.

Any left-over cooked orange veg (à la the orange veg one-tray soup on page 68) can also be blitzed up with the base paste to get another colourway going, too.

Shortcuts

Rather than shaping the different mixtures into balls, simply serve them as dips.

Recipe riffs

You could use the base paste as a vegie dressing. Stir it through blanched chopped cabbage or cauliflower, or cooked beets (which can be kept whole, or halved or quartered, depending on how you like to see them texturally and aesthetically). Garnish with coriander (cilantro) leaves and pomegranate seeds, giving the whole thing one more toss before dishing up on a brightly coloured platter.

Worth it

If you have a hankering for Middle Eastern or North African flavours, pomegranate molasses won't languish long in your pantry. It adds a beautiful tangy sweetness to everything it touches. Many Ottolenghi recipes call for it, and you can also sub some in instead of vinegar in a dressing, splashing in a little extra acid from lemon juice to loosen it up if need be.

Gadget spotlight: Blenders/food processors

There are some extremely nifty blenders and processors on the market, and whether you decide to get one really depends on how often you find yourself needing to blitz stuff, how much cupboard and/or bench space you have at your disposal (is it ever enough??), and whether you feel the need to fork out for a smart machine that also cooks.

At home we have a Thermomix, but mostly use it for steaming with the Varoma attachment, or blitzing as we might in a regular blender. Some people swear by them, like food writer and restaurant critic Dani Valent, who's a whiz at using hers, so if you're looking to get one, it would be worth taking a squiz at her recipes and books.

A stick blender might be a good place to start, and you really can't go past a Bamix for reliability. If choosing a different brand, just pick one with a metal stick, so that you can at least immerse it straight into hot liquids to *zhuzh* them (carefully).

If you're a smoothies and shakes fan, then a Nutribullet or similar might be enough for you, especially if you're swingin' solo. The benefit here is that you tip the cup upside-down to blend, which ensures gravity takes care of every bit for balanced blitzing.

If you already have a food processor, chances are you don't need to fork out for a blender as well. Most processors have a blade attachment that will operate similarly to a blender. Processor slicing attachments are handy if you've got so much to grate or slice in a recipe that you're considering not making it — like when you're banging up big batches of chunky soup or doubling up on zucchini fritters. You can read more about how to get the most out of both in the Blending skills spotlight on page 211.

For pastes and purées like this one, sometimes all you're really looking for is an old-school mortar and pestle. Porcelain is my pick, as it absorbs fewer aromas than granite, which can get 'garlicky' real quick. Indeed, *pkhali* (or *mkhali*, as it's otherwise known) is traditionally mashed by hand using a mortar and pestle, which helps you get the mix just so.

Courgette continuum

Come summer, whether you're a kitchen gardener, a farmers' market meanderer or a specials seeker at the shops, everything's coming up courgettes ... or zucchini, depending on who you ask! Subject to how much heat you apply, or how much acid or salt you add to break it down, or what starch you bind it with, zucchini sits on a continuum of freshness and density. Its spongy texture and fairly neutral flavour means its role in a dish is less about enhancing the taste, and more about helping to build body. Just call it Arnold Gourdznegger.

ZOODLES

Some people regard their suspicion of spiralised zucchini as an aspect of their sense of self, but I remain proudly zoodle-curious. My favourite way to use them is as a half-and-half — half actual pasta or noodle, and half zucchini. That way, it lightens up the carb–veg ratio, adds more colour to your dish, and offers a delightful interplay between *al dente* and *al courge-ente*.

Some people blanch zoodles, but I prefer to scald them. Pop the zoodles into the colander that's about to catch your cooked pasta, and pour the contents of the whole pot over them. Toss with olive oil and your pasta sauce and serve. They're gorgeous mixed through the golden angel hair pasta on page 62 — just add before you pop in the burrata, then whack a lid back on and let the residual heat finish it off.

If you're going the full zoodle, just pour a kettle of boiling water over them to scald. Pouring your hot sauce over the raw zoodle will give you an al-dente result.

Spiralisers don't have to be hefty electrical attachments, either. My favourite kind is like a giant pencil sharpener, with two girths to choose from. Always choose the wider noodle for scalding, and save the skinny version for spiralised zucchini bits to toss into stir-fries, fritters or salads. The acid in your dressing will 'cook' the noodles just enough to soften and slay.

Zucchini pickles
Page 154

Zoodles

Free-for-all fritters
Page 155

Zucchini pickles

1 kg (2 lb 4 oz) medium-sized zucchini
(courgettes), washed and sliced
500 g (1 lb 2 oz) medium-sized salad
onions, thinly sliced
2 cups (500 ml) white vinegar
½ teaspoon ground turmeric
2 teaspoons curry powder
2 teaspoons mustard powder
(Margaret uses Keen's)
1 teaspoon yellow mustard seeds
2 teaspoons salt
1 teaspoon cornflour (cornstarch)
1 cup (220 g) raw sugar

Speaking of softening with an acid, pickling zucchini slices turns them into little sponges for whatever flavours you add. My mate's mum Margaret won first prize at the Maldon show with this mustardy zucchini pickle, so mayhaps you might have similar success. Use a crinkle cutter to get funky, or slice on a mandoline to about a 2 mm (⅟₁₆ inch) thickness.

Pop the zucchini and onion into a large saucepan with half the vinegar. Bring to the boil, then drop the heat and simmer for 30 minutes.

Meanwhile, combine half the remaining vinegar with the turmeric, curry powder, mustard powder, mustard seeds and salt. Mash into a smooth paste.

Add the cornflour and sugar to the last of the vinegar and stir with a fork to incorporate. Pour this mixture into the simmering zucchini, bring back to the boil and stir for about 5 minutes, until the whole thing thickens.

Stir in the mustardy paste, drop the heat again and simmer for 5 minutes.

Scoop into sterilised jars (see page 127) and store in the fridge. The pickles will keep at their best for up to 1 month, then slowly start to soften.

Bonus bits

Skills spotlight: Acid trip

Sourness stimulates saliva and cuts through richness, which is why so many starters and salads are prone to making you pucker, and why rich cheese and desserts are finished with a flourish of astringency. You can harness this effect simply by including optional offsiders such as pickles or lemon or lime wedges. Everyone's penchant for pucker is personal, so these are a great way of optimising the offering for individual palates.

Another reason you'll see lemon cheeks or green pickle on platters comes down to what these colours do for our expectation of taste. Research has shown we associate green and yellow with vibrant, fresh flavours, so including these colours on the plate makes us perceive, and therefore receive, more 'fresh' messaging and increases our enjoyment, especially in hot weather.

From an Eastern medicine perspective, even though lemon — and sourness in general — is acidic in flavour, it actually helps to alkalise the body, which is an excellent state to put yourself in, particularly early in the day. Acid also helps digestion, so not only are you cutting through the richness on the palate, by eating acidic foods you're also helping the food you eat break down.

Speaking of beneficial 'A' things, any time you see the word 'acidulate', you're being called to soak a delicate ingredient in water that is spiked with acid, whether it's a squirt of lemon juice or a splash of white wine or rice wine vinegar. This helps to keep the whites bright in vegies like fennel, daikon and radish, while also helping to set the colour of fruits such as apples and pears.

Free-for-all fritters

/ **Makes**
12–15 fritters

400 g (14 oz) zucchini (courgettes);
    about 3–4 medium-sized ones
½ small red onion
1 teaspoon salt flakes, plus extra to serve
1 cup (110 g) chickpea flour (besan),
    plus extra if needed
1 teaspoon baking powder
3 tablespoons olive oil
sea salt flakes, for sprinkling

These fritters continue to take the internet by storm, after I first shared them on ABC TV's *News Breakfast*. What I love about these fritters is that they're gluten-free, dairy-free, egg-free and nut-free, making them an absolute free-for-all for anyone with dietaries, and everyone who loves a fritter. Not only is chickpea flour (a.k.a. besan) free from gluten, it also behaves like egg when enough liquid is added, and is what makes the liquid you drain from your tin of chickpeas (a.k.a. aquafaba), a common plant-based egg replacement (which you can use in the 'veringues' on page 290). Speaking of water, while many fritter recipes ask you to squeeze the excess moisture from the zucchini before frying, here I'm harnessing its wetness to help everything bind together. Saves on washing a bright-green tea towel, too.

Grate the zucchini and onion on the coarse side of your box grater, into a bowl big enough to hold the entire mixture. Sprinkle the salt flakes on top and stir them through, giving everything a squish to encourage the zucchini to start leaking out liquid. Let the mixture rest for 5–10 minutes to get really juicy.

Scatter the chickpea flour on top, rubbing it through your fingers as you do to eke out any lumps. (Okay, yes, you can sift, but I like to get handsy here.) Sprinkle in the baking powder and stir together with a spatula until well incorporated. The mixture should look and feel like pancake batter … if it feels a little too loosey-goosey, sprinkle in another tablespoon of chickpea flour.

Heat 2 tablespoons of the oil in a large frying pan over medium heat. Once it starts to shimmer, add heaped tablespoons of the mixture in a clockwise arrangement, so that you can remember which fritter needs flipping first.

Flip as the bottoms get golden, which will take 3–4 minutes. Once both sides are cooked, drain on paper towel, sprinkling with salt flakes while hot.

Serve immediately, or allow to cool, refrigerate and pop into lunchboxes for happy eaters. These will store well in the fridge for 4–5 days.

Bonus bits

Tips

These fritters can be frozen, thawed overnight and then reheated. Whack 'em on a lined baking tray in a cold oven, then crank the oven to 160°C (315°F) for about 10–15 minutes. By the time the oven has heated up, the fritters have too.

I've intentionally kept the flavours very neutral, to let you choose your own adventure! Add a pinch of curry powder, za'atar or smoked paprika to take these to a different place.

Depending on how old your zucchini are, they might release more liquid than expected. There's no harm in adding another good helping of chickpea flour into the mixture midway through to help it bind; it's not like these fritters are at risk of being too 'eggy'.

Take the veg factor up a notch with frozen peas or corn. Pour some boiling water over ½ cup (75 g) of one or the other, then drain and add to the mixture. You may need to add a smidge more chickpea flour, depending on how wet your zucchini mixture gets. Other veg that could fit here in a pinch include grated sweet potato, carrot, pumpkin (squash) and beetroot.

Roast zucchini with butter crumbs

6 small–medium-sized
  zucchini (courgettes)
3 tablespoons extra virgin olive oil
½ cup (75 g) currants
juice and zest of 1 lemon
½ cup roughly chopped parsley
60 g (2 oz) parmesan, finely grated
  (preferably with a microplane)

CP butter crumbs
150 g (5½ oz) Cacio e pepe butter
  (page 96), or 100 g (3½ oz) butter
  plus salt and pepper to taste
1½ cups (75 g) sourdough breadcrumbs
  (or panko crumbs)

People usually think of zucchini as a bit player, but here, they're the main act — the stuff of dreams. This recipe is especially handy if you're growing your own, and find one overgrown in the undergrowth. Just remember that the bigger the zucchini, the longer the cooking time will be. This will work as one big roast with a marrow, but as fermentation king Sandor Katz always says: the flavour peaks at the midpoint. As the zucchini grows, the flavour mellows, so just be extra generous with the seasoning and cheese.

Preheat the oven to 180°C (350°F) and line two baking trays with baking paper.

Cut each zucchini in half lengthways. Use a teaspoon to scoop out the fleshy centre that also houses the seeds (a.k.a. 'zucchini guts'), reserving these for later.

Brush the cut side of the zucchini with a little of the olive oil and sprinkle with salt flakes. Place the zucchini on the baking trays, cut side down, and bake for 10 minutes. Take out of the oven, flip each zucchini half over and bake for another 10 minutes.

Prepare the CP butter crumbs by rubbing the butter into the breadcrumbs with your fingers.

Once the zucchini halves are out of the oven, spoon the butter crumbs into them. Feel free to heap the mixture on — height is good, as is a bit of overrun. Pop the tray back into the oven for another 10 minutes, or until the topping is golden brown and crispy.

Meanwhile, sauté the reserved zucchini guts in the remaining olive oil over medium heat for 5 minutes, then add the currants and sauté for another 5 minutes, or until the currants and zucchini innards have softened. Switch off the heat, splash in the lemon juice, stir the chopped parsley through and season to taste with salt and pepper.

Schmear the mixture across the base of a serving platter. Arrange the crumbed zucchini over the top. Finish with the grated parmesan, lemon zest and a drizzle of olive oil.

Bonus bits

Tips

Make these into zucchini parmigiana by sautéing some onion and garlic in a little olive oil, then sploshing in a jar of tomato passata (puréed tomatoes), the zucchini guts and lots of fresh basil to make a sauce. Top the crumbed zucchini with the sauce, plus extra mozzarella or provolone and parmesan, then bake at 190°C (375°F) for about 15 minutes, until the cheese is golden and melted. A smidge of good-quality Parma ham under the cheese will satisfy even the most carnivorous sorts.

Subs

For gluten-free, either use rice crumbs in place of panko, or fry pine nuts in CP butter until just turning golden, then spoon over the crumbed zucchini.

Recipe riffs

Roasted butternut pumpkin (squash) halves would love the last-minute addition of these CP butter crumbs, then being briefly baked again until the topping is golden.

Zucchini & brown butter bread

3 cups (400 g) coarsely grated zucchini
   (courgette), plus some very thinly
   sliced strips for topping if desired
1 teaspoon salt flakes, plus extra
   for sprinkling
150 g (5½ oz) butter, melted,
   plus extra for greasing
1 cup (100 g) grated cheddar
3 spring onions (scallions), finely sliced
3 tablespoons chopped parsley
½ cup (125 g) plain or Greek-style yoghurt
2 eggs, beaten
2 cups (300 g) self-raising flour
   (gluten-free will work here)
1 cup (180 g) instant polenta (or cornmeal)
1 good rasp of nutmeg
2 tablespoons olive oil
¼ cup (40 g) pepitas (pumpkin seeds)
zucchini (courgette) flowers,
   to garnish (optional)

The best part about bakes featuring zucchini is that you can just about guarantee they're going to be moist. While the batter cooks, the shredded zucchini sweats, refusing to yield to neither heat nor starch. Feel free to have a play with your own additions and aromatics for this one. And tip in some chopped soft green herbs, too — parsley, dill, basil ... that sort of thing.

Preheat the oven to 160°C (315°F). Grease and line a 20 cm (8 inch) square cake tin, baking dish or two loaf (bar) tins.

Pop the grated zucchini in a large bowl lined with a clean tea towel and sprinkle with 1 teaspoon salt. Allow to sit for 5–10 minutes, then twist the tea towel into a swag and squeeze to draw out as much liquid as possible. Pour out the liquid and place the zucchini back in the bowl.

Mix the melted butter, cheese, spring onion and parsley through the drained zucchini, then add the yoghurt and beaten eggs.

In a separate bowl, combine the flour, polenta, nutmeg and a good grinding of black pepper. Add half the flour mixture to your zucchini mixture and stir to combine. Add the remaining flour mixture and stir again until everything is incorporated. If using gluten-free flour, feel free to overmix to your heart's content, but be a bit more conservative if using regular flour.

Pour the batter into your chosen vessel. Drizzle the olive oil over and smooth out with a spatula. Decorate with thin zucchini strips if desired, giving them an extra drizzle of olive oil.

Bake on the middle rack of the oven for 15 minutes. Remove the tin from the oven, sprinkle the pepitas and some extra salt flakes over the top, and arrange the zucchini flowers on top, if using. Bake for another 35–40 minutes, or until a skewer comes out clean. Allow to cool in the tin for 10 minutes, then turn out onto a wire rack to cool completely before cutting.

This slice will keep best in an airtight container in the fridge, and will be good for at least a week. Popping a piece in the toaster or oven to crisp up will give it a new lease on life too, and will be most delicious with a dab of butter.

Bonus bits

Tips
Up the veg by lining the tin with strips of roasted capsicum (pepper), sun-dried tomato and/or chopped black olives. You could whack in ½ cup (75 g) thawed frozen peas and/or corn through the mix for extra pops of veg, too.

Recipe riffs
If you're lacking zucchini but swimming in pumpkin (squash), just swap it in, or go half and half.

THE JOY OF BETTER COOKING

You-do-you garlic cob fondue

1 x 200 g (7 oz) bloomy rind soft cheese, such as a camembert-style, nearing its use-by date

1 good-quality cob loaf (a day old, and preferably sourdough)

4 garlic cloves, 3 finely chopped, 1 thinly sliced

½ bunch of flat-leaf parsley, finely chopped

⅓ cup (80 ml) olive oil or melted butter (no need to be too precise)

10 thyme sprigs

¼ cup (60 ml) decent white wine

For this pseudo-fondue you're looking for a brie or camembert-style cheese, but there's no need to splash out — warming any cheese, even if it's on the econo-end, will make it taste way better and bougier than if you serve it at room temp with creaky crackers. Because the heat mellows out flavour, and older cheese is more intense, this is a great way of using up a cheese that's approaching its use-by date; in the shops, these are often discounted for sale — winner! As for the bread, a day-old loaf works best, but if yours is fresh and fluffy, you can dry it out a little first in the oven — 150°C (300°F) for 20 minutes should do it. Day-old breads hold their shape and give you better crunch, so you'll notice that I use stale stuff in recipes quite voraciously. From French toast to cheese toasties to this here cheeseplosion, old bread's still got plenty of love to give.

Preheat the oven to 180°C (350°F). Line a baking tray with baking paper.

If the cheese comes in a box, flip it over and use it as a stencil to cut the same shape into the middle of the cob with a small serrated knife (or cut a round by eye roughly the same size and shape as the cheese). Cut the cob loaf in a crisscross fashion around this central round to form bread soldiers, making sure not to cut all the way through to the bottom. Tear out the central round and reserve these bits of bread.

In a bowl, mix the chopped garlic, parsley and half the olive oil together into a paste. Spoon a little of the mixture between the cracks of the cob soldiers. Pour the remaining olive oil into the dregs of the paste and toss the reserved bits of bread in it.

Place the cheese in the hole and poke in half the thyme sprigs and the remaining garlic slices. Pour the wine over the cheese. Pop the cob loaf on the baking tray, surrounded by the oiled-up bits of bread. Bake for 20 minutes.

Remove the cob from the baking tray and place on a wooden board to serve. Sprinkle the remaining thyme leaves and some cracked black pepper on top. Enjoy with good company and a glass of that wine by ripping the bread soldiers off and dipping into the molten cheese fondue.

THE JOY OF BETTER COOKING

Bonus bits

Recipe riffs

Some CP butter (page 96) would really make the Cheese-Pop. Just sub it in for the garlic paste. Oooft!

You can get pretty creative with the flavouring. Put some Vegemite, Marmite or similar in there to turn it into a cheesy-mite situation, or for a totally different aromatic experience, use tarragon or oregano instead of parsley.

To take this more towards Italy, swap the thyme out for rosemary. Use a square of taleggio instead of brie or camembert, and cut a square into the cob loaf, rather than a circle. Drizzle with a little honey to serve.

Extra extras

Know what goes great with soft cheese and bread? Truffle! If it's truffle season, use a fine microplane to shave some in a cloud over the hot cheese as soon as it comes out of the oven, to elicit max OOOOOHS from all involved. But whatever you do, say nay to truffle oil. That stuff is no good. End of.

Waste knot

You don't need to keep buying hard herbs like thyme and rosemary fresh every time you need to use them, especially if they're going to get roasted or braised in a dish. Pop what you don't need in the freezer and they'll last for ages. Just remember to check the freezer when making your shopping list for dishes such as this one.

Ingredient spotlight: Melty cheese

Melty cheese is one of life's greatest joys, and one that can increasingly be enjoyed by both plant-based eaters and omnivores alike.

For plant-based melty cheeses, look for 'mozzarella-style' or similar; the label will usually tell you what kind of behaviour you can expect with some heat.

For dairy-based cheeses, it's just a matter of working out which cheeses love a blast and which prefer things at room temperature. Check the label or ask the person behind the counter.

If you want your cheese to keep it together, choose one with a high melting point, such as queso blanco, haloumi or saganaki, which are designed to crisp on the outside but maintain composure on the inside.

Other cheeses thrive on pooling into perfect puddles when the mercury rises. Those with lower melting points are ones like provolone, taleggio, mozzarella, gruyère-style cheeses and most cheddars. These are great pizza and toastie cheeses.

You'll often find combinations in cheese pies and classic fondue recipes, as some of the cheese is for stretchiness, and some for sharpness, where you want that balance of both.

Feta is a bit of an in-betweener — it holds together until you give it a poke, and then it may as well be cheese sauce.

Blue cheese is a funny one. It *can* melt, but due to the uneven distribution of mould pockets, the brilliant balance of blue is best kept at room temperature, or you'll have pools of oil in some parts and sharp bitterness in others.

As for brie, camembert and other soft-rind cheeses, these give you the best of both worlds — a bit like fruit. When they're ripe and at their best, room temperature is the best way to serve them, but if things are a bit funky or underdone, heat does wonders for infusing new flavours and bringing out caramel notes. After all, everything tastes better with melty cheese on top ... even cheese.

You-Do-You garlic cob fondue

Page 160

Cauli almond ajo blanco

1 cup (160 g) raw almonds
⅓ cup (80 ml) extra virgin olive oil,
    plus extra to serve
2 French shallots, finely sliced
5 garlic cloves, finely sliced
¼ cup (60 ml) good-quality sherry
    vinegar, plus extra to serve
6 cups (1.5 litres) stock, or 6 cups
    (1.5 litres) water mixed with
    1–2 vegetable stock cubes
1 cauliflower, about 1 kg (2 lb 4 oz),
    cut into florets
100 g (3½ oz) stale bread,
    crusts removed and reserved
1 teaspoon salt flakes, plus extra to taste
⅓ cup (60 g) fresh grapes, cut in half
red-veined sorrel leaves, to garnish

Turn this traditionally chilled Spanish soup into a velvety winter warmer to chase the chills away. Since it's not just bread that deserves to be saved from the compost, you'll be making full use of the cauliflower, leaves and all. This is a great soup to prepare in advance; store the garnishes separately, for sprinkling over just before serving.

Cover the almonds well with boiling water. Leave to soak for about 10 minutes to help the skins soften, then drain and leave to cool. The almond skins should slip off easily with your fingers.

Heat 2 tablespoons of the olive oil in a heavy-based saucepan. Gently sweat the shallot, garlic and blanched almonds for 5–6 minutes, until the shallot is translucent but not coloured. Add the sherry vinegar, stirring to deglaze the pan.

Pour in your chosen stock combo and bring to the boil. Add the cauliflower and cook for 15–20 minutes, until very tender, but not turning greige.

Meanwhile, heat the oven to 180°C (350°F) and line a baking tray with baking paper. Toss the bread crusts in the last of the olive oil, spread on the tray and bake for 20 minutes, until dry and crispy.

Add the torn bits of stale bread innards to the soup and blitz until super smooth and velvety. Season to taste with the salt flakes, some cracked black pepper and a touch more vinegar if needed.

Ladle the hot soup into bowls and garnish with the grapes and sorrel. Finish with an extra drizzle of sherry vinegar and olive oil. Serve with the crusty croutons as well as any other crusty bread you've got in your vicinity.

Bonus bits

Tips

These croutons will work with any bread, from sourdough to sliced white bread to ciabatta. If you're worried yours is a little too hard to blitz, warm up 200 ml (7 fl oz) of the stock and soak the bread in it before blending.

Waste knot

If your cauliflower came with leaves, toss these in oil and season and bake with the bread crusts for a lovely bonus zero-waste garnish. How cheffy of you!

Skills spotlight: Blanching

Blanching is useful for several reasons. Firstly, popping plump fruit and veg such as peaches and tomatoes into boiling water and refreshing in iced water is a sure-fire way to soften skins for removal, without losing the integrity of the delicate flesh within. Nuts such as almonds and hazelnuts benefit from blanching to help peel off their fibrous skins. Blanching also locks in and intensifies the colour of leafy greens.

For a lazy blanch, I'll shorten the time under heat and run under the hot water tap instead — or, for saucing tomatoes, a quick dip in boiling water, then straight into the bowl for peeling does the trick.

THE JOY OF BETTER COOKING

Pan confit tomate

250 g (9 oz) uncooked chorizo
    sausages (see Subs, page 168)
½ cup (125 ml) olive oil
1 red onion, sliced
400 ml (14 fl oz) dry apple cider
a pinch of sugar
500 g (1 lb 2 oz) cherry tomatoes
    (see Subs, page 168)
430 g (15 oz) Turkish pide (or other long
    bread), sliced in half lengthways
1–2 garlic cloves, halved
100 g (3½ oz) manchego,
    or other firm sheep's cheese
a handful of finely chopped parsley
lemon wedges, to serve

Here's a play on a Catalan snack — *pa amb tomàquet*, a.k.a. *pan con tomate* or tomato bread, which is usually as simple as rubbing garlic and then tomato onto crusty bread (see Shortcuts on page 168). Here, though, the tomatoes are given a quick confit on the cooktop in oil and chorizo fat to make them a bit jammy, and slicing and baking the Turkish bread slab the way we do here turns it into a giant tanned and crispy crostini. If you're only making this for a few of you, save the upper crust of the Turkish bread for the toaster — it'll be perfect as an accompaniment to dips and dishes such as the pkhali on page 148. This softer top is also where the expression 'upper crust' comes from — the bit saved for the upper classes!

Preheat the oven to 180°C (350°F).

Pop the chorizo out of its skin in chunks into a large heavy-based frying pan with a tablespoon of the oil, then let it start cooking out its own flaming red fat over low heat for a minute or so. Add the onion and gently sweat for 6–8 minutes, until softened.

Splash in the cider, sprinkle in the sugar and toss in the tomatoes. Bring to the boil, then turn the heat back down to a simmer. Let the mixture bubble away for 25–30 minutes, until it looks syrupy and the oil floats to the top. Season to taste with salt flakes and cracked black pepper.

Meanwhile, place the bread slices on a baking tray, then slip another tray on top to flatten the bread and stop the slices curling up into half-moons. Bake for 25–30 minutes, until the bread is golden brown and crispy as all heck.

To serve, rub some fresh garlic over the open faces of the bread, then arrange on a platter and pour the tomato mixture over them. Shave the manchego over. Sprinkle with the parsley and some more salt and pepper. Drizzle with the remaining olive oil and serve with lemon wedges.

Pan confit tomate Bonus bits

Shortcuts

Rub a piece of toast with garlic and the cut side of a halved fresh ripe tomato for the original version. You could also grate the tomato on the coarse side of a box grater for a saucier fresh version.

Subs

Uncooked chorizo is softer in texture than cooked chorizo, so it can be squashed out of the casings as you might a sausage. Cooked chorizo will need to be cut into discs before adding, which I like to do straight into the pan using my kitchen shears, to save having to wash up a chopping board.

You can easily go plant-based by subbing out the chorizo, adding a few cloves of garlic to the confit tomato mix and upping the oil.

If tomatoes aren't in season, good-quality tinned cherry tomatoes will do the trick. They won't need as long to cook down; just watch for the jamminess to set in.

Recipe riffs

Get cheesy with mozzarella, crumbly ricotta or a plant-based feta-style cheese or go completely cheese free.

For extra kick, sprinkle the toasts with crispy capers (page 84) and/or anchovies or slices of jamón.

For a Mediterranean mash-up, add some good-quality antipasti from the deli, such as roasted eggplant (aubergine), red capsicum (peppers), artichoke hearts and/or mushrooms, tossing these through as soon as the tomatoes get jammy, or just artfully arranging them over the toasts.

Waste knot

If you have left-over stale bread, tear it into chunks, drizzle with olive oil and bake into golden croutons at 180°C (350°F) for 20 minutes.

Blitz any odds and ends in a food processor, place in a bag and freeze for home-made breadcrumbs. Use from frozen!

Gadget spotlight: Speed peeler

Speed peelers — also known as Y-peelers — are so named because the whole blade can pivot rather than being fixed, and is perpendicular to the handle, making it easier to curve across contours and allowing you to apply less pressure to achieve a speedier result.

Speed peelers aren't just for peeling potatoes. You can use them to lift off lemon zest (see the nature-strip cordial on page 124), carrot and pumpkin (squash) skin, shave strips of cheese and curls of chocolate, create stripey cucumbers by peeling lengthways at intervals, and turning zucchini (courgettes) into ribbons.

Speed peelers are an easy way to julienne when you're just learning — hold onto the veg and use the speed peeler to peel ribbons that remain stacked, then use a sharp knife to slice the stack into thin matchsticks. Go slow if you're new, and feel free to shorten the stack to make things easier.

Skills spotlight: Refreshing bread

I'll never tire of introducing people to the wonders of refreshing stale bread — or, as I like to call it, bread-wetting. If your loaf still has some 'give', a quick spritz or dab of water from the tap will do it. For rock-hard hunks, get that bread under the tap and soak it for 3–5 seconds, top to bottom. Chuck the wet bread on a baking tray into a cold oven, then crank the oven to 160°C (315°F). The steam rehydrates the bread, and by the time the oven's warm, the bread will be, too.

Sometimes, if the bread is especially fossilised, I'll find it's still firm, so I run it under the tap and start again, which usually does the trick.

You can refresh any unsliced bread, bagel, crumpet or bun in the same way — even hot cross buns!

Microwaving works, too. For a few bread slices, grab a clean, lint-free tea towel and run it under cold water. Squeeze out the excess moisture from the tea towel, then fold it lengthways to the width of the bread. Wrap the bread slices inside, then microwave for 10 seconds.

Got a bag of bread slices to refresh? Celery sacrifice! Stick a celery stalk into the bag of bread overnight. The moisture from the celery will get soaked up by the bread via osmosis, so while the celery will end up a bit saggy, the bread will be as good as new. Then just chop the stalk into little celery batons and whack them into iced water to refresh these, too. Magic!

'Bread-wetting' helps restore bread to its former glory

Slice bagels against the hole and toast for bagel chips

Blitz or tear bread for crumbs and croutons

Bind stale bread with a little egg, then boil to make bread dumplings

Max bang-for-cluck roast chook

1 large whole chicken,
   at least 1.8–2 kg
   (4 lb–4 lb 8 oz)
2 teaspoons salt flakes
2 tablespoons olive oil
1 lemon
1 garlic bulb (optional)

There are many ways to roast a chicken. There's the brine-and-baste approach, the low-and-slow method … and then there's my way: dry-hot-upside-down. Here, we first dry-age the chicken to help get the skin phenomenally crispy, then, once roasted (breast side down, to protect the delicate meat from drying out), we make full use of every last bit. I'm a firm believer in this approach to any kind of meat-eating, but especially when it comes to chicken, so you get maximum bang-for-cluck. You'll need to start this recipe a day or two ahead to get the best out of the dry-ageing process.

Check the chicken cavity for necks and feet (save these in the freezer for making stock). Pat the chicken dry all over. Place it on a plate, breast side down. Leave, uncovered, on the lowest shelf of the fridge to dry out for a couple of days, or at least overnight. This step is a lot like cultivating the crackling on roast pork. It takes some planning, but the resulting shards of golden chicken skin are well worth the delayed gratification.

Take the chicken out of the fridge an hour before you're going to roast it, so that it's not fridge-cold, leaving it loosely covered.

When you're ready to get roasting, preheat the oven to 240°C (475°F).

Pat the chicken dry, then massage in the salt flakes and olive oil. Chuck the lemon in the cavity with the garlic bulb, if using. This helps distribute the heat more evenly, while also flavouring the chicken.

Put the bird in a roasting tin, breast side down. This protects the delicate breast meat from overcooking, and also exposes the parson's nose (my favourite bit) for maximum crunch-factor. Slide the bird into the oven and immediately drop the heat down to 200°C (400°F). This gives the skin enough time to start crisping up without blistering, meaning that, by the time your chook's cooked, the skin will be evenly golden and the meat as moist as can be.

For the cooking time, roast a bird of this size for around 1 hour 10 minutes. (A good rule of thumb is 40 minutes for the first kilogram, then 20 minutes for every extra kilo.) You can check it's done by poking a sharp knife into the thickest part of the leg and watching for the juice to run clear.

Once the bird is cooked, pull the roasting tin out of the oven. Transfer the chicken to a tray to rest while we harvest the schmaltz (chicken fat) and those roasting pan juices, by pouring the liquid in the bottom of the roasting tin into a clean, wide jar. Store this in the fridge for later use (see Recipe riffs and Ingredient spotlight, opposite).

Once the chicken is cool enough to touch, you can slice in. I prefer to serve the brown meat (legs, thighs, etc.) and leave the breasts on the frame for leftovers, but you do you.

Bonus bits

Double duty

As for the leftovers, there are sandwiches to make, wraps to fold, salads to dress and soups to simmer, not to mention using the carcass to make a stock, and the schmaltz for all manner of things (see right). But the pasta on page 172 is what you should be planning for lunch or dinner post-roast, post-haste — the perfect midweek meal that makes the most of it.

Tips

Find a larger bird if you can, and seek out true free-range, grass-fed and organic where possible. You'll get more bang for your buck, more flavour, and more meals out of the one cook/chook. For smaller birds, you can fake more pan-juice action by drizzling a few extra glugs of olive oil into the bottom of the roasting tin.

Waste knot

Save your roast chook frames for making stock (page 174). You won't get as much flavour out of them as using fresh carcasses, but you'll get a second go out of them.

Recipe riffs

If you do use a larger bird, chances are you'll have quite a yield of pan juices and schmaltz (chicken fat) in your storage jar. Don't feel you have to use all of it for the one meal. Make it go further by bypassing some of the golden stuff on top (that's the schmaltz) and scooping out the brown jelly (that's the pan juices) for the pasta on page 172.

Use the schmaltz for anything from jacking up broths, such as the pressure cooker stock on page 174, to coating parboiled potatoes for roasting, frying zucchini fritters (page 155) or loaded latkes (page 86), and cooking a pilaf or trampoline rice (pages 176–79).

Ingredient spotlight: Schmaltz

Schmaltz is the Yiddish word for chicken fat (or any fat, actually), and if I could get away with writing a book based purely on schmaltzy recipes, I would. You can buy schmaltz from kosher butchers, or harvest it from your roast chicken pan as we do here, or make your own by frying off the fattiest bits of chicken skin, like the scrappy *schmutz* from around the butt. Schmaltz will last for ages in the fridge, as long as you scrape out the jelly from underneath. If you're not sure when you'll use it, freeze it for even later use.

If you've no schmaltz or kosher butcher in sight, duck or goose fat will work at a pinch. You know what? Bacon grease wouldn't go astray, either.

Ingredient spotlight: Plant-based schmaltz

Interestingly, since part of kosher rules dictate that you can't mix meat and milk, Jewish housewives had to get clever with making a neutral, non-dairy/non-meat version of schmaltz — a plant-based one using carrots and onions simmered in Copha (white vegetable shortening) or Crisco, which would then be strained into sterilised jars (see page 127), where it would set like real schmaltz.

You can absolutely apply the same schmaltz-making principles to plant-based dishes. Next time you roast vegies — say, for turning into soup, à la page 68 — double down on the olive oil and toss in some extra juicy vegies such as capsicum (pepper), pumpkin (squash) and sliced onion. When the vegies have roasted, harvest the juices and use them in a sauce for a pasta, such as the one on page 172. Shred in some exotic mushrooms such as lion's mane or shiitake to boost the umami and texture, and proceed as directed in the recipe.

Pan-juice pasta

400 g (14 oz) pasta

6–8 banana shallots, soaked in water (this helps with the peeling), then halved lengthways and peeled

left-over roast chicken meat from page 170 (enough to shred a small handful for each person)

schmaltz and roasting pan juices from page 170

2–3 garlic cloves, finely chopped

1 cup roughly chopped parsley and/or tarragon

⅔ cup (70 g) finely grated parmesan

olive oil, for drizzling

The cool thing about this dish is that you can make the sauce in the time it takes for the pasta to cook — not long at all, in other words. Once you've made this a few times, just set a timer for the pasta and hit autopilot on the rest.

Get the pasta into a big saucepan of well-salted boiling water and bring it back to the boil as quickly as possible. Set the timer for a minute less than the packet tells you to, if you like it *al dente*. If you're a soft pasta softie, stick with the instructions on the pack.

Meanwhile, pop a large heavy-based saucepan on to heat. Pop the shallots face side down in the hot, dry pan.

Shred the chicken using your fingers — or, if you'd prefer to keep yourself tidy, two forks working against each other. (Note: hand-shredding left-over chicken is one of life's joys and well worth the greasy fingertips!)

Add the shredded chicken to the pan and scoop in some schmaltz (that's the golden fat on top, NOT the brown jelly). Check on your golden-faced shallots and flip them over so that the schmaltz sucks up between all the layers. Once the chicken has warmed through and the shallot faces are browned, stir in the brown jellied pan juices (you should have about 2 tablespoonfuls) and the garlic.

If you've used up everything in your pan-juice jar, use it to scoop out a good amount of the pasta cooking water. If you're still packin' schmaltz, use a mug to reserve some pasta water. When the pasta is done, drain it in a colander, then add to the shallot mixture, along with half the parsley and half the parmesan, and gently toss to combine. Pour the reserved pasta water over and stir well so all the flavours get friendly. Taste for seasoning.

Garnish with the remaining parsley, parmesan and a crack of black pepper. Drizzle with another glug of olive oil for good measure. Serve with a side salad.

Bonus bits

Subs

I like using fusili or penne, but any old medium-length pasta will do. You can easily use gluten-free pasta, some of which are top-notch these days; my favourite is made using sorghum.

No schmaltz on hand? You can opt to use olive oil — but once you go chicken fat, you don't go back.

Ingredient spotlight: Shallots

Think of shallots as a cross between a brown onion and a spring onion, with a sweet, mild flavour. French shallots are squat and a little on the knobbly side, come in red and golden varieties and grow in little clusters. Banana shallots — a hybrid of onion and shallot — are a single long thin bulb, easy to slice into uniform rings. Shallot varieties are interchangeable, so pick the one that feels juiciest when squeezed at the bulbiest bit, with skin that hasn't started to shrivel. Crispy fried shallots can be bought at Asian grocers and are awesome as a crunchy salad topping.

THE JOY OF BETTER COOKING

Under-pressure chicken stock

1 generous tablespoon olive oil or
    schmaltz (see Ingredient spotlight,
    page 171)
1 onion, skin left on, roughly chopped
    into large dice
1 kg (2 lb 4 oz) chicken pieces (I like
    drumettes and wingettes, but frames
    or chicken leg quarters/marylands
    work, too, as do roast chicken bones)
1 celery stalk, chopped into
    2 cm (¾ inch) lengths
2 carrots, unpeeled, cut into large chunks
2–3 garlic cloves, roughly chopped
1 thumb-sized knob of fresh ginger,
    peeled and roughly chopped
2 bay leaves
10 peppercorns (black or white)
16 cups (4 litres) water

My mum is of the 'Chuck it in Whole, Skin On, No Sweat' school of stock-making, which certainly has its place if you're whacking the whole thing on to simmer in a big pot on the stove for hours. The onion skin gives extra golden colour to the broth — and means less peeling and chopping, too. BUT, seeing as the name of this game is speed, the smaller the bits, the more flavour you can extract. The schmaltz sure helps, too (more about that on page 171). No matter which way you make this stock — gently burbling on the stove of a Sunday afternoon, or going ballistic in a pressure cooker midweek — your savoury dishes, from soups to stews to risotto, will benefit immensely from the added dimension and flavour that a good stock imbues. Mind you, this 'stock' is *sooo* good, we sip it like broth with the shredded chook and mushy carrots added back in.

In a large stockpot or pressure cooker, heat the olive oil or schmaltz and sauté the onion with the lid on for 8–10 minutes, or until cooked down and translucent.

Place the chicken pieces in a colander in the sink. Pour a kettle of boiling water over them (this really helps reduce the scum that forms on the stock).

Place the chicken in your chosen vessel with the remaining ingredients, ensuring everything is well coated in the oil or schmaltz.

If you are using a stockpot, bring to just before the boil, then reduce the heat and simmer uncovered for 2 hours. Scoop off any scum that rises to the surface, being sure to leave the beautiful schmaltzy fat on top.

If you are using a pressure cooker, seal the lid on, bring the cooker up to high pressure and set the timer for 30 minutes. Turn the heat off, then leave to cool down before opening the lid.

Pull out the chicken and strip the meat from the bones. Strain the stock through a colander into a bowl. Now strain it again, this time through a fine-meshed sieve lined with muslin (cheesecloth) or a clean kitchen cloth. You may wish to repeat this step for crystal-clear stock. (I wash the cloth in-between to get any gunk out, then strain again through the same side.)

Once cooled, pour or ladle into 2 cup (500 ml) containers and store in the fridge or the freezer. The stock will keep for up to a week in the fridge, and up to 6 months in the freezer.

Bonus bits

Tips

I use filtered water because the flavour is more neutral, but tap water is also fine.

How much water you actually need will depend on the size of your pot — only fill to the maximum line so you don't have an overflow.

I freeze any left-over stock in ice-cube trays for MYO stock cubes. Simply add two or three frozen cubes as your base stock (no need to thaw), then supplement the additional liquid required with water. The larger-sized silicon trays work especially well for this.

Recipe riffs

This is a tradish chicken stock, but there's nothing stopping you making this with roasted beef bones, roasted chicken frames, fish bits or even straight-up veg. Beef stock will take 4 hours in a stockpot, and fish or veg an hour. If using a pressure cooker, you can quarter those times — 1 hour for beef stock, and 15 minutes for fish or veg.

I like to add mushrooms to my vegetable stock, as well as whatever's hanging about in my freezer stock bag — from leek tops and fennel stalks to celery hearts and squashy tomatoes.

Gadget spotlight: Pressure cooker

Pressure cookers got a bad rap for a while there, because the old-school ones had a tendency to flip their lid, literally. These days, the tech is fairly fail-safe, whether you're utilising a multi-cooker or a stovetop pressure cooker (which is my preference, but only because we've got a handy small one that's perfect for our little family).

The method is pretty foolproof, and great when you're in a hurry, but there are a few things to note.

Firstly, pressure cookers divide your cook time by four, so if you're converting a conventional stovetop recipe, just divide by four and be mindful of the liquid — it should cover any meat or veg, but not be overflowing, since unlike an open pot on the stove, pressure cookers retain all of the moisture inside.

Give the pressure cooker at least 5–10 minutes to cool down before releasing the pressure slowly, one stage at a time. Face the steam hole towards a wall rather than yourself — this is not the time for a steam facial.

If your sauce feels a little on the runny side, scoop out the meat/veg and let the sauce bubble away over medium–high heat until it thickens.

Ingredient spotlight: Chicken

The number-one tip I can give you for great chicken soup is to use the best-quality chicken you can afford. Wingettes and/or drumettes are a relatively inexpensive option, and they provide a clear, rich broth. You can opt to include organic free-range chicken carcasses also.

Well-reared chickens taste so much better than battery hens. You're rewarding best practice, AND it's more sustainable because you can extract a lot of flavour using less. A bag of free-range chicken carcasses from a good butcher is a great place to start if you're on a budget.

I harvest schmaltz (page 171) every time I roast a chicken. Once the chicken is out of the pan, I very carefully pour the golden liquid into a sterilised jar (see page 127) and store it in the fridge, where it solidifies.

Trampoline rice

Think of this as a jumping-off point ... wheel out the trampoline! These next few pages are absolutely designed to help you see the potential in the rice that's still left in the pot once everyone's had their fill. In fact, like mash, it's another base I like to cook up as a double batch, knowing that it means I can accelerate another meal later — whether that's a quick fried rice for breakfast, a rice salad for lunch, a pilaf for dinner or a rice pudding for dessert. The type of rice will often dictate what the dish becomes, but you're welcome to play with them interchangeably to see which textures and combinations your household likes best.

A WORD OF WARNING: There's a bit of a 'Mission Impossible' element to cooked rice, as its farinaceous nature means it only has a very short fridge-life for safe consumption (which can certainly be extended with the vigorous heat of frying). When reusing cooked rice, it's important to cool, store and reheat the rice safely in order to prevent contamination. Have a google for the most up-to-date information, and in the interests of getting dinner done before this message self-destructs, let's get to it!

There are over 40,000 rice varieties in the world, and depending on where you live, you'll have access to some more types than others. The main varieties I cover here are grouped by grain size: short, medium and long, which determines cooking time, flavour and texture. The choice is yours!

As well as these more common varieties, black rice, red rice, wild rice and other varieties that aren't as readily accessible are worth having a play with if you can track them down, particularly if you're feeling in a ricey funk. Most of these are still a whole grain, so they'll take longer to cook. Making note of the length of their grain will ensure you end up with the desired result — whether that's in a black sticky rice dish, red rice risotto or wild rice salad.

Short-grain rice

These include arborio, short-grain brown and sushi rice. They are the stickiest and stubbiest varieties, which is why you'll find arborio thickening up risottos and rice puddings such as the Greek *risogalo*. Try stirring left-over cooked arborio through a sweet custard (page 258), then pouring it into a tart case and baking until set — like rice pudding, in a pie!

Short-grain brown rice has more chew because the bran is still intact, but it's still way stickier than its longer-grained counterpart, and is best used like a grain — cooked in stock and finished with plenty of fat, such as butter or olive oil.

Sushi rice is fab because it's just sticky enough to hold its shape, but still offers a good bite as a counterpoint to any soft fillings or toppings. Taco rice (page 76) is one thousand per cent my favourite way to serve sushi rice, and I'll often put enough in the rice cooker to guarantee a few spare serves to roll into sushi for lunch the next day.

✦ BOUNCE

Second-day risotto is easy to turn into arancini (see the risotto Double duty on page 97), flavouring with whatever seasonings, cheese, aromatics and veg you have at your disposal. You can even turn rice pudding into sweet arancini balls, drizzling with honey to serve.

Second-day brown short-grain is equally as helpful as a binder for fried balls and fritters, loaded up with veg, tinned tuna, smoked fish, seaweed and/or mushrooms.

Consider popping the mixture into a greased muffin tin and baking rather than frying, for a one-pan solution that's lighter on the oil.

Sushi rice is traditionally served cold or at room temperature, so use any leftovers for bonus sushi on day two. If you're a bento-box wielding family, creating little shapes and creatures with left-over sushi rice, and decorating them with chopped nori (seaweed sheets), is absolutely on the cards for you. Make up some sushi rice seasoning with rice wine vinegar, sugar and salt to taste. Pour boiling water over the cold sushi rice to reinvigorate it, then drain it, before gently stirring your sushi rice seasoning through. You may like to sprinkle this with shichimi togarashi or furikake as a bonus topping before serving alongside a bowl of miso soup and pickled veg.

Sushi rice can also be coated with sesame seeds and baked or fried into excellent lunchbox snacks — just add enough rice seasoning to taste, shape into balls (or the more tradish *yaki onigiri* triangles), then fry in a non-stick pan until golden on both sides. Namiko Hirasawa, of *Just One Cookbook* fame, has a fab step-by-stepper online.

Medium-grain rice

These rice varieties, including carnaroli and bomba, are far more toothsome than their shorter counterparts. So while carnaroli gets used in risotto, its finish is far more *al dente* than if you'd used arborio — which is why carnaroli is referred to as 'the caviar of rice'.

Bomba rice is best for paella, soaking up twice as much liquid as long-grain varieties, without losing its shape and chew. The paella cooking process is a lot like making risotto, but more of the liquid gets cooked out, and the burnt crust at the pan's base is something to aspire to rather than scrape into the compost.

✦ **BOUNCE**

You can absolutely use carnaroli as you might arborio, so arancini (page 97) is a natural fit.

Carnaroli or bomba also make a cracking good tart crust. Squash the cold rice into a lined baking dish, then top with something that will bind everything together in the bake, such as egg or cheese. It's a great gluten-free option, and can also be kept plant-based by subbing silken tofu in for the eggy filling component.

If you're not game to try the tart track, mix the cooked rice *into* the eggy mixture for a frittata — or jazz up the mix with plenty of veg, such as carrot, zucchini (courgette) and corn, then fry in blobs to make fritters. Keep these ideas in mind for most of the long-grain varieties too, mind you …

If you want to find common ground with almost anyone in the world, ask them how they cook their rice.

Long-grain rice

The long-grainers are jasmine, basmati and brown. Jasmine is my go-to rice for soaking up South-East Asian curries and soups. It's fragrant, fine-textured and a real catch-all. Jasmine rice is surprisingly seasonal, so picking one that's furthest from its expiration date will guarantee the most aromatic results. Speaking of 'guaranteed results', rice cookers are the BEST for fluffy rice! (You can read more about these on page 77.) I love to spike my jasmine rice with caramelised shallots and pandan leaf for even more aroma and flavour.

Basmati is another favourite in our household, cooking to gondola-like grains that are glorious for South Asian, African and Middle Eastern cookery. Basmati is supremely fragrant, particularly porous, and enjoys being infused with extra spices and aromatics, such as turmeric, saffron or paprika, and easily elevates to the main event when cooked in stock for a pilaf (or pulao or plov, depending on who you ask), crispy-bottomed for tahdig, or jazzed even further with tomato passata (puréed tomatoes) or tinned tomatoes for the African red rice dish known as jollof.

Long-grain brown basmati behaves similarly to shorter-grained ones, but is texturally more interesting, as far as I'm concerned. It's considered a wholegrain rice, and has more nutritional benefits than the more refined varieties. Its flavour is nutty, its texture chewy, and colour homely. Do I love it? Not really. Will you? Depends whether you're into that sort of thing. Just remember that when cooking brown rice, it will require twice the cooking time and slightly more water.

✦ BOUNCE

Now that I've talked you out of brown rice, I *will* say that I do enjoy it served as part of mujadara– a caramelised shallot and lentil salad hailing from the Middle East (see page 184).

Basmati is wonderful reinvigorated into a pseudo-pilaf with left-over roast veg and/or meat. Splash in some extra stock, some spice (curry powder is always an easy add) and fat — be it oil, butter or schmaltz — then whack a lid on and let it bubble away until the liquid gets sucked up. Flipping this into a biriani is simple — add saffron to half your left-over rice (more on saffron on page 61), then layer the rice into a wide greased saucepan or deep baking dish with veg, cooked meat (if using) and herbs.

Any left-over jasmine rice in my fridge knows exactly where it's going: into a very hot wok! Fried rice is absolutely my favourite way to use left-over rice in general, particularly when that rice gets a bit burnt and crispy from the heat. Use this as an opportunity to use up any sad-looking veg in the crisper, or add half a cup or so of frozen corn and/or peas for a boost of colour. For easy flavour and extra veg, I also love adding kimchi or other ferments into the rice once it's started sizzling. Some egg never goes astray, so I'll fry a few beaten eggs in a separate pan to chop through at the end. Finish with fresh green stuff such as coriander (cilantro) and spring onion (scallion) and you will be one happy breakfast-er.

All three long-grainers are fab as bulk for rissoles and cabbage rolls — and I actually prefer to use cooked rice to shorten the cooking time.

There are over 40,000 known varieties of rice on the planet

Wash your rice until the water runs clear

Cover with a knuckle's worth of cold water

Leave to steam out with the lid on for 5, then fluff with a fork

Eggplant kharcho with Georgian gremolata

800 g (1 lb 12 oz) eggplants (aubergines)
2 teaspoons salt flakes
grapeseed or rice bran oil, for deep-frying
250 g (9 oz) cherry tomatoes
6 garlic cloves, thinly sliced
a handful of walnuts, toasted (optional)
coriander (cilantro), to garnish
good olive oil, to serve

Khmeli suneli paste

100 g (3½ oz) walnuts, toasted and chopped
1 tablespoon finely chopped parsley stems
1 tablespoon finely chopped coriander
   (cilantro) stems
1 tablespoon finely chopped mint stalks
1 tablespoon finely chopped dill stalks
1 tablespoon ground coriander
1 teaspoon salt flakes
1 teaspoon ground fennel seeds
1 teaspoon ground fenugreek
½ teaspoon cayenne pepper
1 tablespoon olive oil

Soup base

2 tablespoons olive oil
1 brown onion, diced
2 carrots, diced
1 celery stalk, diced
5 garlic cloves, sliced
1 red chilli, seeded and roughly chopped
⅓ cup (75 g) medium-grain white rice,
   or 1 cup (185 g) cooked rice
2 tablespoons tomato paste
   (concentrated purée)
2 stock cubes (see Subs, page 182)
1 teaspoon pomegranate molasses,
   plus extra if needed
2 potatoes, peeled and diced
2–3 bay leaves

Georgian gremolata

½ cup chopped parsley
½ cup chopped coriander (cilantro)
½ cup chopped dill
½ cup chopped mint
zest and juice of 1 lemon
1 garlic clove, finely grated
1 tablespoon walnuts, toasted
   and finely grated

Kharcho (like a sneeze!) is Georgia's answer to congee, a gloriously gloopy, soupy mix of rice and broth that usually has a lamb or beef base. I've turned it totally plant-based by using one of nature's meatiest veg: eggplant. You could stir any left-over wet-fried mushrooms (page 113) through instead, or as well as. Layered with cooked, crispy and raw garlic, this soup is hot and spicy, the kind of combo that'll knock a cold right out of your nose. For a PG version, go easy on the cayenne and garlic. The walnut cloud is a technique I love implementing to fancy up soups and salads, grating the walnuts over like parmesan, perfect for vegans. Try the technique with other nuts, too.

Slice the eggplants into 1 cm x 3 cm (½ inch x 1¼ inch) wedges. Sprinkle the salt over the exposed eggplant faces, rubbing it in a little, then leave the eggplant in a bowl to sweat. Meanwhile, using a mortar and pestle, pound all the khmeli suneli ingredients to a well-combined paste.

To make the soup base, heat the olive oil in a large heavy-based saucepan and sauté the onion, carrot and celery for 10 minutes, or until the onion is translucent and starting to caramelise. Stir in the khmeli suneli paste, garlic, chilli and rice. Sizzle for 2 minutes, or until aromatic. Stir in the tomato paste, stock cubes and pomegranate molasses. Add the potato, bay leaves and 10 cups (2.5 litres) water. Bring to the boil, then simmer for 45 minutes, or until the potato is fork-tender and the flavours are starting to develop, skimming off any froth that rises to the surface.

While the soup is simmering away, heat 5 cm (2 inches) of oil in a large saucepan over medium–high heat to 180°C (350°F), or until a cube of bread dropped into the oil turns golden in 15 seconds.

Grab handfuls of the eggplant and squeeze the liquid out. Fry the eggplant in batches for 8–10 minutes, or until golden and crisp on the outside, yet soft in the middle. Remove with a slotted spoon and drain on paper towel.

Use a slotted spoon to drop the cherry tomatoes into the hot oil, being careful to only use tomatoes with their skin fully intact; stand back as the oil may spit. Remove from the oil once they pop to the surface. Drain on paper towel; the skins will slip right off as soon as they're cool enough to touch. Set aside.

Fry the garlic slices in the oil for 1 minute, or until golden and crisp. Remove with a slotted spoon and drain on paper towel.

Combine the gremolata ingredients in a bowl and set aside.

After the soup has been simmering for 45 minutes, check the seasoning. Add extra salt and black pepper to taste, and extra pomegranate molasses for more acid if needed. The soup should have a bit of an agrodolce vibe — a little tangy, a bit sweet, and spicy and aromatic.

To serve, ladle the soup into bowls, blob in some gremolata, then arrange the tomatoes, crispy garlic and eggplant on top. If you like, grate the toasted walnuts over the top to create a fluffy cloud, then finish with fresh coriander and a glug of olive oil.

Eggplant kharcho Bonus bits

Shortcuts

You can make this soup in a hurry, using pre-cooked rice, roasted veg, tomato paste, stock and roughly chopped herbs. Finish with crispy fried shallots and call it a day.

Subs

Instead of using stock cubes, you can use 10 cups (2.5 litres) home-made or good-quality stock as the soup base.

I've tried to keep the *khmeli suneli* ingredients as light-on as possible, but if you're low on spices you can use a teaspoon or so of madras curry powder instead of the mixed ground spices, plus an extra tablespoon of ground coriander.

Ingredient spotlight: Nuts about nuts

You may be surprised to see nuts being used *in* a soup, rather than just on top, but some classic soups, such as Turkish walnut soup and Spanish *ajo blanco* (see my take on page 164), do feature nuts as a thickener.

Plant-based eaters are increasingly relying on nut milks to replace cow's milk and cream in creamy soups; you can make these yourself by soaking, blitzing and straining nuts for a finer result, or leaving the nutty meal in for chunkier soups like this one. Nut meals such as almond meal are also a convenient option if you're seeking to add body to a batter, particularly if you're trying to keep said batter gluten-free. You'll also see nut meals used in cakes and slices that are designed to be dense but moist, such as Persian love cakes, or supplemented with flour and semolina to lighten up the mix, as in the honey cake recipe on page 278.

As with spices, the flavour of nuts changes with toasting, releasing more of their natural oils and making them taste richer and warmer. If nuts are baking on top of a cake or slice, there's no need to pre-toast them, because they'll get their time in the sun come oven time. Do keep an eye on nut toppings, though, and if they're toasting too quickly, a little tinfoil hat for the last 15 minutes or so of baking will stop them burning.

If you're using nuts for a crust or crumb — and *especially* for a stuffing, where there's no direct heat — it's an idea to toast the nuts first, particularly older nuts, to help mask any rancidity with notes of buttered toast. Some people like to roast their nuts in a moderate oven, but I prefer the control that a stovetop can offer in terms of eyeballs — a watched nut never burns, I say.

If you've no time or headspace to watch said nuts, preheat your frying pan to smoking, turn off the heat, *then* add the nuts and give them a few tosses in the pan before walking away. The residual heat will be enough to impart a golden glow, without taking the colour too dark — something that's less likely with denser nuts like almonds and macadamias, but a classic conundrum for pine nuts, walnuts, pecans and peanuts (an honorary nut!), which are oilier and more delicate. Frying nuts such as pine nuts in oil or butter infuses the fat into the nuts and crisps them up.

If you're operating a nut-free household, you can toast seeds instead; the same rules apply. Sunflower seeds are one of my favourite subs — toasting them is about as close as you'll get to peanut butter on toast, in teeny-tiny morsels. Who needs molecular gastronomy when Mother Nature's done most of the work? Nut butters are handy in the pantry for adding to bliss balls, stirring through salad dressings and soups like this kharcho or popping into dips.

Making your own nut butters is as simple as tossing nuts into a blender and giving them a blitz. A pinch of salt helps to bring out their natural sweetness and enhance their creaminess, so don't forget to season, whether you're making nut butter or nut milk.

I don't usually take the skins off nuts unless I absolutely have to, but if need be, nuts like hazelnuts can go into the oven with the skins on until golden, then you can bundle them into a tea towel and rub the skins off. Blanching is the alternative, about which you'll find more in the Skills spotlight on page 164.

Crushing the spices and nuts together releases the oils and aromas and intensifies the flavours

Toasting nuts in a pan means you can keep a closer eye on the fine line between burnished and burnt

The deep-fried tomatoes look like little golden snitches!

Use a sharp knife to chop the herbs finely, but still retain their shape

Pumpkin wedge mujadara

1 cup (210 g) Puy lentils

1.25 kg (2 lb 12 oz) jap pumpkin,
cut into 8 wedges, seeds removed

3 tablespoons olive oil,
plus extra for drizzling

4 large brown onions,
halved and thinly sliced

2–3 star anise

½ cup (125 ml) grapeseed oil

½ bunch of kale, stems removed,
leaves shredded

1 cup (200 g) long-grain rice

1 bay leaf

1 garlic clove, peeled and smashed

¼ cup (40 g) pepitas (pumpkin seeds)

¼ cup (40 g) sunflower seeds

½ bunch of coriander (cilantro), stems
finely chopped, leaves reserved

1 pomegranate

2 tablespoons pomegranate molasses

My babushka Raya and I didn't always see eye to eye. She'd say, 'Your room should be like a candy', when it more resembled a wasteland of discarded wrappers, but one thing we both loved was thrifting. In my teens, I'd walk with her to the op-shops down the road, where they'd know her by name, but in my twenties, I'd treat her to a drive down the highway to the biggest op-shop within a 100 km radius: Savers Frankston. Two storeys of second-hand shmatters that we would both enthusiastically trawl for mohair cardigans and plaid skirts. We'd cap off the trip by visiting the teeny Turkish cafe next door, for the jewel in the weekly crown: a tub of mujadara. Sweet with caramelised onion, with chewy lentils and fluffy rice, this was another thing we could both agree on. She's no longer with us, but those cardigans and skirts still hang in her room, which remains tidy like a candy. My housekeeping skills never improved, by the way … but I make a mean mujadara.

Preheat the oven to 200°C (400°F) and line two large roasting tins with baking paper.

Boil a kettle, put the lentils in a bowl and pour in enough water to cover the lentils by 1 cm (½ inch), then leave to languish.

Brush the pumpkin wedges with 2 tablespoons of the oil and sprinkle with salt flakes and pepper. Place standing up in one of the roasting tins and bake for 45 minutes, until golden and soft, turning the tray halfway through cooking.

Meanwhile, put the onion in the other roasting tin with the star anise, grapeseed oil and a sprinkle of salt. Give the onion slices a good massage, then roast for 30 minutes. Once they start to caramelise on the edges, give them a little stir to let the ones underneath come up for hot air. They're ready once coloured, softened and very sweet.

Using a slotted spoon, scoop the onion out of the roasting tin and set aside. Add the shredded kale to the roasting tin, tossing it through the left-over oil in the pan. Roast for 10–15 minutes.

Meanwhile, drain the lentils in a fine-meshed sieve. Add the rice, rinsing under cold water until the water runs clear. Tip them into your rice cooker, or a medium-sized saucepan with a tight-fitting lid. Add the bay leaf, garlic and 3 cups (750 ml) cold water and stir. If using a rice cooker, walk away and live your life (see page 77 for why this is one gadget worth investing in). If using the absorption method in a saucepan, stir the mixture occasionally until the water comes to the boil, turn the heat down, put the lid on and cook for 15 minutes, then turn off the heat and leave to rest for 5 minutes more. Whatever route you took, once cooked, fluff up the rice mixture with a fork, and fish out the bay leaf and garlic.

Heat a dry frying pan until smoking. Add the pepitas and sunflower seeds and toss about for a minute or two, until slightly toasted.

THE JOY OF BETTER COOKING

Toss the roasted onion and kale into the rice and lentils with most of the toasted seeds and nuts, chopped coriander stems, and any oil left in the onion baking tin. Taste for seasoning.

Cut the pomegranate in half. Knock the seeds out of one half, add some of them to the rice mixture and toss well. Juice the remaining pomegranate half and mix the juice (and any extra juice from the seeds) with the pomegranate molasses, to make a dressing.

Place the mujadara on a serving platter. Arrange the pumpkin wedges on top. Scatter with the remaining pomegranate seeds and toasted seeds and nuts. Pour the pomegranate dressing over with an extra drizzle of olive oil, garnish with the coriander leaves and serve.

Bonus bits

Tips

I like to use basmati (white or brown) for this. Brown basmati takes longer to cook, so check the packet instructions. You could also use wild rice, but remember to up the cooking time according to the packet instructions, as wild rice takes even longer to cook.

Subs

If pomegranate is not in season, use dried barberries, or lemon cheeks.

Any whole lentil — green, brown or black — will work for this dish. Save your split lentils for daals and soups.

Shortcuts

If you have left-over roast veg and cooked long-grain rice in the fridge, toss them through a rinsed, drained tin of lentils with some crispy fried shallots. Freshen it all up with some herbs, a squirt of lemon juice and a good drizzle of oil.

Worth it

Buying a pack of star anise won't cost the earth, and will also last for ages in the pantry due to its woodiness. I use star anise in both savouries and sweets; it has a unique liquorice warmth, without overpowering. You'll find it in everything from Chinese five-spice and Middle Eastern pilaf to classic roasted or poached fruits such as the pears on page 258.

Star anise can also help to activate the compounds in other ingredients – such as making onions taste 'meatier', according to Harold McGee, author of the food science bible *On Food and Cooking*. That's why they're often used in tandem, and why star anise is a main component of savoury spirits such as ouzo, Pernod and pastis.

Ingredient spotlight: Tinned legumes

Stocking your pantry with tins of beans and lentils is an easy pathway to ensuring that you have protein-rich, plant-based texture and bulk at your fingertips. Look for cans that explicitly state that they're BPA-free, and ideally containing organic legumes — and best yet, that they've been pre-soaked before cooking.

Bougie beans will occasionally also come in glass jars, which taste great, but you'll have to accept some casualties when trying to extract the lot out of the jar's narrower neck.

Remember to rinse and drain well before using, as the liquid the beans are stored in can be gluggy, will throw your seasoning out, and make you even more susceptible to beans' powers of wind-breaking. If you're using tinned chickpeas, however, consider saving the liquid they come in — the aquafaba — for use as a plant-based egg white replacement in desserts such as the veringues on page 290.

Because they're already cooked, tinned beans and lentils can go straight in towards the end of cooking to give extra body to braises and broths (like the kharcho on page 181) and to turn salads into substantial planty protein-rich meals (à la the crispy, sprout lentils on page 54), or to pulse up a treat into purées or dips ... hello, hummus!

Pumpkin wedge mujadara
Page 184

Loosen your shoulders

For weekend pottering and entertaining

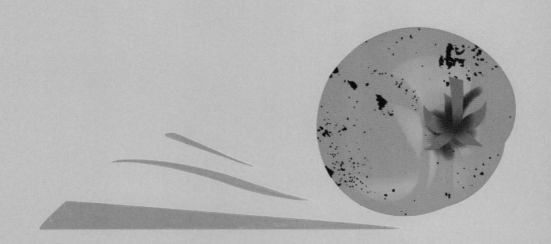

Shimmy, shimmy, shake it out

Cooking can elicit all manner of emotions and physical reactions from people. Some see it as restorative and relaxing, while others feel more of a pit-of-the-tum terror at the prospect, like being involuntarily buckled into a rollercoaster.

Maybe it's a good time to check in with where you're at, physically. Are your knuckles gripping onto the edges of this book for dear life, or are you thumbing through with glee? Tap your fingertips on the sides of your jaw, and just check if you can't unclench some tension. Wiggle your toes. What's your breathing like? Are your shoulders up around your ears? Time to loosen up.

Loose-shouldered cooking is a lot like any mindfulness practice.

Food — both the process of cooking it and eating it — taps into all of our senses, so there are no better moments in the day to practise being deeply present. This may read a little woo-woo at first, but there's a method to the madness, I promise.

Learning to look at an ingredient — really look at it — and giving it the odd gentle prod, will help you begin to identify what traits the best examples of said produce possesses, which makes shopping easier.

Your nose is your best asset during the procurement process, too — something I save for days when I can take my time. A truss of really ripe tomatoes, or the honey-sweetness of a radioactive-orange carrot, tells me I need to have them in my basket. At home, tapping into what you're smelling is particularly useful when heat is applied, as the natural sugars starting to caramelise and smelling like toffee will often tell you when something is just about done.

Bakers will often attribute their knowledge of 'doneness' in the oven to the sound the batter makes — from a bubble to a fizz, to the quiet of being ready to exeunt.

Take a breath, turn your head, stretch yourself — physically and culinarily.

The importance of tasting goes without saying, but it's something we can often forget to do enough of, trusting a recipe's measurements rather than actually sticking a teaspoon in to make sure everything works together just-so. Remember, different salts, vinegars — even honeys — will vary slightly, so it's up to you to fine-tune the volume using your own senses.

The recipes in this section can absolutely be made midweek, if you have the bandwidth, but they've been annexed here because they take a different kind of sense and sensibility.

Sundays are a good day for making up batch-y stuff that'll last you into midweek lunches and dinners, too.

Unlike midweek meals, which can and should be prepared on autopilot, weekend cooking is intentionally intensive. Whether it's the repetitive motion of a prep-heavy dish, or a multi-process meal made for dinners with friends, these are the techniques designed to drop you deeply into your body, out of your head, and into the warm embrace of your simmering pots.

Ahhhh, that's better already.

Chocolate cloud French toast

1 challah loaf
6 eggs
1 cup (250 ml) milk
50 ml (1½ fl oz) single (pure) cream
½ teaspoon salt flakes
1 teaspoon vanilla extract
   or vanilla bean paste
100 g (3½ oz) couverture
   dark chocolate, chopped
3 tablespoons butter
3 tablespoons neutral-flavoured oil
   (I like grapeseed oil)

To serve
icing (confectioners') sugar, for dusting
maple syrup, for drizzling
salt flakes, for sprinkling
zest of 1 orange (optional)
crushed toasted hazelnuts
   (optional, but excellent)

Challah, the plaited brioche that graces Jewish dinner tables every Friday night, makes for the most opulent French toast base, because of its eggy, buttery fluffiness. You can also use brioche, which is eggy bread that isn't as fancy, but just as buttery. To track down your town's best challah, head to your local bagel belt on a Friday morning and follow the queues.

Cut your challah loaf into slices about 2 cm (¾ inch) thick.

In a bowl big enough for soaking your slices in, whisk the eggs, milk, cream, salt and vanilla together.

Using a sharp paring knife, slice a pocket horizontally into the middle of each piece of challah, deep enough to bury some chocolate, but not all the way to the bottom — like a chicken kiev. Carefully pop bits of chocolate inside each pocket. Lay your choc-laden challah pockets in the eggy mixture for at least 10 minutes, carefully flipping them over halfway through.

Heat a tablespoon of butter in a frying pan over medium–low heat, then splash in a tablespoon of oil. Working in batches, fry your challah slices for 3–4 minutes, until the underbelly turns a glorious shade of golden brown, then carefully flip them over with a spatula to cook the other side. Your French toasts are ready to remove from the pan when the chocolate has just started to ooze out of the pockets, indicating that the eggy bits inside have cooked through as well.

Fry the remaining challah pockets in the same way, adding more butter and oil to the pan each time.

Serve warm, dusted with icing sugar, drizzled with maple syrup, sprinkled with salt flakes and maybe some orange zest and toasted hazelnuts.

Chocolate cloud French toast Bonus bits

Stuffed with gooey chocolate and left to soak up a bowl of custard, this challah is the kind of brekkie that lets you float away with your eyes in the back of your head.

Tips

The key here is to slice the challah thick enough so that you can cut a pocket into them. You could ask your bakery to do the slicing for you, but it's not an exact science. Find a serrated bread knife, imagine you've taken two slices of bread out of a packet for a sandwich, then slice off that amount.

Shortcuts

The smaller your challah bits, the quicker they'll fry. If you're in a hurry, cut the bread into soldiers for soaking, and rather than stuffing them with chocolate, serve them drizzled with maple syrup or a chocolate sauce instead.

Recipe riffs

Instead of stuffing the pockets with chocolate, you could just whack in a heaped teaspoon of a good gianduja or choc hazelnut spread and call it a day.

If you're a bit chocolate-d out, these challah toasts would be amazing stuffed or topped with the sour cherry compote from the oladiki pancakes on page 129.

Swap the challah for brioche, or even shokupan — the fluffy sandwich loaf that's sweeping social media with its fluffiness, and stuff the pockets with kaya jam (a rich coconut egg jam) or anything else pandan, with which I am obsessed.

Waste knot

Old bread — even the mouldy kind — isn't beyond help. Just chop out any fuzzy bits and use everything else as you might fresh. The heat from toasting or frying or baking will help to kill any doubts about whether it's still good.

Worth it

Proper genuine maple syrup, made from the sap of maple trees in North America, is an investment piece for your pantry. It has herbaceousness and a savoury woodiness (surprise!) that you just won't get in an imitation maple syrup. Use it in place of honey for plant-based sweetness in both sweeties and savouries. In this book you'll see it come up a lot in salad dressings and drizzles. I love it on pancakes, but also tossed in with soy sauce for burnished brussels sprouts.

Skills spotlight: French toast

French toast actually works best with a day-old loaf, hence its French name, *pain perdu* ('lost bread'). You can cheat by drying your slices out a little in a 150°C (300°F) oven for 10–15 minutes before soaking.

The key to a really fab French toast result is in how long you leave the bread to soak in your eggy mixture. You should soak for at least 5 minutes each side — better yet, 10 minutes each side — then cook over a lower heat for a longer time, rather than higher and quicker. Cooking in a mixture of butter and oil will help stop the butter burning, but still give you that extra buttery flavour.

Pain perdu is only one step removed from bread and butter pudding. Make some extra egg/milk/cream mixture — custard, essentially — and pour it over stale bits of challah, brioche or shokupan in a greased baking dish, then cover and bake on low until the custard sets.

Thrupple butter crumpets

2 teaspoons dried yeast (1 x 7 g sachet)
1 teaspoon sugar, plus extra for sprinkling
300 ml (10½ fl oz) warm water
100 ml (3½ fl oz) buttermilk
2 cups (300 g) self-raising flour
1 teaspoon sea salt flakes
1 teaspoon baking powder
¼ butternut pumpkin (squash),
    seeds removed
vegetable oil, for brushing
25 g (1 oz) butter, melted

Walnut ripple butter
(makes a 300 g/10½ oz roll)
125 g (4½ oz) unsalted butter, softened
¼ cup (90 g) honey
¼ cup (35 g) walnuts, toasted
    (see page 182), then roughly
    chopped or crushed
½ teaspoon ground cinnamon,
    plus extra for sprinkling
¼ teaspoon sea salt flakes

You *know* I can't resist a triple-up, especially where 'butter' AND word play is concerned. Here, we're making our own crumpets, which may seem a daunting task, but isn't too hard once you get the hang of it. Rather than getting too cultured, we're leaning on our ol' pal food science to help lift and lighten the batter — namely, acid + alkaline AND yeast ... butter-*bing*, butter-BOOM! If you don't have crumpet rings or egg rings, don't worry. You can fashion your own out of medium-sized tuna tins (or any tins of that size), which are conveniently the perfect shape for forming fantastic crumpets. Make sure the tins are labelled BPA-free, of course, and get them scrupulously clean before using.

In a small bowl, dissolve the yeast and sugar in 2 tablespoons of the warm water. Leave for 10 minutes, or until foamy.

Pour the buttermilk and remaining warm water into a bowl. Add the flour and salt and whisk by hand for 5 minutes, or for half that time if using an electric mixer.

Stir the baking powder into the yeast mixture, then add to the batter and beat for 30 seconds, or until combined.

Place a tea towel over the mixture and leave in a warm place for 1 hour.

Meanwhile, preheat the oven to 180°C (350°F). Line a baking tray with baking paper. Brush the pumpkin with oil, place face down on the baking tray, then roast for 40 minutes, or until completely softened. Remove from the oven and leave to cool.

While the pumpkin is roasting, make your walnut ripple butter. In a small mixing bowl, squish together the butter, honey, walnuts, cinnamon and salt flakes. Spoon out onto a sheet of baking paper and make a sausage shape. Roll the paper up, twist the ends to enclose, then store in the freezer.

Scoop out the softened pumpkin flesh and squash it into a mash, then fold it through the crumpet batter.

To cook the crumpets, heat a cast-iron pan for 10 minutes over medium heat. Use some baking paper to grease your pan and well-washed medium-sized crumpet/egg rings/empty tuna tins with the melted butter. Place the crumpet rings in the pan and spoon about 2 tablespoons of batter into each. Leave for 5–10 minutes and watch the bubbles come to the surface; once the crumpets look almost set on top, you can help the bubbles pop with a skewer.

Once cooked and set, flip the crumpets over to seal the top. Remove the rings and marvel at how clever you are. Now repeat the process until the batter is used up.

The crumpets are delicious straight from the pan, slathered with the walnut ripple butter, and perhaps an extra sprinkle of cinnamon and sugar.

THE JOY OF BETTER COOKING

Butternut for moisture, buttermilk for puff ... and butter, because, BUTTER!

Tips

Crumpets store surprisingly well for a few days in the fridge. You can reinvigorate them by whacking them in the toaster or under the grill (broiler) until golden and warmed through. They're also great to take on a camping roadtrip, because they fry up a treat on a barbecue hotplate (perhaps on a sheet of foil or baking paper if the hotplate looks a bit grubby).

The crumpets can also be frozen for up to 6 months, when you can celebrate your crumpet cleverness once more. Thaw in the fridge overnight and then warm in a pan or low oven to revive. You could also freeze the batter, but if you're already on the pans, you may as well cook the full batch and freeze as crumps to speed up the process on the other end.

The walnut ripple butter can also be frozen for up to 6 months, or will keep in the fridge for a couple of weeks.

Recipe riffs

Take the crumpets in a savoury direction by topping them with the sorts of ingredients you'd put on a blini ... I'm talkin' cream cheese and caviar.

You can schmear the walnut ripple butter liberally on toast, for a good time always.

Subs

Turn this recipe plant-based by subbing out the buttermilk and upping the water to 400 ml (14 fl oz). Use a neutral-flavoured oil instead of butter, and maple syrup to serve.

Shortcuts

If you have any left-over vegie mash — from carrot to sweet potato to potato — all or any of these can be subbed into this batter. A cup's worth should do it, and you don't even need to fold it through at the end — just mix it in when the dough is being whisked.

So, you didn't get round to making that walnut ripple butter? Just pile on some honey and butter!

Skills spotlight: Compound butter

Compound butter combines (or 'compounds') the creamy richness of butter with the flavours and colours imbued by whatever fresh and dried ingredients you fancy, anything from Chinese five-spice to curry paste, to cocoa powder or even salted caramel — this is the butter of your wildest imagination! You can stick to savoury classics such as herbs, garlic or mustard, or go wild with lavender or black truffle, or even crispy chopped-up chicken skin, which was such a THING at a particular Melbourne restaurant a while back. (The restaurant has gone, but the schmaltz remains!)

Soften a block of butter (see page 273), fold in your chosen ingredient/s, form into a log, wrap in baking paper and stash in the fridge or freezer.

Just remember that compound butters are often best incorporated once the heat is off, particularly where fresh ingredients are concerned, to keep their flavours bright.

Try dobbing savoury compound butters over jacket potatoes, pastas or roasted vegies, or in your toasties. Stuff it inside a chicken breast, or let it melt into a pool of golden garlicky garnish on top of your steak!

Thrupple butter crumpets
Page 196

Hubba-babaghanoush

/ **Serves 4–6 as a dippy starter, or as part of a main meal**

1¼ cups (250 g) dried chickpeas, soaked overnight (see Ingredient spotlight and Shortcuts, page 203)
2 strips dried kombu (optional, but good if you're gassy)
2–3 medium-large eggplants (aubergines), the glossier the better
1 massive handful of parsley, roughly chopped
1 massive handful of coriander (cilantro), roughly chopped
4 garlic cloves, peeled
juice of 2 lemons
3 tablespoons extra virgin olive oil, plus extra to serve
2 tablespoons tahini (see Subs, page 203)
1 tablespoon salt flakes
1 teaspoon ground coriander
½ teaspoon ground cumin
¼ teaspoon sweet smoked paprika, plus extra to serve
1–2 ice cubes (see Tips, page 203)

Pickled pink cauli

1 cauliflower, washed, dried and cut into florets (see Tips, page 203)
1 medium beetroot, peeled and roughly chopped
½ tablespoon caraway seeds (optional, but excellent)
2 bay leaves
1 cup (250 ml) white wine vinegar or apple cider vinegar
4–5 garlic cloves, peeled and bruised
3 tablespoons salt flakes
1 teaspoon caster (superfine) sugar

To serve

parsley, roughly chopped
coriander (cilantro), roughly chopped
pomegranate seeds
falafels (page 208)
soft pitta breads

You know those ads for tacos where the little girl says, 'Why not have both?' Well I *am* that girl, asking, if you're deciding between making hummus or babaghanoush, why NOT have both? In this mash-up of the two, the chickpeas help make the baba even smoother and creamier, while the eggplant makes the hummus infinitely more interesting. And the pickled cauliflower florets just cap it all off — like chewed-up bits of purple Hubba Bubba bubble gum. On toast with avocado, as a 'purée' with Middle Eastern mains, or straight from the fridge, this dip is just hubba-hubba.

Drain the soaked chickpeas and place in a large saucepan with 12 cups (3 litres) cold water and the kombu, if using — but no salt! Bring to the boil, then simmer for about 1½ hours. Once the chickpeas are soft enough to squash between your fingers, drain and allow to cool slightly, removing the kombu. At this point I like to peel the chickpeas for the smoothest hummus, but you are SO welcome to skip this step. I'm already asking a lot.

While the chickpeas are simmering, roast the eggplants over a gas cooktop (see Tips, page 203) or barbecue over medium heat, rotating occasionally, for 30–45 minutes, until blackened on all sides and completely soft in the middle. Alternatively, pop the eggplants on a rack over a baking tray and roast in a 200°C (400°F) oven for an hour or so, until the skin has charred, and when poked seems more balloon than eggplant. Leave until cool enough to handle, draped over a clean sink to leak out a whole lot of *schmutz* that will otherwise make your baba way too watery.

For the pickled cauli, bring a large-ish saucepan of well-salted (preferably filtered) water to the boil. Add the cauliflower florets and beetroot and bubble away for 3 minutes to soften slightly. Drain, reserving 3 cups (750 ml) of the now magenta-coloured water. Divide the veg among two sterilised containers (see page 127), each about 300 ml (10½ fl oz) in capacity. Sprinkle the caraway seeds evenly on top, finishing with a bay leaf.

Pour the reserved poaching water back into the pan. Add the vinegar, garlic, salt and sugar and bring to the boil. Pour this mixture over the veg to cover and seal. If there isn't enough liquid, boil a little more vinegar and pour over the top. The cauli and beet will get even better after a day of hanging out in the pickling liquid, and will last comfortably for up to a month in the fridge.

Scoop the eggplant flesh into a food processor. Toss in the chickpeas and remaining ingredients (including the ice cubes) and blitz until smooth and velvety, adding more olive oil if you want it even creamier. Taste for seasoning.

Serve warm or cold, topped with the pickles, extra herbs and pomegranate seeds, with falafels and soft pitta breads to round it all out. The hubba will last for up to a week in the fridge in an airtight container — just cover with olive oil to help stop a skin forming, and give it a good stir before serving, if need be.

200 **THE JOY OF BETTER COOKING**

THE JOY OF BETTER COOKING

Hubba-babaghanoush Bonus bits

Tips

The ice cubes help the hummus become extra fluffy — a very cool trick I learned from Noor Murad at Ottolenghi Test Kitchen. If you're worried your food processor or blender can't handle it, skip this step.

If using a gas cooktop to char the eggplants, use some foil as a splatter guard. Take the trivet off your chosen burner. Poke a hole in a sheet of foil, so it will skirt around the heat source, and place it over the top, to cover the rest of your cooktop. This will catch the eggplant weepings and make for easier clean-up.

If you're roasting the eggplant in the oven, to save on energy, bake something else in there too — like, say, a halved butternut pumpkin (squash), or some veg for the orange veg soup on page 68.

To cut the cauli into florets, place upside-down on a chopping board, and hold onto the stalk end while you twist or snip away at the florets from the base. Cut the florets in half again so that they're all roughly the same fork-friendly size.

Shortcuts

To speed up the chickpea-soaking process, pop them in a big saucepan and pour in enough cold water to cover them by a good inch or so. Bring to the boil, reduce the heat and simmer for 5 minutes, then turn off the heat. Leave to soak in this water for 1 hour, then drain and cook as per the instructions on page 200; they'll cook in around half the time!

A pressure cooker is another option, if you have one — once it comes up to pressure, 15 minutes is enough time to cook the chickpeas, once soaked.

In even more of a hubba-hurry? Go the tinned route, of course, but please do rinse them — keeping the aquafaba (see page 185) if you like — and consider popping the chickpeas out of their skins for the smoothest finish.

Subs

If you're out of tahini, you can use sesame oil instead.

Ingredient spotlight: Dried legumes

I'm not here to can the can — no sirree. Indeed, I have all kinds of tinned beans, lentils and chickpeas on the shelf for those emergency 'bulking' situations where a dish is missing some oomph and I've forgotten to soak something leguminous from scratch.

BUT if you're not already on the dried legume wagon, here's a little secret: not every dried bean needs a soak every time. In fact, the soak is less for texture than for digestion. An overnight soaking is useful if you're prone to the percussive predilections of prebiotic-packed produce … and we all are, actually. Soaking helps to tame the toot, by breaking down the oligosaccharides (complex sugars) that our bodies don't produce the right enzymes to break down. Left unsullied, these sugars ferment in our gut and goad the gas.

Soak dried legumes overnight in lots of cold water (I use filtered water, or you can add a teaspoon of bicarb of soda/baking soda to alkalise it), allowing for them to double in size. If you don't have time to soak, slip a strip or two of kombu (kelp) in with your legumes when cooking from dry. Seaweed has magical enzymes that accelerate the breakdown of those stubborn sugars before they reach your gut. It may add a faint savoury funk, but if you like miso soup (which seaweed is a key ingredient in), you'll be A-OK with kombu, which you'll find at Asian grocers and health food stores.

When cooking dried beans and chickpeas from dry, avoid salting until the very last half hour or so. Salting too early can toughen the outer layer of the legumes and impede the cooking process.

Overnight garden focaccia

Overnight dough
3 cups (450 g) strong white flour
  (see Worth it, page 207)
2 teaspoons dried yeast (1 x 7 g sachet)
1½ teaspoons salt flakes
1½ cups (375 ml) lukewarm water
1 tablespoon olive oil

Garden toppings
(think of your favourite pizza
toppings and go wild!)
multi-coloured capsicums (peppers)
  and mild chillies, thinly sliced
multi-coloured tomato slices
red onion or spring onions (scallions),
  thinly sliced
mixed herbs, such as marjoram, basil,
  chives and parsley, chopped
olives and/or other pickled goodies
  such as capers, artichokes
  or sun-dried tomatoes
olive oil, for drizzling
sea salt flakes, for sprinkling

Tradish toppings
a small handful of rosemary leaves
olive oil, for drizzling
sea salt flakes, for sprinkling

Focaccia translates to 'hearth bread', which is handy, because while most overnight doughs are hoping for a high rise, this one's all about the chew. It utilises the no-knead method popularised in *The New York Times* by Jim Lahey and Mark Bittman over 15 years ago, and improved upon by Kenji López-Alt (see Skills spotlight, page 207), but with a wetter dough and olive oil for a chewier crumb, à la Samin Nosrat's. Lahey aptly credits this technique as being the one originally used to bake bread in ancient Rome ... the home of, you guessed it: focaccia! And the best part? Focaccia can totally be way flatter than a regular loaf, so even if yours doesn't rise quite right, the satisfaction and aroma of freshly baked bread, from your own hand, is just *belissima*. It's up to you whether you go the glorious garden route or keep yours more traditional. Just see how you feel come Sunday morning.

Place all the overnight dough ingredients in a bowl. Mix with a wooden spoon or spatula to combine, until you have a wet, sticky dough. Cover with a clean damp tea towel and leave in the fridge for at least 8 hours, preferably overnight; you can even leave the dough for 48 hours or more, to really develop the flavour.

About 4 hours before you want to bake it, take the dough out of the fridge and let it come to room temperature; during this time, it should rise a little more. Punch the dough down — which is exactly how it sounds! — and give it a little knead to bring it all together into a ball. The oil in the dough will make it easy to handle.

Line a 25 x 30 cm (10 x 12 inch) baking tray with baking paper. Place the dough on top, stretching and pressing it out with your fingers into whatever shape you like — round, oval, square or rectangle. Allow the dough to rise again in a warm spot for 1–2 hours, covered again with a damp tea towel.

When ready to bake, preheat the oven to 180°C (350°F). In a bowl, toss your garden topping ingredients (or rosemary leaves if you're going tradish) in a few tablespoons of olive oil, so they don't go dry too quickly and burn.

Using your fingers, press dimples into the dough, then squish the topping ingredients into your creation. Scatter with salt flakes and freshly cracked black pepper.

Pour water into a heatproof mug or baking dish and sit it on the bottom of the oven to create steam (this helps the focaccia expand before forming a crust). Bake the focaccia on the middle shelf of the oven for 35–45 minutes, or until golden and cooked through. Some of your vegies might char a bit, but that's cool — these can even be the most delicious aspects of the bake.

Once cooked but while still HOT, drizzle with a little more olive oil, and garnish with more fresh herbs if you like. Then either show off your creative genius as a whole loaf at the table, or cut into jaunty pieces to serve.

THE JOY OF BETTER COOKING

After

Before

Leavening dough is like cultivating a garden. You need to give it every chance of success, but it's capricious, and it won't always grow the way you expect. That's the magic.

Tips

This dough is super easy to make and can be used for terrific puffy pizza bases as well.

Shortcuts

Use store-bought pizza dough, straight out of the fridge, or even thawed puff pastry (à la the Bus stop tarta on page 226). Shape into an oiled and lined baking dish, drizzle with plenty of olive oil, poke in some holes with your fingertips, then plant your garden, sprinkle with salt flakes and black pepper and bake as described.

Double duty

Slice stale bread or focaccia thinly, brush with extra virgin olive oil and bake in a 140°C (275°F) oven until golden brown and crunchy.

Alternatively, tear the bread into chunks and toss with olive oil, dried herbs and/or garlic before baking.

Worth it

Thanks to the recent uptick in sourdough baking at home, you should be able to find strong flour, also called 'bread flour', at most supermarkets these days. Strong flour has a higher level of protein, and therefore gluten, which helps with a nice open crumb (that's the holes or 'alveolation' in the middle of the bread).

If you plan on baking lots of bread or focaccia, investing in a bag of strong flour (with 11–13% protein) and storing it in the fridge between bakes is worthwhile. Otherwise, plain (all-purpose) flour is totally fine, too — it might not rise quite as high, but if you're only baking loaves on the odd occasion, you'll be right.

Skills spotlight: Bread leavening

Overnight, no-knead or minimal-knead breads and focaccias are the easiest way to bake bread at home — short of buying a bread-maker, that is. The best part is, there's no need to maintain a sourdough starter, or get your hands dirty, and the smell of fresh bread in the morning is just ace!

Some points to consider. The best ratio of ingredients, according to food writer and innovator Kenji López-Alt, is 100 parts flour, 1.5 parts salt, 1 part dried yeast and 70 parts water. Dried yeast is more stable than fresh yeast, but if fresh is all you have, you'll need to hold the salt until after the dough has had a chance to form overnight, otherwise it will kill the yeast. There's also no need to add sugar to a bread dough — especially an overnight one — if using dried yeast, but fresh yeast could always use a little extra sweetness to feed the yeast and help the dough grow to its full power.

A cast-iron casserole dish and/or tray are great for baking loaves and focaccias, because you want as much heat underneath the dough as possible for a great crusty bottom. If going down the tray route, rather than proving the dough in a casserole dish, preheat the tray along with the oven to give your bread an even crustier bum.

Fried green falafels

oil, for deep-frying (I like grapeseed oil)
salt flakes, for sprinkling

Falafels
2½ cups (500 g) dried chickpeas
(see Subs, page 211), soaked in
plenty of cold water overnight
(see Shortcuts, page 211)
2 brown onions, roughly chopped
2 tablespoons ground coriander
2 tablespoons ground cumin
1½ tablespoons garlic powder
2 teaspoons fine salt
1½ bunches of parsley, about
150 g (5½ oz), roughly chopped
(see Tips, page 211)
1½ bunches of coriander (cilantro),
about 150 g (5½ oz), roughly chopped
1 teaspoon bicarbonate of soda
(baking soda)

Cauli tabouleh
1 small head of cauliflower, cut into
florets, stalk roughly chopped
½ salad onion, finely diced
2 roma tomatoes, diced
1 garlic clove, bruised
2 tablespoons olive oil
½ bunch of parsley, roughly chopped
½ bunch of coriander (cilantro),
roughly chopped

Dressing
4 tablespoons plain yoghurt
juice of ½ lemon
1 tablespoon honey
1 tablespoon tahini

To serve
soft pitta breads
Hubba-babaghanoush (page 200)
or store-bought hummus
Pickled pink cauli (page 200), optional
lemon wedges

I learned to make this falafel care of Emi from Egypt, a vivacious woman whose childhood in bustling Cairo could be contained within these fragrant footballs. Emi told me that once I tasted her falafel, I wouldn't want it any other way. I was struck by her confidence, but thought I'd best reserve comment until we'd completed the demo of this very dish. Dear reader, it really *is* the best falafel recipe, and I'll never make it any other way. Emi uses dried fava beans though, and if you can find them, I'd recommend you sub them in for the chickpeas — but I'm trying to remove every possible excuse in the book, so checkout chickpeas it is!

To make the falafels, drain the soaked chickpeas and set aside.

Place the onion, ground spices, salt and half the parsley and fresh coriander (in that order) in a blender or food processor. Blitz until the onion starts to break down to a sludge, and the herb stalks have yielded to the blades. Add the chickpeas, bicarbonate of soda and the remaining herbs (reserving a handful for garnishing, if you like). Blend to the consistency of a smooth paste.

Heat the oil in a medium-sized saucepan with high-ish sides; 8–10 cm (3¼–4 inches) of oil should be plenty.

Use your tablespoon measure and another tablespoon to scoop and press the mixture into football-looking oblongs. Working in batches, gently drop them into the oil, from as close to the oil as possible, and let them fry for a minute before turning to do the other side. Sometimes they'll stick to the bottom of the pan, but just let them sit there and they'll float up with a little agitation from your spider skimmer or long-handled tongs. Fry for another 2 minutes or so, until each is the colour of leather. Drain each batch on paper towel, sprinkling with salt flakes while still hot for good measure.

While the falafels are frying, make your tabouleh. Pop the cauliflower florets in a bowl and cover with freshly boiled water from a kettle. Let them sit for 5 minutes in the water to soften slightly. Combine the salad onion in a bowl with the tomatoes and season with salt and freshly ground black pepper.

Mix the dressing ingredients together in a jug, ready for pouring.

Blast your blender with water to dislodge any hop-ons, then pop in the cauliflower florets, garlic clove and olive oil. Blitz until the cauli is finely chopped to the size of couscous.

Toss the chopped cauli through the tomato mixture. Finish the tabouleh by stirring through the parsley and coriander just before serving. Drizzle with the yoghurt dressing to finish.

Serve the falafels in a pitta bread, with your hubba-babaghanoush, cauli tabouleh, pickled pink cauli, if using, and lemon wedges.

Fried green falafels Bonus bits

Shape these to your will. Roll them into soccer balls with your hands or an ice-cream scoop if you like. I prefer an oblong shape, because of the crunchier tips.

Tips

You can store any left-over mixture overnight in the fridge, or even freeze it. You can also fry the balls and freeze for reheating straight from frozen later.

Depending on what stalk-to-leaf ratio you have in your herbs, this falafel mixture might end up wetter than desired — which you'll be able to tell immediately with the first falafel, as it will frizzle heaps and start to *schmutz* everywhere. Pop the mixture back into the food processor and blitz in two tablespoons of chickpea flour (besan). The added starch will help bind them right up. And never fear — any *schmutz* will make a great crumb on poached or soft-boiled eggs, or sprinkled over soups or dips.

For deep-frying tips, check out page 57. For more about working with dried legumes, go to page 203.

Shortcuts

I know you came here for a shorty, but please accept this cautionary tale instead. DO NOT attempt to make the recipe with tinned chickpeas. They are nowhere near starchy enough, and your falafel mixture will quite literally disappear before your very eyes as it fries. There are recipes out there with tinned chickpeas that supplement with flour and other starches, and you're welcome to go hunting ... or, just remember to soak your chickies the night before — I promise you it's worth it!

If you don't have time to make the tabouleh, make a simple leaf salad (page 26) and drizzle with the lemony yoghurt dressing instead.

Subs

As an alternative to chickpeas, try using dried lima beans or fava beans. Texturally, it doesn't hurt to pop these legumes out of their skins. Once soaked for long enough, the skins should slip right off.

Double duty

Left-over falafels can be wrapped in pitta bread or mountain bread and then flattened in a sandwich press to form a chickpea burger or kebab. Slip a few slices of tomato in, and maybe some onion, too, and any fresh herbs you happen to have.

Skills spotlight: Blending

Have you ever chucked a bunch of stuff in the blender, flicked the switch, and heard ... crickets? That's probably because there wasn't enough moisture in your mixture. Blenders and food processors create a vortex with their whirring blades, but if you don't give them something sloppy to slosh around, they'll just circulate air among the solids that are clinging to the sides.

Circumvent the crickets by chucking the wet stuff in first, chopping things finer than you think before you begin, and occasionally even splitting the mixture into batches. Herbs are particularly challenging to blitz, so be judicious with chopping — and blitz for long enough to allow the stalks to get sucked into the vortex too. If you're trying to decide what kind of *zhuzher* you need, check out the Gadget spotlight on page 151.

Five-spice tempura with MYO chilli oil

6 cups (1.5 litres) grapeseed oil,
   for deep-frying
½ cup (75 g) plain (all-purpose) flour,
   for dusting (see Subs, page 214)
500 g (1 lb 2 oz) bougie brassicas,
   such as caulini and broccolini
   (see Subs, page 214), chopped
   into fork-friendly chunks
1 teaspoon salt flakes
1 teaspoon Chinese five-spice
lemon cheeks, to serve

Tempura batter
a few ice cubes
½ cup (60 g) cornflour (cornstarch)
   (see Subs, page 214)
½ cup (75 g) plain (all-purpose)
   flour, plus extra for dusting
   (see Subs, page 214)
1 teaspoon salt flakes
1 cup (250 ml) chilled sparkling mineral
   water or soda water (club soda) — or
   even just chilled tap water at a pinch

MYO chilli oil
2 cups (500 ml) grapeseed oil
1 thumb-sized knob of fresh ginger,
   peeled and grated
20 g (¾ oz) sichuan peppercorns
20 g (¾ oz) chilli flakes (see Tips,
   page 214)
100 g (3½ oz) crispy fried shallots
   (see page 172)
1 tablespoon grated fresh garlic
1–2 spring onions (scallions),
   finely chopped
1–2 star anise
1 teaspoon Chinese five-spice
¼ cup (60 ml) sesame oil
2 tablespoons sesame seeds, toasted
1 tablespoon tomato paste
   (concentrated purée)
1–2 tablespoons light soy sauce
1 tablespoon black vinegar
   or rice wine vinegar

Here we make the most of the mild, sweet flavour of brassicas, blossoming buds on top, with more stalk for the fork. You can use this tempura batter for any of the bougie brassicas, or just your usual suspects such as regular cauli or broccoli (with the florets split in half lengthways to help accelerate the cook), as well as tofu, mushrooms or even seafood, if you're so inclined. You'll notice I've popped some tomato paste in the chilli oil, which may seem wild at first glance, but once you try it with this decidedly inauthentic umami-rich addition, you won't go back. For best effect, make the chilli oil at least the night before.

Start by making the chilli oil. In a small saucepan, bring the oil and grated ginger to 170°C (325°F). This takes about 10 minutes over low heat; the oil will be shimmering but not smoking.

In a large heatproof bowl, mix together the peppercorns, chilli flakes, fried shallots, garlic, spring onion, star anise, five-spice, sesame oil, sesame seeds and tomato paste. Set a fine-meshed sieve over the top. Being careful of spitting, pour the hot oil over the lot. Add the soy sauce and vinegar to taste, then leave to infuse. Once cool, pull out the star anise. The longer the oil stands, the more intense the heat and flavour will be. Store in the fridge, in a clean sealed jar.

When ready to cook, prepare the tempura batter. Find two bowls that can nestle into each other. Pop a few ice cubes into the bottom bowl and pour in just enough cold tap water so that it won't overflow with the other bowl on top. Combine the cornflour, flour and salt flakes in the top bowl. Pour in your cold fizzy water in a steady stream, stirring with a fork or whisk to get rid of any lumps. Allow to stand for 10 minutes.

While the batter is resting, heat the frying oil to 180°C (350°F) — you don't need a thermometer, just drop in a small speck of batter and if it immediately curls into a ball and turns golden, you're all set. (Or you can use a cube of bread; see the Skills spotlight on page 57.)

Set up a plate or tray lined with paper towel as a draining station. Add the plain flour to a bowl as your dusting station. Working in batches, pop the brassicas into the flour, then the batter and pull them out, allowing any excess batter to drip off, before submerging in the oil for 2–3 minutes, or until golden. Drain each batch on paper towel.

Crush the salt flakes with the five-spice using a mortar and pestle, or crush the flakes between your fingertips and toss through the five-spice to combine.

Sprinkle the hot battered tempura with the salty spice sprinkle and serve immediately, with the chilli oil for drizzling, and the lemon cheeks for squeezing over.

Five-spice tempura Bonus bits

Tips

Some varieties of chilli flakes are sweeter and milder than others. Look for terms like 'mild' or 'hot' on the packet, although they're not always expressly labelled.

Shortcuts

The chilli oil is infinitesimally scrumptious, but if you don't have time to MYO, store-bought will do the trick. My preference is for any that say 'crunchy', because they contain roasted peanuts and/or sesame seeds.

Alternatively, you can serve this with sriracha or similar chilli sauce, a squirt of Kewpie mayo or even just a few artfully placed lemon cheeks.

Subs

If caulini and broccolini aren't available, slice a head of regular cauli or broccoli into fork-sized bits, stem included.

If you don't have cornflour, just use straight-up plain (all-purpose) flour (or its gluten-free equivalent), though I do enjoy the lightness and golden colour that cornflour brings.

To go gluten-free, use gluten-free cornflour, and swap the plain flour for gluten-free plain flour.

Recipe riffs

The great thing about tempura batter is that once you've got it down pat, you can batter and fry whatever you like. I love frying ribbons of zucchini (courgette), discs of sweet potato or pumpkin (squash), little button mushrooms, green beans, lotus root, and of course seafood such as prawns (shrimp), whitebait and chunks of firm-fleshed white fish.

Consider swapping the five-spice for sweet paprika, or adding a teaspoon of curry powder to the batter for a whole new ballgame.

Waste knot

If you have any left-over tempura batter, coat the frizzy roots of the spring onion and deep-fry them — they'll be gloriously sweet and people will be *shooketh* that these can be eaten!

Allow the frying oil to cool completely, then strain into a jar or bottle and label clearly to use again. Frying oil is still good to go for at least a couple of times — you'll know it's spent when it changes colour to a darker shade of brown.

Ingredient spotlight: Bougie brassicas

Have you noticed the proliferation of some decidedly gentrified green stuff lately? Bog-standard broccoli booted for broccolini; cauliflower heads in hues of yellow and purple strutting round like they've been to the hairdresser for a rinse; romanesco broccoli fractals formed in lurid acid green, thinking they're all that because of a cameo in *Star Wars*; kalettes, little frilly-skirted brussels sprouts, looking like mini Marilyns perched atop a grate in *The Seven Year Itch*. And then there's caulini — my pick for fancy brassica supreme. If you're wondering what's with all the new varieties, I have news: brassicas are the new black! Ever since Eyal Shani started burning cauliflower heads and Ottolenghi sliced his into steaks, growers have been jostling for position in the produce aisle with new-fangled florets to capture consumers keen to try something new.

Coloured caulis will lose their tinge when cooked, but pickling caulis with beetroot (page 200) will turn them hot pink, which looks fantastic in shawarmas and the like.

Broccolini (or baby broccoli) is a hybrid of broccoli and kai-lan (a.k.a. Chinese broccoli), so recipes are interchangeable between the three — just blanch broader broccoli for slightly longer.

The MYO chilli oil looks like a lot of work, but you'll be hooked

Whatever brassica you use, cut or tear into bite-sized chunks

Using an ice bath means your batter won't dilute

No need for a thermometer — use the batter or crumb test

Not quite niçoise

4–5 eggs, at room temperature
400 g (14 oz) new potatoes
    or kipfler (fingerling) potatoes
3 tablespoons extra virgin olive oil,
    plus extra for drizzling
sea salt flakes, to taste
200 g (7 oz) green beans,
    topped, leaving the tails on
200 g (7 oz) cherry truss tomatoes
a handful of your favourite olives,
    pitted (see Tips, page 219)
5–6 radishes, thinly sliced and
    refreshed in cold water until needed
1 small red onion, or 1 French shallot,
    thinly sliced into rounds
½ cup roughly chopped parsley
250 g (9 oz) good-quality tinned tuna in
    spring water (see Ingredient spotlight,
    page 35)
6 anchovies (optional)
caper berries, to serve
lemon wedges, to serve

Sauce gribiche
2 tablespoons mayonnaise
    (see Tips, page 219)
2 tablespoons extra virgin olive oil
1 tablespoon dijon mustard
1 tablespoon red wine vinegar
1 tablespoon lilliput capers in salt,
    rinsed and drained
16 cornichons (75 g/2½ oz),
    finely chopped
1 cup finely chopped parsley
1 tablespoon finely chopped tarragon
    or Thai basil (weird, but it works!)

Niçoise salad is steeped in tradition, with strict rules around what goes in and what stays out. But here's the thing: even on the French Riviera, which is where the dish originates, tourists will be surprised to discover a multitude of interpretations from the modern chefs of Nice. That's the nature of cuisine — it's a moveable feast. And so, this version is full of twists and turns, which I think makes the salad even Nice-r.

Pop the eggs into a pan of boiling hot water from as close to the water as possible. Leave to cook for 6–8 minutes, depending on how runny you like them; 8 minutes will be hard-boiled (see Skills spotlight, page 219). Run under cold water and set aside. Peel when cooled.

Parboil the potatoes in plenty of well-salted water for 20–25 minutes, or until they're fork-tender. Drain well, chop them into fork-friendly shapes, place in a large mixing bowl and gently toss with 2 tablespoons of the olive oil and a pinch of salt flakes.

To 'tiger' the beans and tomatoes, place them in a bowl together and toss with the remaining 1 tablespoon of olive oil. Heat a large, heavy-based frying pan over medium heat. Once smoking hot, add the beans and leave for a minute or two to get some burnished tiger stripes, then toss and leave for another couple of minutes. Do this for 8–10 minutes, adding the tomatoes at the 5-minute mark. The beans need to be bright green with stripes of brown and black, and still have a bit of crunch. In the last couple of minutes of cooking, add the pitted olives to warm through. Add the whole lot to a bowl.

At this stage, if you would like to crisp up the potatoes, add them to the hot pan for 5 minutes or so over high heat to get some colour. Pop the green bean mixture back into the pan to soak up every last bit of juiciness and retain some heat while you make the sauce gribiche.

Grate or finely chop two of the eggs. Place in a bowl with all the gribiche ingredients, except the herbs. Mix well and season to taste with salt and black pepper, then mix in the herbs. Set aside until ready to serve.

To assemble the salad, choose a large serving platter or chopping board. In a large mixing bowl, give the cooked veg a gentle toss with the radish, onion, parsley, broken-up tuna chunks and anchovies, if using, seasoning to taste with salt and pepper before tumbling it all onto the platter without a care in the world. Splodge the sauce gribiche over the top.

Cut the remaining two eggs into quarters, or finely grate them over the top (if you're a hard-boiled kinda gal or guy). Scatter some caper berries over, and an extra drizzle of oil. Squeeze the lemon wedges over just before serving.

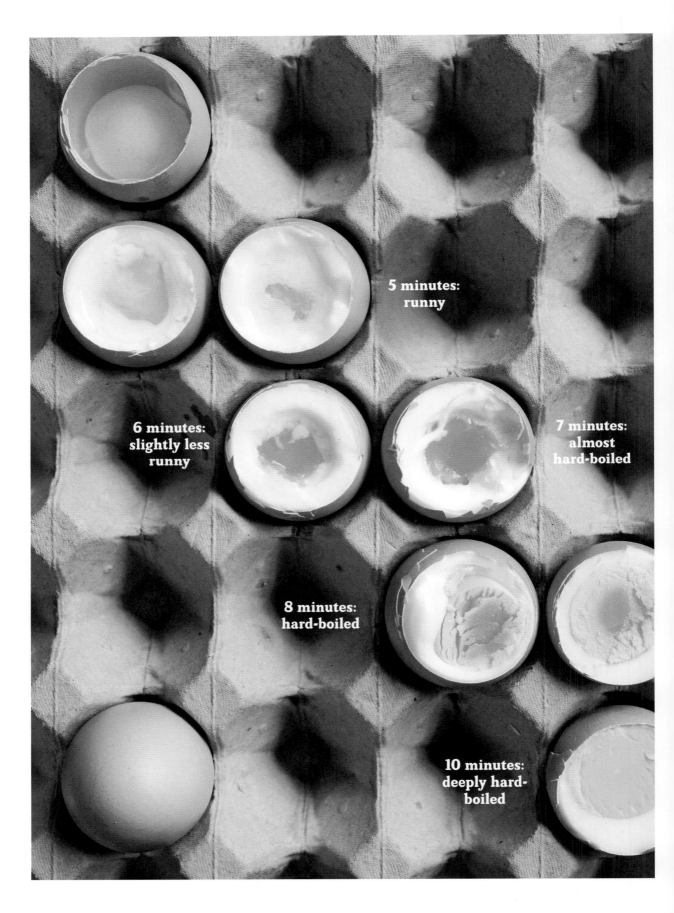

5 minutes: runny

6 minutes: slightly less runny

7 minutes: almost hard-boiled

8 minutes: hard-boiled

10 minutes: deeply hard-boiled

Getting a handle on history and tradition is part of being a better cook. The more you understand the rules, the easier it is to crack them in ways that work.

Tips

I use Kewpie mayonnaise for extra umami, but whole-egg mayo will do, too.

Pit the olives by placing them on a chopping board and squishing each olive with something sturdy like the base of an olive oil bottle, the flat of your chef's knife or even between your fingers!

All of the ingredients can be prepared a few hours in advance and chilled, but need to be brought back to room temperature before being assembled and served.

Shortcuts

If you're making the salad in summer, barbecue the beans and tomatoes, or just blanch the beans and leave the tomatoes raw. Instead of the sauce gribiche, use a simple Kewpie dressing.

Double duty

Sauce gribiche is absolutely glorious served with steamed greens such as broccolini or asparagus, and works beautifully as a type of tartare for fried fish. It also makes a rad dressing for a baby potato salad.

Extra extras

Make the salad go further by adding some perfectly prepared cos lettuce wedges.

Sear actual tuna steaks, then slice into fork-friendly morsels against the grain for a gorgeous EXTRA element. If you can, leave the tuna steaks out of the fridge for an hour to take the fridge chill off. Get your pan searing hot, then pop a piece of baking paper down and the oiled tuna steaks on top, and 2 minutes on each side should be plenty. You still want the steaks to be raw through the centre, and they'll keep cooking for a little while regardless.

Skills spotlight: Boiling eggs

Have you ever heard of someone say they can't even boil an egg? Believe it or not, there is an art to it, and once you learn how to do it properly, you'll start including boiled eggs in all manner of things, whether it's to grate hard-boiled eggs on top of salads and soups like a cheese, or leaving them runny and artfully arranged to sploodge forth their yolk when dug into.

Pop your room-temperature eggs into a pan of boiling hot water from as close to the water as possible. Drop to a simmer and leave to cook for the desired time, then run under cold water and set aside. Peel when cooled.

Here's a guide to cooking times:

5 minutes: runny
6 minutes: slightly less runny
7 minutes: almost hard-boiled
8 minutes: hard-boiled
10 minutes: deeply hard-boiled.

Braised leek with blue cheese crumb

3 leeks, about 750 g (1 lb 10 oz) in total
1 cup (250 ml) chicken or vegetable stock
1 cup (250 ml) decent white wine
   (if you can't drink it, don't cook with it)
½ cup (75 g) currants
10 thyme sprigs
100 g (3½ oz) butter
2 tablespoons snipped chives

Blue cheese crumb
100 g (3½ oz) of your favourite
   blue cheese, crumbled
¾ cup (45 g) panko
   breadcrumbs
½ cup finely chopped parsley
½ teaspoon garlic powder
   (optional, but excellent)
2 tablespoons olive oil

This feels like a super retro combo ... because it IS! Leek, with its pungency and sweetness, really loves a bit of crumbly blue cheese action, and the sweet currants are like little pops of syrupy surprise, capped off with a crispy panko crumb. Here, most of the prep time is spent swanning past the oven, wafting the aromas towards your nostrils and rubbing your hands together with glee. The flavours will only intensify overnight, so it's perfect for a lazy Saturday bake, with a luscious Sunday lunch finish. Bake the leek the day before, and the next day finish it off by adding the crumb, covering with foil and popping into a preheated 180°C (350°F) oven for 10 minutes, then removing the foil and exposing the crumb to the elements for the last 20 minutes to get some burnish. Leftovers will happily languish in the fridge for up to a week, so you really can't go wrong with this dish. It will go gloriously as a side with fish or chicken, or stand on its own as a vego main.

Preheat the oven to 180°C (350°F).

Meanwhile, remove the green tops from the leeks (see Waste knot, page 223) and cut the pale parts into 1.5 cm (⅝ inch) chubby discs. Soak the leeks in a salad spinner or bowl filled with cold water to get rid of any grit, then drain and spin, or wash them really well under the tap.

Snuggle the leek, cut side up, in a 20 x 30 cm (8 x 12 inch) baking dish. Add the stock, wine, currants and thyme. Dab the butter over the top, cover with foil and bake for 2 hours.

Combine the crumb ingredients in a bowl by stirring vigorously together with a spatula or wooden spoon. (You could also use your hands, if you're a fan of finger-lickin-blue — but no more touching the mixture once any licking has ensued, of course!) You want to end up with a nice chunky crumb.

At the 2-hour mark, remove the dish from the oven. Flick off the foil, fish out the thyme stalks and submerge the currants into the braising juices. Sprinkle with the crumb and bake, uncovered, for a further 30 minutes, until the top is golden and the juices have reduced to a syrupy consistency.

Serve in the baking dish or a serving bowl, drizzled with the juices and sprinkled with snipped chives, salt flakes and freshly ground black pepper.

Bonus bits

Subs
To go plant-based, use olive oil instead of butter. Instead of the blue cheese, finish with fried capers (page 84), or the herby almond picada from the mussels on page 100.
   For gluten-free, use rice crumbs instead of panko.

Shortcuts
Slice the leeks into thin rounds to halve the braising time.

Recipe riffs
For a more substantial dish, add chunks of parboiled potato into the braising liquid at the 2-hour mark.

Soak sliced leeks to help dislodge any dirt

Leeks like to soak up aroma ... and butter

Keep your blue cheese crumb chunky

No need to splash out on fancy blues for this one

THE JOY OF BETTER COOKING

Braised leek Bonus bits

Double duty

Turn any leftovers into a big leek tart by spreading them atop a piece of puff pastry. Cut a shallow 1 cm (½ inch) indent all around the pastry edge to make a crusty border. Crumble some more blue cheese over and bake as per the pastry packet instructions until golden and puffed.

If you've gone the leek and potato route, blitz any leftovers, add stock and/or cream and you have yourself a magnificent soup.

Waste knot

Keep the green ends of the leek for the freezer. Just remember to wash them well first. It may require some elbow grease and a good soak, but the bonus flavour you'll get into your stocks and soups is way worth the effort.

Worth it

Panko crumbs are a finer flake with more surface area than traditional breadcrumbs. Generally, if you panko-crumb and deep-fry anything — from chunks of cheese to scoops of ice cream — you're going to win fans. Rice crumbs will yield a similar (but ever-so-slightly less satisfying) result for gluten-intolerant guests.

Panko will last for yonks in the pantry, and can be subbed in as a filler any time you need to bulk out minced (ground) meat or thicken up a loaf.

Check the packet to make sure there's no palm oil in the ingredients list, as some brands, bafflingly, continue to show zero regard for rainforests and orangutans.

Ingredient spotlight: Blue cheese

Blue cheese has mould in it ... that's what makes it taste good. The origin story of blue cheese — Roquefort, to be exact — has all the makings of a Hollywood blockbuster. A young shepherd abandons his lunch of bread and fresh cheese in a French cave for a couple of weeks when he spots a beautiful damsel, comes back and discovers that the cheese has blue'd itself! So the youth does what any sensible individual would do and takes a bite, only to discover the most magnificent funk, which continues to be a stalwart of cheeseboards and salads to this day.

Some blues are intentionally injected with the blue-forming bugs, while others are pierced and exposed to the elements, which you can see clearly in the skewer marks through a wheel — and then it's up to the type of milk that is used, and where and how the cheese is aged, to determine the end result.

Gorgonzola is a robustly flavoured Italian blue made with cow's milk. Blue stilton hails from the actual village of Stilton in England (and thereabouts), with a sharp aroma and tighter crumble, while Danish blue is creamier again. What's most notable about all of these is that the sharpness and funk of the mould helps to balance out the richness of the cheese itself, making it a terrific body-builder for dishes.

Blues come alive with sweetness when paired with fruit, either dried or fresh. They're also great additions to rich soups and cheese bakes. I'd usually warn you off cooking with it, but will make an exception for a recipe like this baked leek one, where the breadcrumbs soak up any of the escaping oil and flavour, and reincorporate it into the dish.

Skills spotlight: Great gratins!

Gratinating, or 'gratin', is the process of grilling (broiling) the top of something creamy or crumby to bring on the burnish. You can do this by cranking up the heat in your oven for 10 minutes or so, or switching to the grill (broil) setting (if your oven has one) for 5 minutes. Just watch it carefully for a bronde rather than a burn — some ovens are a little too efficient.

If your dish has straight-up cheese topping, it'll glow up slower than if there's a bread-crumb involved, so be extra vigilant if the recipe is a traditional *au gratin* with a crusty top. For an even bake, it might pay to get the crumb on for the very last 10–15 minutes rather than keeping it there the whole time.

Panais, pommes au poire anna

/ Serves 4–6

3 large parsnips, peeled
4 Dutch cream potatoes, peeled
1 large onion, peeled
2 firm pears, peeled and cored
¼ cup (60 ml) extra virgin olive oil
4 garlic cloves, sliced
1 teaspoon sea salt flakes
½ teaspoon freshly ground black pepper
8 sage leaves, finely shredded
a few scrapes of fresh nutmeg
150 g (5½ oz) oat cheese
   (or any other melty plant-based
   cheese, vegan or otherwise), grated

Sauce vierge
⅓ cup (80 ml) olive oil
2 tablespoons white wine vinegar
1 teaspoon dijon mustard
   (although any type will work)
1 teaspoon chopped tarragon leaves
4 tablespoons chopped parsley

Doesn't this description sound so much better than a Parsnip, potato and pear bake? The French are good like that. Made with scalloped (i.e. thinly sliced) potatoes, this dish has its origins in a region near the French Alps, where it's cold enough to justify baking big trays of buttered-up and/or cheesed-up root veg, be you *après skiing* or *après* wandering the shops on the weekends. This is a show-stopping standalone dish if served with a sharply dressed salad of leaves (page 26), or as the side hustle of a larger meal. These scalloped bakes are often a bit fiddly, so if you're just learning to slice, a mandoline will come in handy. What you'll love most about this dish is that not only is it a one-trayer, but we've also swapped out the butter for olive oil, and the cheese for planty cheese, so this is also THE dish your vegan friends will French-kiss you over. Speaking of switches, any root veg loves a cheese sauce, vegan or otherwise. I'm talkin' 24-carrot gold.

Preheat the oven to 200°C (400°F).

Using a mandoline (with the guard attached!), slice the parsnips, potatoes, onion and pears, keeping them in their separate piles.

Brush a heavy-based casserole dish or skillet pan with some of the olive oil. Layer half the parsnip and potato on the bottom, then half the onion and garlic. Sprinkle with some of the salt and pepper, sage and nutmeg. Now add a layer of pears, half the cheese, a drizzle of olive oil — then repeat in reverse, finishing with the parsnip, potato and cheese, and drizzling with any left-over oil.

Cover with foil or the lid and bake for 1 hour. Remove the foil or lid and bake for a further 30 minutes, until golden and saucy. Remove from the oven and leave to rest for 5 minutes.

In a blender, blitz the sauce vierge ingredients until vivid green, then season to taste with salt flakes and freshly ground black pepper.

Either turn the dish out onto a serving platter, bottom side up, or just serve in the pan, drizzled with the sauce vierge and lots of black pepper.

Bonus bits

Shortcuts

For even more speed than a mandoline, use the slicing blade of a food processor on a thin setting to slice all the veg.

Got an air-fryer at home? Layer the veg in a baking dish that fits inside, and it'll be ready in just 20–25 minutes, with a 5-minute rest.

Ingredient spotlight: Plant-based cheese

These days you can get everything from crumbly feta made of almonds to gooey soft-rinds made of cauli. Check the label to see how the cheese will behave under heat, as some may split, while others will stretch. 'Mozzarella' or 'cheddar' styles should be fine here.

Bus stop peperonata burrata tarta

Serves 6
with leftovers

375 g (13 oz) packet wholemeal spelt
   butter puff pastry (see Ingredient
   spotlight opposite)
3 red capsicums (peppers), halved
   lengthways and deseeded
2 long red chillies, halved lengthways
   and deseeded
¼ cup (60 ml) olive oil,
   plus extra for drizzling
1 onion, finely sliced
4 garlic cloves, finely sliced
6 anchovies (optional)
1 tablespoon red wine vinegar
1 cup (250 ml) tomato passata
   (puréed tomatoes)
1 teaspoon sugar
¼ cup (45 g) sultanas
¼ cup (50 g) capers, drained
100 g (3½ oz) cheese-stuffed
   mini peppers, cut in half
100 g (3½ oz) large stuffed
   green olives, cut in half
250 g (9 oz) truss cherry tomatoes
⅓ cup (50 g) pine nuts
1 egg, beaten with a splash of water
8 basil sprigs
250 g (9 oz) ball of burrata
   or torn buffalo mozzarella

Why 'bus stop'? Because it's up to you where you get off! Let's start with the shape of the pastry. You could decide to fold in the sides and get galette-y, or keep it as one big rectangle (as we've done), in which case it's more like a giant vol-au-vent. Speaking of, you could also cut the pastry into individual tarts — be they square like Danishes, or cookie-cutter round. Then, with the filling, you can elect for every optional extra (like my dad does when buying an SUV), or keep things simple and dip a toe in with a purer version. This makes a perfect festive appetiser, and is also great as the main event with a bitey leafy salad (page 26).

Take the pastry out of the freezer for at least 40 minutes before cooking and leave in a cool-ish place in the kitchen, or in the fridge if the weather is hot.

Line a baking tray with baking paper. Place the capsicum and chilli halves on the baking tray, cut side down, and drizzle with a little olive oil. Place into a cold oven, then set the temperature to 200°C (400°F). Cook for 20 minutes, or until the skins start to blister, then remove from the oven, cover with foil and leave to steam for a while, which will make it easier to slip off the skins.

Unfurl the pastry onto a large lined baking tray and use a sharp knife to cut a 2 cm (¾ inch) border around the whole sheet, without cutting all the way through. (TBH, it's no drama if you do that every now and again, either.) With the tines of a fork, prick small holes all over the pastry, inside the border.

Put the pastry into the very hot oven and bake for 30 minutes.

Meanwhile, heat the olive oil in a heavy-based pan. Sweat the onion and garlic for 10 minutes over medium heat, until the onion is super soft but not coloured. Smoosh in the anchovies, if using, and deglaze the pan with the vinegar. Stir in the passata and sugar and cook down for about 10–15 minutes, until the mixture starts to go jammy.

Slip the skins off the cooled capsicums and chillies. Shred the flesh with your fingers, then add to the tomato mixture with the sultanas and capers.

When the pastry is golden all over, and the base is cooked and beginning to flake, take the tray out of the oven. Your pastry may puff quite a bit, in which case you might need to use a clean tea towel to push the centre of the pastry down, leaving the border raised.

Season the capsicum mixture with salt and pepper if needed, then spoon it onto the pastry, right to the corners. Top with the stuffed pepper halves, olives and cherry tomatoes, scattering the pine nuts around.

Brush the pastry edges with the beaten egg for a shiny finish. Turn the oven down to 180°C (350°F) — no need to wait for it to cool down, though — then bake the *tarta* for another 10 minutes, or until the tomatoes start to blister.

Pull the tart out of the oven and place on a serving board. Scatter with the basil leaves. Either put the burrata ball in the middle, ready to tear open when serving, or dot the torn mozzarella all around. Cut into pieces to serve.

THE JOY OF BETTER COOKING

Bonus bits

Tips

You'll find stuffed peppers and olives at a continental deli or in the deli section at the shops.

Shortcuts

Use store-bought vol-au-vent or tart casings. Fill them with the jammy capsicum mixture (or even just some caramelised onion jam), plus whatever deli fillings you have handy. Top with a smidge of cheese, then bake under the grill (broiler) until it melts a little.

To make things even quicker, smoosh on some ready-made onion jam or pesto, use cherry tomato halves, bocconcini, fresh basil and a drizzle of olive oil and call it a day.

Ingredient spotlight: Playing with puff

I thought long and hard about whether to inflict a recipe for MYO puff pastry on you in this book, but having done a straw poll within my team, as well as searching deep within my soul, I realised that the last time I made a puff from scratch was … a decade ago. So I'm here to say: Normalise Shop-Bought Puff!

Check the back of the packet and make sure it has the same ingredients that you would use if making regular pastry from scratch: flour, butter, eggs, water … that sort of thing. Get creative — there are fabulous options like spelt pastry, and even gluten-free. In Australia, Carême is a reliable brand, and in the United States, Dufour gets great reviews; wherever you are, 'all-butter puff' is what you're looking for.

If the pastry is in a roll, let it thaw before rolling it out, to avoid cracking (this can be done on the bench, and shouldn't take longer than an hour). If it's already flattened, pop it on a tray and allow to thaw completely before using (this takes about 40 minutes on the benchtop, or 4 hours in the fridge). You can absolutely roll your pastry thinner to get more bang for your buck (a classic Mum move if she wants to get an extra layer out of her puff for her multilayered Napoleon on page 267).

To keep the puff the 'puffiest', abstain from 'docking' (that's hole-poking). For crispier puff, poke some holes in it with the tines of a fork — this will help steam escape, creating pockets of puffy parts and a flakier result. For the crispest, flattest puff result, dock as above, then flatten the pastry by sandwiching it under another sheet of baking paper with another baking tray on top.

While we're at it, try other store-bought frozen pastry sheets, like filo and shortcrust. Life is almost always too short to make your own — even on weekends — and having an arsenal of frozen sheets means you're already halfway to dinner just by opening the freezer door.

**Bus stop peperonata
burrata tarta**

Page 226

Gnudi rudey with hazelnut brown butter

1 cup (315 g) rock salt
    (see Tips, page 232)
4 large carrots, about 800 g/1 lb 12 oz
    (see Tips, page 232)
½ orange
2 cups (480 g) ricotta
    (see Tips, page 232)
1 cup (100 g) finely grated parmesan,
    plus extra to serve
1 egg yolk
1 teaspoon salt flakes
a pinch of freshly grated nutmeg
3 cups (540 g) fine semolina
    (see Subs, page 232)
3 tablespoons olive oil
200 g (7 oz) cold butter, cut into cubes
½ cup (75 g) raw hazelnuts
4–5 fresh thyme sprigs
honey, for drizzling (optional)

This dish epitomises 'weekend project', because you can kick it off on a Saturday, and serve it up for a triumphantly terrific late Sunday lunch. Gnudi are a bit like gnocchi, in that the letter 'G' is silent, and they're both dumpling-y. But while gnocchi rely on starchy stuff such as flour or spuds, gnudi are like naked ravioli (hence the name) — mostly made up of ricotta and the boundless optimism that their thin semolina skin will hold up under the pressure of a rolling boil. Like a skinny-dipping pasta.

Preheat the oven to 200°C (400°F).

Make a bed of rock salt in a baking dish. Place the carrots on top and bake for 1 hour, until blistered and wrinkly. Once cool enough to handle, rub the skins off the carrots using a clean tea towel, then trim the stalk ends.

Using a food processor or blender, blitz the carrots to a purée. Zest the orange, reserving the orange. Add a teaspoon of the zest to the blender with the ricotta, parmesan, egg yolk, salt and nutmeg and blend until combined. Scrape the mixture into a bowl; it will be quite wet.

Place half the semolina in the bottom of a clean baking dish.

Depending how big you want your gnudi, scoop out a heaped teaspoon or tablespoon of the carrot mixture at a time and gently roll it between your palms to form a ball. If the mixture is sticking, pat your hands in the semolina between rolls, or have a bowl of water at the ready and use damp hands.

Drop the balls into the baking dish and roll them about until fully covered in semolina. Give each another pat with your palms before rolling in the semolina again for good measure. Sprinkle the remaining semolina on top, then cover and leave in the fridge for at least half a day, preferably overnight — the longer the better. The semolina forms a protective layer or skin, allowing the gnudi to be billowy inside when cooked.

Segment the reserved orange following the instructions on page 41.

When ready to serve, warm your serving bowls or platter and drizzle with the olive oil. Pour 10 cups (2.5 litres) water into a large saucepan, add some salt and bring to the boil, then reduce to a simmer. Add one-quarter of the dumplings to the pan at a time, cooking for 2–3 minutes, or until they start to float to the surface. Fish them out straight away and gently pop onto the warmed bowls or platter. Repeat with the remaining batches, reserving a mugful of the cooking water for the sauce.

Heat the butter and hazelnuts in a frying pan. Once the hazelnuts have coloured, scoop these out, leaving the butter to foam until it turns a lovely deep brown and the kitchen smells like cookies. Splash in a few tablespoons of the reserved pasta water to loosen the mixture, and when this starts to bubble, toss the hazelnuts back in to warm through, along with the orange segments and thyme sprigs. Pour over the gnudi and finish with a sprinkling of freshly ground black pepper, some extra parmesan and a drizzle of honey if desired.

THE JOY OF BETTER COOKING

Gnudi rudey Bonus bits

Subs

If you want to go gluten-free, use fine polenta instead of semolina.

If you want to go fancy, crack open some honeycomb and scoop bits of it across the top. The comb itself is entirely edible (though a little chewy).

Tips

Sniff your carrots — the freshest ones will smell of honey and the skin will look quite fine, while older, ashen-looking carrots will have started to turn fibrous and bitter.

The rock salt will help to draw moisture out of the carrots, intensifying the flavour and making them more mealy as the gnudi base. You can do the same with other root veg, too — it's a good trick if you want to make the world's best mash.

Grab your ricotta from the deli section, where it'll be lopped off a big wheel, rather than reaching for a tub from the fridges. It will have a far more interesting flavour than the long-life stuff, and won't be as grainy.

Waste knot

Save your baking rock salt to use again for baking potatoes or other root vegetables.

Freeze your egg white for the next time you need a quick shiny egg-wash.

Skills spotlight: Browning & caramelising

You'll often see recipes encouraging you to 'brown' butter or 'caramelise' veg, which may seem an unusual prompt for savouries when there's no actual 'caramel' involved ... and YET! Both really benefit from the magic of the Maillard reaction, which activates the natural sugars in the veg and the milk proteins in the butter with prolonged or high heating until they literally caramelise. This changes the colour (in the same way white sugar, when cooked, turns to brown toffee), intensifies the sweetness, and adds bonus complexity in the form of slight bitterness, which our tastebuds find exciting.

It's often the biggest difference you'll experience in restaurant veg, from gourds such as pumpkin and zucchini (courgette), to brassicas like cabbage and broccoli. Chefs are willing to take them to just before burnt, which creates gorgeous juxtaposition with the soft, milder-flavoured flesh within.

If you're worried about overcooking the veg, parboil or even par-steam them first, then finish with a blast of heat — either in a hot oven, or in a hot pan with plenty of oil or butter.

Caramelisation turns onions jammy, but it's a process that takes much longer than you think. You can speed up the process of caramelisation for vegies by sprinkling in some actual sugar, or adding a splash of maple syrup or honey. Just remember that these will heat much quicker than the natural sugars in the veg, so watch that it doesn't all end up on the wrong side of burnt.

Ingredient spotlight: Butter & ghee

Butter is the chocolate of savoury cooking. It adds dimension to dishes, and can even be tempered for a crack — a mind-blowing discovery I made courtesy of Antoni from *Queer Eye*! If you've ever tried to cook with crappy chocolate, you'll know that this is one area where you just don't skimp. It splits, it curdles, it's grainy, it throws out the flavour ... you get the picture. It's exactly the same with butter. (For more on chocolate, head to page 282.)

It may feel like a stretch to fork out a tenner for a log of over-whipped cream, but the difference it can make to a dish's overall slam-dunk factor is astronomical. Generally, the best butter you can buy is the cultured stuff that's made within your vicinity. They take it to art galleries, teach it a language, encourage it to take up an instrument ... well, actually, the 'culture' here is bacterial in nature, cultivated in the cream (usually overnight) before it's churned. As with kimchi, cheese, salumi and wine, the magic is in the microbes.

Cultured butter has a way more interesting flavour profile than the non-cultured variety. It's slightly acidic (great for cutting through its higher butterfat richness), and has a heavenly hazelnutty aroma. That nuttiness is only enhanced with cooking, and I like to highlight this, as I do in this gnudi recipe, by incorporating *actual* hazelnuts.

Because it's brimming with bugs, cultured butter is much more temperamental in terms of shelf-life, *especially* if it's unsalted, as salt acts as a natural preservative. If you don't plan on using all your cultured butter within a couple of weeks, pop it in the freezer and slice off shards as needed.

Unsurprisingly, French butter — cultured or otherwise — is a good choice no matter where you are in the world, because of its high butterfat content, and because the French take their *beurre* extremely seriously.

I'll often have a better butter on hand for spreading in a butter bell or butter dish, and a more cost-effective butter for cooking with that lives in the fridge. Occasionally, we'll also have a compound butter log or two in the freezer (more on this on page 197), and potentially some home-made ghee for high heat cookery.

Ghee, or clarified butter, is butter that has had the milk solids removed (as these burn at high temperatures), whereas ghee, sans milk solids, has a far higher smoking point of around 250°C (480°F), making it perfect for high-heat cooking to bring out the flavours of spices and aromats in curries. Milk solids, incidentally, are also what make burnt butter sauce taste so incredible ... so, we take the good with the bad. The best thing about ghee is that once you've made some, it lasts in the fridge for ages, since it's also the milk solids that turn rancid, while the actual butterfat is surprisingly stable, even at room temperature.

Making your own ghee is pretty darn easy, too. Buy a nice chunk of local butter; I usually go for 400–500 g (14 oz–1 lb 2 oz) at a time, which makes enough to last me about a month. Melt the butter in a small heavy-based saucepan over a super-low heat; you don't want the mixture to boil, as this will displace those aforementioned milk solids. When the whole thing has liquefied, turn off the heat, allow the butter to cool completely, then place in the fridge overnight. The next day, you'll have a pot of solid yellow stuff — this is the ghee! Use a knife to gently ease the solid block out of the pot. Underneath will be a layer of whitish-creamish liquid (ironically called the milk 'solids'); wipe these off with a paper towel, or scoop off and save for the next time you're making oladiki (page 129).

Store your ghee in a container (preferably glass) in the fridge and use as needed.

Excellent eggplant lasagne

1 brown onion, finely diced
3–4 garlic cloves, finely chopped
3 tablespoons olive oil, plus extra
   for brushing and drizzling
1 tablespoon red wine vinegar
a chef's pinch of salt flakes
   (see Skills spotlight, page 236),
   plus extra for salting the eggplant
a chef's pinch of brown sugar for
   the onion, and another chef's pinch
   for the sauce
2 x 400 g (14 oz) tins whole peeled
   cherry tomatoes (see Subs, page 236)
1 cup (250 ml) tomato passata
   (puréed tomatoes)
½ teaspoon dried oregano
½ bunch of parsley, finely chopped
½ bunch of basil, finely chopped
3–4 medium eggplants (aubergines),
   about 1.5 kg (3 lb 5 oz), cubed
375 g (13 oz) fresh pasta sheets
   (see Subs, page 236)
crusty bread, to serve

MYO pizza cheese
⅔ cup (100 g) shredded mozzarella
1 cup (100 g) grated cheddar
½ cup (50 g) finely grated parmesan

Béchamel sauce
50 g (1½ oz) butter
¼ cup (35 g) plain (all-purpose) flour
2 cups (500 ml) milk
a fresh scraping of nutmeg
½ cup (50 g) finely grated parmesan
ground white pepper, to taste

One of the first things you learn at culinary school is how to make béchamel sauce. It might seem strange to wait until the very last savoury dish in the book before we tackle that skill, but by now you'll have absorbed the idea that learning to cook is not a linear process — it's a journey, and a personal one at that. The puff of béchamel, the silky, slippery eggplant, the fact that you can make this gluten-free and/or plant-based with a few simple changes, finding shortcuts like cooking the onion in the preheating pan and using fresh pasta sheets instead of dried to save on washing up... all of these make this recipe a perfect bookend, and a whole lot of reasons to loosen your shoulders. And, as with most slow-cooks, it's a weekend project that only tastes better by Monday night (see Tips).

Pop the onion, garlic, olive oil, vinegar, salt and sugar in a large high-sided baking dish. Whack into a cold oven, then crank the temperature to 190°C (375°F) so it starts to cook as the oven heats up (about 20 minutes).

Once the onion is translucent and starting to caramelise, scoop the whole lot out into a bowl. Add a pinch of brown sugar and the tinned tomatoes, rinsing the tins out with a tablespoon of water and pouring the dregs in, too. Stir in the passata, oregano and most of the parsley and basil, leaving some herbs for garnishing. Taste for seasoning and set aside.

Add the eggplant to the baking dish, drizzle with 2–3 tablespoons oil and toss to coat. Roast for 40–50 minutes, until super caramelised, then remove from the dish and set aside.

Meanwhile, make the béchamel sauce. Melt the butter in a medium-sized saucepan, add the flour and stir for 2–3 minutes. Start pouring the milk slowly into the buttery flour mixture (roux), while stirring with a wooden spoon and scraping the roux from the edges of the pan. Add the nutmeg. Change over to a whisk and cooking until the mixture thickens and comes to the boil (around 7–10 minutes), whisking from time to time to help break up any lumps. Once thickened, add the parmesan and turn off the heat, still whisking until the parmesan melts in. Season to taste with salt and white pepper.

In a bowl, toss together your pizza cheeses to combine.

To assemble, spread a spoonful or two of the tomato sauce over the bottom of the baking dish. Place a layer of pasta sheets on top. Spread one-third of the tomato sauce over, then half the eggplant, and sprinkle with one-third of the pizza cheese. Cover with another layer of pasta sheets. Add another layer of tomato sauce, the remaining eggplant, then cheese, then pasta. Finish with a final layer of the tomato sauce. Pour the béchamel sauce over and sprinkle over the remaining cheese. Bake for 50 minutes, or until the cheese is melty and bubbling at the edges.

Serve drizzled with a little olive oil and garnished with the remaining herbs, with plenty of crusty bread to mop up all the saucy bits. Some peppery rocket (arugula) leaves would be an ideal side here, too.

THE JOY OF BETTER COOKING

Excellent eggplant lasagne Bonus bits

Tips

This dish portions and freezes really well. While still hot, transfer serves into heatproof containers, then let these cool a little before storing in the fridge for up to 1 week, or the freezer for 2–3 months.

To reheat fridge leftovers, whack in a cold oven and crank the heat to 140°C (275°F) — that way the inside warms through without the outside drying out. Thaw freezer lasagne in the fridge overnight, then cook as above.

Subs

If you only have dried lasagne sheets, there's no need to par-cook them. Just add a whole 400 ml (14 fl oz) tin of tomato water to the sauce to help it fully cook through.

To ditch the gluten, use gluten-free pasta sheets, and make the béchamel with gluten-free flour.

For a vegan version, use plant-based cheese, and make the béchamel with olive oil and a non-dairy milk.

It really pays to find good-quality tinned cherry tomatoes for this, but you can also use fresh cherry tomatoes. Just blanch the skins off by dropping the toms into boiling water and pulling them back out again; the skins should slip straight off once cooled.

Shortcuts

For a cheat's béchamel sauce, whisk 2 cups (500 g) smooth ricotta, 1 cup (250 ml) milk and ½ cup (50 g) finely grated parmesan until smooth.

Double duty

We love the MYO pizza cheese for its deep umami, stretchy fun and oozy fat content. It makes the best cheese toasties, and is great scattered over vegie gratins for added melty goodness — and, of course, pizzas!

Recipe riffs

Make a parma tray bake by leaving out the pasta sheets and sprinkling the top with panko crumbs.

When you're layering in the eggplant, add some cooked minced (ground) meat to your lasagne, or even slow-braised beef.

Waste knot

If you have any left-over fresh pasta sheets, cut them up into pappardelle or rag pasta and cook them the following night with a simple sauce like the gnudi rudey's burnt butter on page 230.

> ## Skills spotlight: A chef's pinch
>
> If you've ever seen a chef seasoning, you'll probably know that 'a chef's pinch' really is a thing. A chef's pinch is using all four of your fingers and thumb; a normal pinch is a thumb and pointer finger. The first is good for seasoning, the second for finishing. To help evenly distribute the seasoning, sprinkle the salt from a height (like Salt Bae!) and let gravity do its thing.

THE JOY OF BETTER COOKING

Ingredient spotlight: Salt

Have you ever tasted a dish and thought, 'something's missing?'. That something is more than likely salt. It's no wonder that it's salt we are being referred to when we're told to 'season to taste'. Just like seasons in general, and how some people prefer colder weather and open fires, and others sunshine and margaritas, salt is a very personal affair.

With a toddler at the table, I choose to under-season when I cook, and have a well-stocked pinch bowl of salt flakes on the table so that we can help ourselves. She has now learned to pinch a little salt in at a time, then taste, then go again; it's very cool. But layering seasoning, and knowing which salt is which, is still super important.

Many cookbooks (particularly those from North America) will tell you to use kosher salt, which is a fine-granule salt that's traditionally used for koshering meat, and can be found at specialty delis and shops. Its fine grain means it melts easily, and its weight and salinity doesn't tend to vary between brands, which is why cookery writers like to have it as an option when precise salt levels are needed, especially in baking.

I prefer to use flaked sea salt, because of how it behaves on the tongue. Chef Neil Perry taught me to have a thicker-flaked salt like Maldon for seasoning steak and pan-bound veg — it goes on the bottom of the dry pan while it's heating up, and when the salt starts popping like popcorn, it's hot enough to help form a crust. The finer salt flakes he and I save for seasoning salads and sprinkling on top of dishes. Having more salty surface area for the tongue to register means that you get an interplay of texture and saltiness with every bite, and it makes the eating experience more interesting to keep coming back in for.

Everyone has their preference. Mine is for pink salt flakes for salad-seasoning, and the thicker flake for steaking, but you can have just the one good salt and be just as happy.

Skills spotlight: Béchamel sauce

Béchamel is also known as one of the 'Mother Sauces' in French cookery, but so many cuisines have their own version. It's used in moussaka, in mornay, in chowder, in cauliflower gratin and, in this case, a very fluffy vego lasagne.

For all of these, starting with equal parts flour and butter, then cooking out the resulting roux — a fancy way of saying flour + fat — in a pan until the flour turns golden and smells a bit cookie-like, before pouring in the milk, will give you the best roux base. You can flavour the milk (the weight of flour x 10) by pressing some cloves into half an onion and simmering that for 10 or so minutes first to infuse. Bay leaves and nutmeg are great partners to the sauce, regardless of cuisine — and for me, the addition of a cheese such as parmesan can never be overstated.

A béchamel can be enriched and made into a savoury choux pastry by adding double the weight of eggs as flour/butter, and with extra cheese, into gougères, or can be folded through other ingredients for all kinds of croquette fillings.

If you're wondering whether you can make it gluten-free and/or plant-based, modern technology has made this possible, too! Use the same proportion of gluten-free flour and butter or olive oil, then add 10 times their individual weight in either dairy or plant-based milk.

Seriously good sweeties

Like, *seriously* good

How sweet it is ...

Are you the kind of person that flips their menu over to plan for dessert before deciding on mains? Do you flick through cookbooks back-to-front to see what sweeties await? Well, then, I might have caught you right here first — welcome!

You would already know that sweeties slide along a scale from fresh-fruity-fizz to decadently-dense-dark-chocolate. I've organised the recipes in this chapter from easy to hard, but I've left the easy easy *easiest* one out, because honestly, my favourite dessert is often simply whatever fruit is most in season and ripest, chopped chunky and shared.

If you're going to a friend's place for food and being asked to bring dessert, particularly if it's for a large contingent, a box of seasonal fruit from a quality greengrocer or a fresh food market — like cherries, or mangoes, or even a really ripe watermelon (which should be heavy for its size, and sound like a basketball when you tap on it) — will give you exceptionally good ROI. However, if you're up for working a little harder for your honey, this section includes recipes across the scale, from simple fruit poaching and custard through to classic meringues and rich, fudgy chocolate cake.

Sugar has had a bad rap over the past few decades, with some people quitting it entirely, and others seeking alternative sources for sweetness. And sure, there is definitely a case for being mindful of the amount of refined sugar in our lives. Mindless eating isn't great for any food group. If you're going to make something — savoury, sweet, show-stopper — take your time to savour it, and you'll find you end up eating a more moderate amount regardless. Not that I'm advocating for 'moderation' ... sustainable satisfaction, maybe.

My stance is all about fit-for-purpose. For example, I'm not about to bake profiteroles with agave syrup, because even the size of a sugar granule will impact the end result. A cookie's chew depends on the moisture content in its sweetness source. A honeycomb *can* be made with stevia, but it just won't have the same bubbly mystique. Other sweeties, however — particularly ones that call on sugar for syrupy-ness or balance, rather than structural support — can be far more flexible. I've offered alternatives where it feels natural to do so, but if you look at a recipe and wonder, 'Can I still make this with maple syrup?', give it a whirl and let me know.

A word on kids and sugar: they're going to eat it. No matter if you're a carob-counting household, or you try to vet their friends based on the odd side-eye into a bouncing schoolbag, our kids are going to be faced with sweeties in their day-to-day lives. There's no use demonising sugar, or calling it a 'sometimes food'. The only thing all this moralising is going to do is make them feel ashamed for enjoying something that human biology has created a desire for by design. In fact, current research suggests that there's no need to hold off on serving up dessert until 'after you're done with dinner', or to treat the sweet as a reward for finishing the 'proper' meal. This will only serve to elevate it to 'forbidden fruit' status (pun always intended!) and make it all the more tempting to gorge with guilt rather than actually openly enjoy with relish. Sometimes serving up all the courses on the table together is the simplest way of equalising the entire meal and nipping any negative connotations in the bud.

The best that we can do is to normalise being fussy with food. Chocolate IS special — not because it's an 'occasional treat', but because it's *an occasion*. The Mayans served cocoa ceremonially, as sacred ritual. Buy the best chocolate you can afford, which means smaller quantities, and savour it, in a mindful, joyful way, free of puritanical guilt or shame. Fruit is *fantastic*! Nature's lollies! Teach kids to smell for ripeness, to know what's in season, to anticipate

with enthusiasm the return of their favourites. Bake together when you can, not because you want them to 'see how much sugar goes in' (which they will, don't you worry), but because when *they* make it, it's more special, and they'll do their best to make it last, and to share it around.

After all, that's my favourite part of seriously good sweeties: they're designed to be shared. Whether to cap off a meal, as a bonbonnière, or in a tin by the doorstep, cakes and cookies and bakes are a love language for many — and that's what cooking, in general, should be all about.

The bostocks here

4 croissants (day-old ones
    are good — better, even)
⅔ cup (70 g) flaked almonds
1 tablespoon apricot jam
1 tablespoon boiled water

Frangipane

1 heaped cup (110 g) almond meal
125 g (4½ oz) unsalted butter, softened
⅓ cup (75 g) caster (superfine) sugar
1 egg
1 teaspoon vanilla extract
⅛ teaspoon almond extract
    (optional, but soooo great)
a pinch of salt

I take croissants very seriously. Not the baking, mind you; the *eating*. My most memorable birthday ever was a Paris croissant crawl, where we ate our weight in flaky pastry ... which only served to reinforce that if you're going to have croissant fresh, it's gotta be great. But you can take any shop-bought croiss from good to great with one fell swoop of frangipane (almond paste) and apricot jam. A bit like a pseudo-Bostock (a French mash-up of brioche and croissant, which usually has apricot jam under the frangipane), but we've flipped the two because it's quicker, and 'cos apricot jam makes a brilliant glaze, too.

Preheat the oven to 175°C (340°F). Line a baking tray with baking paper.

To make the frangipane, use a wooden spoon to beat the almond meal, butter and sugar in a bowl until well mixed. Add the egg, vanilla, almond extract (if using) and salt, then use a whisk to beat until light and creamy. Or, you can blitz all the ingredients together in a food processor or small blender.

Split the croissants through the top like a hotdog. Spoon some frangipane into the centre and allow it to squish out over the top. Spread more frangipane on the tops. Spread the flaked almonds on a deep plate or bowl, turn the croissants upside-down and press the frangipane into the flaked almonds.

Place the croissants on the tray, right side up. Bake for 20 minutes, or until the tops are golden and bubbling. Some of the topping mixture will slip off and become crunchy, caramelised bits around the base — the best bits, really.

While the croissants are still hot, combine the apricot jam and hot water and brush over the croissants to glaze.

Bonus bits

Tips

MYO almond meal by blitzing whole or blanched almonds in a food processor. You could even use walnuts or hazelnuts.

The frangipane recipe is easily doubled, and can be frozen for use as you need it.

Recipe riffs

For a Danish-ish version, slip roasted pear (page 258) into the split croissants.

Ditch the croissants for slices of brioche.

Subs

To go dairy-free, make the frangipane with 200 g (7 oz) almond butter, ⅓ cup (80 ml) maple syrup and 1 egg and use dairy-free vegan croissants from specialty stores. Or, use the dairy-free frangipane with a butterless pastry such as filo, rolled into cigars!

For a fully plant-based frangipane, use a vegan butter, and instead of the egg use aquafaba, the drained liquid from a tin of chickpeas.

Ingredient spotlight: Almond extract

I know this seems like a niche purchase, but a tiny jar of almond extract will last you for ages, because you really only need a tiny thimbleful in recipes. If you're doing lots of baking, especially with nut meals or coconut, you will love what almond extract does for the all-round rounding out of the flavour. Think of vanilla, but more like cherries and apricots and dark chocolate. The aroma alone is worth forking out for.

I especially love adding a smidge to Belinda Jeffery's flourless coconut and almond cake — one of the best gluten-free cakes ever, and one of the easiest to bake!

Coffee jelly

4 cups (1 litre) hot (but not boiling)
    black coffee, brewed to your taste
4 teaspoons powdered gelatine
best-quality single (pure) cream,
    to serve
coffee sugar crystals, to serve

Jelly is enjoying a resurgence, and for grown-ups there's so much more on offer than just jelly shots! This genius recipe is so refreshing, and so easy, with a hit of caffeine and joyful jiggles. Considering how coffee-mad we are, I'm surprised it's not more popular here. It was certainly popular in England in the 1960s, when a friend's mum worked as a young nurse for an *actual* lady, by the name of Lady Vivienne, whose Irish cook would make this dish often. You would serve yourself from the jelly bowl, and sugar and cream (occasionally spiked with Irish cream) would be passed around the table. The Japanese have kept coffee jelly alive, replacing the gelatine with kanten, a seaweed-based gelling agent that makes it perfect for planty people.

Decide what receptacle to set your jelly in (see Tips).

Pour ¼ cup (60 ml) of the hot coffee into a small bowl. Sprinkle the gelatine over and whisk with a fork. Once the gelatine starts to dissolve, add the mixture to the remaining hot coffee and gently stir until completely dissolved.

Transfer to a jug and pour into your mould/s, then set in the fridge for at least 7 hours, or preferably overnight.

Serve drizzled with cream, topped with a scattering of crunchy sugar crystals.

Bonus bits

Tips

You can set the jelly in individual moulds, latte glasses, a large jelly mould, or even a gorgeous fridge-to-table ceramic, glass or crystal dish. Or, you can set the jelly in a baking tray (make sure it's not too shallow) and cut into cubes for serving.

To make the jelly easier to turn out, line the moulds with plastic wrap. (Note: you can get biodegradable plastic wrap these days, so seek this out whenever you can.)

Subs

To turn this recipe plant-based, use agar agar or kanten instead of gelatine as the gelling agent. For agar agar, the proportion of liquid to powder is pretty similar; for kanten it's a straight swap.

If you can't find coffee sugar crystals, grate some good dark chocolate over the cream instead, or just use raw sugar granules.

Extra extras

For an adults-only version, splash some Irish cream liqueur into the cream itself before serving.

Ingredient spotlight: Setting in jelly

When using gelatine for setting jellies and desserts, the general rule is 1 teaspoon powdered gelatine OR 1 gold-strength gelatine sheet per 1 cup (250 ml) liquid. Allow gelatine sheets to 'bloom' (soften) in lukewarm water first; squeeze out the excess water before using.

Jelly shots do have their place. Just remember booze makes gelatine harder to set, so add 1½ times the amount of leaves or powder than noted above. I love using champagne or prosecco as the base to set fruit in for a festive dessert — white cherries in golden sparkly jelly are absolutely heavenly.

Traditionally, gelatine is made by harvesting animal collagen (skin, gristly bits, bones), then its processed, dried and ground. Agar agar and kanten are plant-based options. (Agar is used in the Japanese ube raindrop cake, a vibrant purple bubble that looks like a raindrop in a bowl.) These seaweed products have a higher melting point than gelatine, so they do have a different mouthfeel, with a bit of chew to them.

Gadget spotlight: Moulds & ramekins

For individual serves, I use dariole moulds, available from most kitchenware shops. You can get plastic or metal ones (which can be washed and reused), if you're making moulded desserts often. If you'd prefer ramekins, they're one of those kitchen 'nice-to-haves' that you'll buy for something like this ... and then they'll sit in the drawer for way too long, gathering dust. Check your local op-shop before buying some new.

Grate apple & raspberry crumble cake

125 g (4½ oz) salted butter,
  plus extra for greasing
  (see Subs, page 248)
1 cup (180 g) coarse semolina
1 cup (220 g) caster (superfine) sugar
1 cup (150 g) self-raising flour
  (see Subs, page 248)
1 teaspoon ground cinnamon
½ teaspoon salt
2–3 large granny smith apples
1 teaspoon vanilla bean paste
  or vanilla extract
juice of 1 lemon
400 g (14 oz) frozen berries
  (see Tips, page 248)
1 cup (100 g) shelled pecans,
  roughly chopped
thick (double) cream or
  plain yoghurt, to serve

It would be remiss of me not to include this recipe in our collection of sweeties, as it throws everything I thought I knew about cake-baking out the window, and because when I first shared it with the people of Australia on morning telly, it went absolutely ballistic. It's Bulgaria's gift to baking, where the most complex process required is grating. Like the ostentatious arrangement of animal print-on-print at Russian restaurants, this cake probably shouldn't work … but somehow, it does. Here's why: as the grated apple mixture stews and bakes, it releases just enough liquid to bind the dry ingredients together into a crumbly consistency that yields a surprisingly light, logic-AND-gravity-defying crumble-cake mash-up.

Place the butter in the freezer for at least 2 hours or preferably overnight (see Tips, page 248).

When you're ready to bake, preheat the oven to 180°C (350°F). Line the base of a 20–22 cm (8–8½ inch) springform cake tin and grease the sides with butter (or cooking spray).

Combine the semolina, sugar, flour, cinnamon and salt in a bowl. Toss about with your hands to evenly distribute, or use a wooden spoon if you must.

Peel, quarter, core and coarsely grate the apples into a separate bowl, stirring in the vanilla bean paste and lemon juice to stop the apple browning, and to add to the juiciness. Stir in the frozen berries to combine.

Take the butter out of the freezer and coarsely grate one-third of it across the base of the cake tin. Scoop out a cup of the dry ingredients and sprinkle these across the bottom of the cake tin. (Yes, it will look like the weirdest thing you've ever put in your cake tin.)

Spread half the apple mixture on top, then sprinkle with another cup's worth of dry ingredients. Grate another third of the butter on top (if it feels like it's starting to melt, consider using some baking paper as a handle, or popping the butter back into the freezer for 15 minutes or so).

Spread the remaining apple mixture over the top, then the remaining dry ingredients. Scatter the pecans over the top. Finish with the last of the butter.

Pop the cake tin on a baking tray and bake for 50–55 minutes, or until the top of the cake is slightly burnished, just before the nuts begin to burn. Remove from the oven.

Allow the cake to cool in the tin, before releasing and removing the tin.

Serve the cake with cream or yoghurt. Prepare for it to be crumbly, yet light, and for your guests to be amazed.

Grate apple & raspberry crumble cake Bonus bits

Tips

You can use frozen raspberries, blueberries, even strawberries here. Frozen berries hold their shape well in baking recipes, but you can totally use fresh if need be; just be prepared for more in the way of mush.

Freezing the butter makes it far easier to grate. If you've started on the recipe and realise you forgot to freeze some, then all is not lost! Chop the butter as small as you can and pop it into the freezer as soon as it's chopped — that way it'll be far easier to handle and distribute evenly.

If all this 'layering' talk has you confused, the order into the tin is: butter, dry, apples, dry, butter, apples, dry, pecans, butter.

If your oven has a problem with uneven heat (like mine!), once the cake is cooked, turn the oven off, turn the cake tin around 180 degrees and leave it in the oven for an extra 5 minutes, to let the residual heat help even out the browning on top.

You don't have a springform cake tin? Use a pie dish and scoop the cake out as more of a crumble.

Subs

No self-raising flour? You can using plain (all-purpose) flour instead, subbing 2 tablespoons of the flour with baking powder.

If your butter is unsalted, add an extra ½ teaspoon salt flakes.

For a plant-based cake, you could use olive oil spread or even just oil instead of the butter, but you'll end up with a crumblier result.

Ingredient spotlight: Vanilla

Vanilla and cinnamon are my go-to combo for desserts of any kind, perhaps because they evoke memories of all manner of childhood sweets, from fruit compotes heady with warming cinnamon, to cool orbs of vanilla ice cream, dotted with little black flecks.

Those gorgeous little black flecks are the vanilla seeds from inside your vanilla bean, and they're the reason why I recommend investing in some vanilla bean paste rather than extract or essence.

Vanilla extract is certainly welcome as an alternative, as it's made with real vanilla, but I'd steer clear of imitation essence, which is the synthesised flavour of vanilla rather than the real thing.

Considering how little vanilla bean paste you'll need to use in a recipe — a teaspoon is equivalent to a whole vanilla bean — and how long it lasts, buying a little tub of it will always be worth it in the long run.

If using the real thing, split the bean lengthways, scoop the seeds out with a teaspoon, then pop the seeds and bean into your mixture to infuse. Unlike the extracted versions, the bean itself needs heat to unlock its flavour, so it works best when infused into a warm custard or poaching liquid.

You can rinse off the used, disembowelled bean and pop it into a jar of caster (superfine) sugar to infuse the sugar with its flavour — a few spent cinnamon sticks wouldn't go astray in there either.

To read more about cinnamon, head to page 287.

Coconut rough semifreddo

800 ml (28 fl oz) coconut ice cream
   or gelato (I like Pana)
½ cup (30 g) flaked coconut, toasted
   (see Skills spotlight)

MYO choc coconut rough
1 cup (250 ml) coconut oil
1 cup (100 g) unsweetened cocoa powder
1 cup (250 ml) maple syrup
½ cup (35 g) shredded coconut, toasted
   (see Skills spotlight)

A semifreddo is a no-churn ice cream that is usually made by creating a whipped custard first. In this instance, you're letting someone else do all the work of whipping air into the mix by using a store-bought vegan ice cream. Peruse the ingredients list and you'll note that this one is also very plant-friendly. You might even call it a Veganetta, because it so resembles that very nostalgic dessert log that used to get rolled out for every fancy family do. And you won't hear a peep out of even the most discerning vego — except maybe the odd hum of delight.

Grease a 5 cup (1.25 litre) loaf (bar) tin and line with two layers of plastic wrap. Our loaf tin was 17.5 cm (7 inches) long, 7.5 cm (3 inches) wide and 8 cm (3¼ inches) deep.

To make the choc coconut rough, melt the coconut oil in a saucepan. Stir in the cocoa powder and maple syrup until combined, then divide between two bowls. To one of the bowls, add the toasted shredded coconut, stirring to unite into a gritty goop I like to call 'mocklate'. The bowl without the coconut will be destined to become the drippy sauce when you're ready to serve, so cover it and set aside in the fridge until needed.

Take the ice cream out of the freezer and let it soften enough to be pliable. Spoon one-fifth of the ice cream into your lined loaf tin, smoothing the surface. Add 2 tablespoons of mocklate and use a small palette knife or spoon to spread it evenly. Repeat the layering four more times, finishing with ice cream. Place in the freezer overnight.

When ready to serve, gently warm the remaining chocolate sauce in a small saucepan over low heat to loosen it a little, then allow to cool slightly.

Turn out the loaf onto a serving platter (I find chilling the platter helps to stop the bottom edges getting soupy too quickly) and remove the plastic wrap. Drizzle the sauce over and crown with the toasted flaked coconut. Slice and serve immediately.

> **Skills spotlight: Toasting dried coconut**
> Place the dried coconut in a cold frying pan over low to medium heat and toss or stir continuously for a minute or so, until it becomes a light golden colour. Once it starts to colour it will do so very quickly — it might even be worth switching off the pan and letting the residual heat finish things off.

Bonus bits

Recipe riffs

Make the coconut rough with an extra ½ cup (35 g) toasted coconut. Place teaspoons of the mixture on a sheet of baking paper and pop into the fridge to set. Get the kids to help with this, and serve up as little treats.

For home-made chocolate-coated ice-cream sticks, pour the melted coconut ice cream into icy pole moulds on a stick. Coat with the coconut rough crackle and refreeze until needed.

You can also simply pour the melted coconut rough straight into a lined baking tray and tilt the pan to spread it out. Place in the fridge to chill, then snap into shards of choc-coconut bark. Or, pour into a jar and store at room temperature for some simple home-made coconut ice magic.

Shortcuts

For an even quicker version, make a bowl of ice cream with MYO ice magic, using store-bought ice cream or gelato AND store-bought chocolate. (Wowzer!)

Just use 200 g (7 oz) dark couverture chocolate chips, or a block of good-quality dark chocolate, broken into pieces. Place in a heatproof bowl over a pan of simmering water with 100 g (3½ oz) coconut oil. Stir together until melted and smooth. (You can read more about melting chocolate on page 297.)

Use right away, drizzled on top of a few scoops of your favourite ice cream or gelato.

Ingredient spotlight: Coconut

Coconut is such a versatile ingredient — from the flesh, to the inner reservoir of sweet tasty water, to the tough outer shell that's used for everything from jewellery to clothing to hipster Buddha bowls. Nifty! The magic is in the flesh's fat content, which can be manipulated based on how much water is added.

Coconut oil is of course another gift from the coconut, and is excellent as a cooking oil with a high smoke point (as long as you're incorporating other coconut components or complementary South-East Asian, Polynesian or tropical flavours, as the taste is not what I would call neutral).

Young coconuts — the ones that can be bought whole and chopped into from the top to form a lid for sipping — can be quite juicy inside, with the water sweet and refreshing. The flesh in young coconuts is wonderful scooped out and served on jelly or with fruit, or blitzed with a little of the water and some honey or maple syrup to make a light whipped mousse.

Don't skip on it for savouries, however. Check out the Double duty tip on page 114, where strips can be added to a coconut water broth for bonus creaminess and texture.

As coconuts age, they dry out, and the flesh becomes firm and a little starchy. It's this flesh that is milled, moisturised and magicked into coconut milk and cream, or dried further then desiccated, shredded or flaked. You can make your own coconut cream from the dried bits by blitzing with water, at a pinch. Different brands of coconut cream and milk vary in their processing methods, but my preference is for the ones in cartons like Kara, which are always creamy and don't separate as much as some of the tinned varieties. However, if you open your tin and it has separated, you can either bring it back together by heating gently and mashing together, or, if it's going into a hot dish like a curry or soup, just scoop it all in as is, and as the liquid simmers away, the components will reunite.

You can also buy coconut milk powder and rehydrate as needed. It's something I like to have in the pantry to sprinkle into my daughter's gluten-free porridge with water for an easy gluten-free, dairy-free breakfast.

**Coconut rough
semifreddo**
Page 250

Puffy plum muffins (pluffins)

Makes 12

125 g (4½ oz) salted butter, softened

¾ cup (150 g) raw brown sugar
   (see Subs, page 256)

2 teaspoons ground cinnamon

2 teaspoons vanilla extract
   (see Subs, page 256)

½ teaspoon almond extract

2 eggs

½ cup (125 ml) buttermilk
   or plain yoghurt (see Subs, page 256)

1 cup (100 g) almond meal
   (see Subs, page 256)

1 cup (150 g) self-raising flour, sifted
   (see Subs, page 256)

6 plums, cut in half, stones removed

½ cup (50 g) flaked almonds

icing (confectioners') sugar,
   to serve (optional)

honey, for drizzling (optional)

The beauty of muffins is that they're like teeny individual cakes. Each muffin hole acts like a mini cake tin, heating the batter faster and forcing it to puff in half the time that cake batters usually take. But for every benefit, there is an equal and opposite disadvantage — and in this case, that's the dreaded dry muff. That's why the best muffins always contain bits and bobs of sustained moisture, in the form of berries, grated zucchini (courgette), or melty cheese or chocolate chips. These pluffins are actually more like a friand/muffin hybrid, where we're using almond meal and flour in equal measure, which loosens the crumb and gives you a richer, nuttier finish. Speaking of nuts, almonds in any capacity always go fabulously well with stone fruit, because they're marzipan-y, so feel free to sub in nectarines, peaches, apricots or even pitted cherry halves.

Preheat the oven to 180°C (350°F). Line a 12-hole muffin tin with paper cases.

Cream the butter and sugar, either by hand or using a stand mixer. Add the cinnamon and the vanilla and almond extracts. Scrape down the bowl, then add the eggs one at a time, beating well after each addition.

Add the buttermilk and almond meal and mix until well combined. Fold the flour through using a flexible spatula until just mixed — you shouldn't be able to see any white blobs bobbing around, but try not to overmix.

Using an ice-cream scoop, spoon equal portions of the batter into the muffin cases. Lightly press a plum half, cut side up, into each muffin hole, then top with the almond flakes.

Bake on the middle shelf of the oven for 20–25 minutes, or until the pluffins bounce back when gently touched. Stick a skewer into a cakey part and see if it comes out clean-ish; I prefer to leave mine ever so slightly under-done. Finish with a dusting of icing sugar and a drizzle of honey to serve.

These muffins will keep for 4–5 days and are best stored in an airtight container on the kitchen bench.

Puffy plum muffins Bonus bits

Rich with fruit and nuts, this is the kind of muffin that's never dry or stodgy. More like a Friand with Benefits, really.

Tips

This is a fantastic recipe to make with kids — there's no machinery involved if you don't use a stand mixer, just plenty of egg-cracking, measuring, bowl-stirring, spoon-licking and the like. They'll just need you to take care of the oven fussing, and to remind them to wait until the pluffins have cooled a little before running about with their proud creations.

Subs

Instead of raw brown sugar, you can add a teaspoon of molasses to regular granulated sugar, or use the sweetener you'd prefer. Just remember that different sugars will compact differently — and the wetter a sugar is, the looser it'll sit in the cup.

Vanilla extract or vanilla bean paste will both be perfection in this. I try to avoid vanilla essence if I can (see Ingredient spotlight, page 248), but since it's mostly the aroma that you're using it for here, you may as well use it up if it's already in the pantry.

If you don't have any buttermilk or yoghurt, use milk with ½ teaspoon lemon juice stirred in. It'll curdle, but you'll be right once the muffins come out of the oven.

To keep these nut-free, you can use oat flour or desiccated coconut, and then rolled oats or shredded coconut on top.

These muffins can absolutely be made with gluten-free flour. I like to add 50 g (1½ oz) milk powder (a tip I learned from the *Women's Weekly* cooking team) to help the proteins bind without the gluten.

Recipe riffs

Frozen berries are a fantastic alternative here — blueberries and raspberries are especially excellent, as they splotch their way through the batter. Since berries are so delicate, using them frozen rather than fresh means they hold their shape and colour better under the duress of folding and baking.

Poached fruits — apple, pear, rhubarb — are also wonderful additions, and even tinned fruit works well.

Chocolate bits never go astray, or try a choc–miso combo. Cream some miso paste in with the butter and sugar, then fold choc chips or chunks through the batter just before scooping into the muffin cases.

Banana would work well too. Instead of freezing squashy bananas whole, chop them into little chunks for freezing, so you'll have individual portions to fold through the batter once the flour has been mixed in.

Savoury muffins are a fab option for grab-n-go snacks! In place of the plums, use fresh or frozen peas and/or corn, a handful of grated cheddar or bits of bocconcini, with sun-dried or even halved cherry tomatoes.

This batter would also do seriously well in a loaf (bar) tin. Just double the cooking time; you'll know it's baked when the sides shrink away from the pan.

Shortcuts

Scoop the batter into the holes of a mini muffin tin. They should bake within 15–20 minutes, but check on them after about 12 minutes, just to be safe.

Skills spotlight: Greased lining!

Most baking vessels these days are coated with some form of non-stick coating, but it never hurts to give them an extra greasing, as they develop a natural patina over time. And if a recipe tells you to grease and line your baking tin, then do go ahead and grease and line — it'll save you much heartache on the other end.

My favourite grease goop is butter, of course, because it enhances the flavour and helps to encourage an extra glossy crust. For plant-based, or convenience, you're welcome to go down the cooking spray route. Just be mindful that olive oil sprays will impart a grassy flavour that can overpower sweet baked goods, and instead consider a more neutral-flavoured oil if need be.

If you're going down the butterfingers route, you can encourage a more even rise by applying the soufflé principle and greasing in the direction that you want the baked ingredients to go — so, for things like soufflés, grease with your fingers sliding up the tin. And for soufflés, an added layer of security between the batter and the grease from a dry ingredient is never a bad idea. For savoury ones, try flour or finely shaved parmesan, while for sweet soufflés, cocoa powder (for chocolate ones) or sugar or flour will do it. Just remember to shake out the excess before pouring in the batter.

When greasing a ring (bundt) tin, you'll get the smuggest turn-out by greasing generously, then freezing the tin for at least 15 minutes before scooping the batter in.

For lining purposes, the flatter you can get your baking paper, the neater the end result. Counterintuitively, it helps to scrunch the paper up a bit, to make it more malleable and help coax it into every corner of the baking vessel. (And a splash of water, or a dab of butter on the bottom of the tray or tin, either in the middle or on each corner, will help glue the paper down before the batter weighs it down.)

You can make patty cases out of squares of baking paper. Just squeeze each square in your palm to make it easier to mould, then squash down into the muffin holes.

If I'm using a round springform tin, I don't tend to cut my paper into a circle. I just lay the square sheet down across the bottom, then squash down with the sides and secure with the spring. Once the cake ring locks into place, it automatically shapes the paper into a circle anyway, saving you a tedious technical step.

Baking paper can be reused — either flipped over if it's a bit messed-up from its first stint in the oven, or kept right side up if it's not too crumby from baking cookies and the like. You can also find reusable baking sheets, which might be worth investigating if you're doing a lot of oven work.

Honey & ginger pears with nutmeg custard

8 firm pears, such as corella
   or beurre bosc
1 cup (200 g) soft brown sugar
1 cup (350 g) honey
½ cup (110 g) chopped glacé ginger
1 cinnamon stick
100 g (3½ oz) butter, cubed
Golden granola clusters (page 133),
   optional

Nutmeg custard

2 cups (500 ml) milk
2 teaspoons vanilla extract (preferably
   with seeds), or use 1 vanilla bean,
   split, seeds scraped
2 eggs
2 tablespoons cornflour (cornstarch)
2 tablespoons caster (superfine) sugar
2 scrapes of nutmeg

This dessert plays an enchanting trick of kitchen alchemy — as the pears cook, they soften to fork-tender, and yet as the custard heats and cools, it gets thicker. Magic! What is also magic is that the ratio of ingredients in the custard recipe is so easy to remember. For a good time, just dial 222222.

Preheat the oven to 200°C (400°F).

Peel the pears, cut in half and scoop out the cores using a teaspoon or melon baller (retro!), then arrange in a large shallow, lidded cast-iron pan.

In a saucepan, combine the sugar, honey, glacé ginger and cinnamon stick. Pour in 650 ml (22 fl oz) water and stir until everything combines. Bring to the boil over medium heat, then quickly pour over the pears in the cast-iron pan and place the lid on.

Transfer to the oven and poach for 20 minutes. Remove from the oven, then carefully pour off the liquid into a saucepan. Drop the butter cubes around the pears and roast for another 30 minutes, until golden and burnished, basting the pears with the melted butter if some are looking glossier than others.

Meanwhile, boil the reserved poaching liquid vigorously until reduced by half into a syrup.

To make the custard, warm the milk and vanilla (including the pod if using a vanilla bean) in a saucepan until just before boiling. As the milk gets close to a simmer, whisk the eggs, cornflour and sugar together in a large heatproof bowl. Pour the hot milk mixture over the eggs and whisk together until incorporated, then pour the whole lot back into the pan and place back over low heat. Stir continuously with a wooden spoon for 7–10 minutes; the key here is to get the mixture hot, but not to let it boil, or the eggs will curdle. To check when the custard is ready, run your finger through the custard on the wooden spoon — if the line you've drawn in the custard stays straight, and the custard doesn't immediately drip back into the pan, it's ready to go (see page 260). The custard should be the consistency of silky pouring cream, and will thicken up more as it cools.

When the custard is ready, pour it through a fine-meshed sieve into a bowl, to get rid of any pesky lumps, and to catch the vanilla pod, if using. (Note: you don't want to leave the custard in the hot pan, as the residual heat will continue to cook it.) Taste for sweetness and stir in the nutmeg.

Serve the poached pears generously drizzled with custard and finish with the syrup. For extra value, add some crunch by crowning with a spoonful of golden granola, if you like.

Generally, 1 teaspoon vanilla extract or paste = 1 pod

Straining catches any curdles and chunks

A coated spoon means the swipe stays put

Firm pears are best for poaching and baking

THE JOY OF BETTER COOKING

Honey & ginger pears Bonus bits

Tips

The pears can be prepared a day ahead to the end of the poaching stage. To serve, gently reheat in the oven, covered with foil.

If you're not using the custard right away, you can stop a skin forming on top by placing some plastic wrap directly onto the mixture. You can absolutely make it ahead and reheat on low temperature with the odd stir when ready to serve.

Shortcuts

The oven-poached pears are delicious simply served with cream, perhaps sprinkled with chopped lightly toasted nuts such as almonds or pecans.

Double duty

Any left-over poached pears make a beautiful addition to breakfasts such as French toast (page 193), and served atop porridge (page 132) with some plain yoghurt and a drizzle of honey.

Leave the cornflour out of the custard, double the batch and use it to make a crème caramel (page 274), or as an ice-cream base by chilling and churning in an ice-cream maker.

Worth it

You'll find glacé ginger in the dried fruit section of supermarkets. It's usually added to desserts more for the sweetness it brings than any actual gingeriness (its gentle heat notwithstanding), and because there's so much sugar involved, it's like a dry jam, so will last for ages in the pantry. You can add it to cakes, cookies and use it any time you're roasting fruits of any kind.

Ingredient spotlight: Nutmeg & mace

More nut than meg, these spherical orbs of spicy warmth can be used to add a woody aroma to everything from mashed potatoes to the top of your chai latte. Anything creamy, whether savoury or sweet, will benefit from a bit of nutmeg.

Buy your nutmeg whole, rather than ground, as it does lose its spicy intensity as soon as it's ground. To use whole nutmeg, just 'rasp' it by running a fine grater over it as needed. As a measure, a 'rasp' of nutmeg is about as specific as a pinch of salt, because it does depend on the intensity of the nutmeg you've purchased. Usually, grating enough nutmeg to be visible (two or three back and forths with the grater) is plenty, as nutmeg is very aromatic, and the flavour can lean towards medicinal if you add too much.

Nutmeg's sister spice is mace, which is a bit like the nut's leathery jacket. It has a sharper flavour than nutmeg — slightly smoky, less sweet, yet still heavily aromatic with a blend of black pepper and pine needle. You can use it whole to flavour dishes cooked low and slow, such as braises and curries, and in sweet fillings for pies and crumbles. As with nutmeg, if you buy it ground, be sure to use it fairly quickly, as its compounds are highly volatile and dissipate quickly.

Lady Marmalade melting moments

⅓ cup (40 g) icing (confectioners') sugar
250 g (9 oz) unsalted butter, softened
1½ cups (225 g) plain (all-purpose) flour, plus extra for dusting (see Subs, page 265)
½ cup (75 g) custard powder (see Subs, page 265)
1 teaspoon baking powder
¼ teaspoon salt flakes

Marmalade buttercream
100 g (3½ oz) unsalted butter, softened
⅔ cup (85 g) icing (confectioners') sugar, plus extra for dusting
zest and juice of ½ orange

You know that version of the song 'Lady Marmalade', where Christina Aguilera pumps out that EPIC note as she begins her verse? What a MOMENT, right!? That's what these melting moments remind me of. The slightly bitter tang of the marmalade in the buttercream is enough to splice through the richness of the biscuit and filling, and as it melts on your tongue, you'll find yourself having a moment, too. I've adopted the custard powder of the classically Aussie yo-yo biscuit, because I like the colour and flavour it provides. Most melting moments recipes use cornflour (cornstarch) — either of these additions stop the flour and fat binding too tightly, which means the biscuit will, quite literally, melt in your mouth.

Line two light-coloured (see Tips, page 265) baking trays (ideally biscuit trays) with baking paper.

If your icing sugar is lumpy, pop it into a food processor and blitz, or into a zip-lock bag and mash with a rolling pin.

Using a stand mixer with the paddle attachment, beat the softened butter until uniformly soft, then add the icing sugar and beat until the mixture is pale and creamy (more is more here).

Sift together the flour, custard powder and baking powder. Add to the butter mixture, along with the salt, and mix with a wooden spoon until just combined.

Use a teaspoon measure dusted with a smidge of flour to scoop out 2 level teaspoons of the mixture, rolling into walnut-sized balls between your hands. If your hands are hot, pat a little flour onto them to stop the mixture sticking. Evenly space the balls out on the baking trays. Don't worry if they're a bit mangy; you can always smooth them out once chilled.

Pop the trays in the fridge to chill for 15 minutes, or even overnight.

When ready to bake, preheat the oven to 150°C (300°F). Use a floured fork to press each dough ball into a 2 cm (¾ inch) disc. Bake for 15–18 minutes, until the biscuits are set enough to be dislodged with a gentle prod, are custard-yellow in colour and the bottom is still blonde. Allow to cool for 10 minutes, then cool completely on a wire rack before filling.

Make your buttercream in the stand mixer by creaming the butter and icing sugar together until super pale. Add the orange zest, juice and marmalade and beat until incorporated.

To fill the biscuits, either transfer the buttercream to a piping bag and squeeze it over half the biscuits, or spread a teaspoon of filling over them. Pop the unfilled biscuits on top of the filled ones like hats, squashing ever so slightly to more evenly distribute the filling.

Give the whole lot one last dusting of icing sugar as a final flourish.

The biscuits will keep in an airtight container in a cool place for up to 5 days. They can also be frozen (filled or unfilled) for up to 3 months; thaw for at least 30 minutes before serving.

THE JOY OF BETTER COOKING

If your icing sugar's clumpy, whiz it or bash it in a bag

As soon as the batter looks like this, stop mixing

Smooth any lumpy balls out just before forking

The juice will flavour and loosen the buttercream

THE JOY OF BETTER COOKING

Lady Marmalade melting moments Bonus bits

Tips

Place any left-over dough on a piece of baking paper, roll up into a log (twisting the edges so it looks like salami) and stash in the freezer. When you have a hankering, simply slice off 1 cm (½ inch) pieces and bake as normal.

There are entire books and blogs dedicated to tweaking the various variables on the biscuit/cookie caper, but some tricks of the trade are so tried and true that you simply must capitulate — after all, it's science!

For evenly coloured biscuits, using an aluminium or lighter-coloured biscuit tray will make all the difference — the darker the tray, the more heat it absorbs, which leads to toasty bottoms (not in a good way, sadly). Biscuit trays are also almost entirely flat, which means that the heat can access each side of the biscuit evenly.

The more butter/fat you add to the dough, the 'shorter' your biscuit will be, meaning the more easily it crumbles.

Subs

You can use cornflour (cornstarch) if you don't have custard powder; if so, add 1 teaspoon vanilla extract or vanilla bean paste PLUS an extra 1 tablespoon icing sugar to your biscuit mixture.

Amazingly, gluten-free flour is just as good here!

Recipe riffs

You can mix and match these riffs, but just remember, whatever goes in must come out — so if it's dry, pull back on the flour and sugar. For aromatics such as vanilla or citrus and the like, watch that the flavours play well together, and add just enough to make them sing without shouting.

Biscuit flavours:
- Chocolate — sub in ¼ cup (30 g) unsweetened cocoa powder for some of the flour
- Pistachio — use ¼ cup (35 g) blitzed pistachios instead of some of the flour
- Go floral with ½ teaspoon dried lavender

- For a citrus twist, add 1 teaspoon grated zest — anything from lemon to Tahitian or makrut lime to yuzu would be sensational.

Buttercream options:
- 1 tablespoon passionfruit pulp
- Zest + juice of 1 small lemon
- 1 tablespoon cocoa powder + 1 tablespoon milk
- Chocolate hazelnut spread (+ hazelnut meal in the biscuit dough)
- 1 tablespoon fresh raspberries or mulberries
- Peanut butter (+ raspberry jam to sandwich the biscuits together).

Melting moments are essentially shortbreads, so there's no real need to sandwich with icing if you're not in the mood. Just serve with a cuppa, or spread the filling on just one biscuit.

Conquering Napoleon

2 square sheets of butter puff pastry,
    cut in half, or 1 x 375 g (13 oz) roll
    of butter puff pastry, cut into thirds
600 ml (21 fl oz) thickened
    (whipping) cream
2 x 150 g (5½ oz) store-bought crème
    caramels (see Tips, page 268)
1 teaspoon vanilla bean paste
a pinch of salt flakes (optional)
icing (confectioners') sugar,
    for dusting

Every family has 'a cake', and Napoleon is ours. It's the Russian version of a French mille-feuille ('one thousand layers') or the Aussie vanilla slice, which makes sense, because the many *many* layers of cream and pastry in a traditional Napoleon are a bit like a Babushka doll crossed with a mille-feuille, and just as complex to make. Of course, by now you'll know that my mum is the shortcut queen, so hers is the cheat's version — because ain't nobody got time for 18 layers. Instead, she blends the best bits — flaky puff pastry and a custardy crème pâtissière — with a sprinkling of icing sugar and spare pastry flakes to finish (because she also doesn't believe in waste). Speaking of blending and shortcuts, instead of making crème pâtissière (French pastry cream; see Longcuts, page 268) from scratch, Mum simply blends store-bought crème caramels with cream to help set it, and for bonus flavour, which I discovered only very recently.

You could say this is 'an old family recipe', but really, it's more of 'an old family philosophy': find the shortcuts to success, leave nothing behind, and always say 'yes' to a second piece of Napoleon.

Preheat the oven to 200°C (400°F). Line one or two baking trays with baking paper, and have another baking tray or trays at the ready.

Place the pastry pieces on the lined baking trays, without overlapping, then poke the pastry all over with a fork. Top with another sheet of baking paper and place another baking tray on top. The pastry will want to puff up, but the trays will keep it flat, which is what you're after here.

Bake on the middle rack of the oven for 30 minutes. Remove the top baking tray and baking paper sheet. Flip the pastry over and bake for another 10 minutes, or until the pastry is very golden (bordering on 'lightly browned'), and evenly cooked all the way through. Cool completely on a wire rack.

Meanwhile, whip the cream until soft peaks form, then add the crème caramels, vanilla paste and salt flakes, if using. Whip again until stiff.

Use a serrated knife to carefully trim the edges of the cooled pastry; reserve these for the top of the Napoleon. If you used square pastry sheets, leave three intact and crumble the fourth into flakes (or embrace a four-layered Napoleon and use less cream on each layer).

Place a pastry piece on a serving plate. Spoon just under half of the pastry cream on top, before topping with another layer of pastry and another half of the pastry cream. Add the last layer of pastry, then top with the remaining pastry cream and any broken-up pastry flakes, if you've ended up with any. Dust liberally with icing sugar.

Leave in the fridge overnight to soften for a traditional Napoleon, or serve immediately for more of a mille-feuille vibe. Both will make you feel a million bucks at the table!

This just gets better overnight. Napoleon himself might've baked it of an evening, rebuffing premature nibbles from his empress: 'Not tonight, dear Josephine.'

Tips

You'll find crème caramels in the refrigerator section at the shops, in the vicinity of the chocolate mousse cups. You could use a tin of condensed milk with similar success, though it'll be sweeter. If you'd prefer to go the traditional route and make your own crème pâtissière, see Longcuts, right.

You can also use left-over crème caramel (page 274) if you have any handy — you clever planner, you.

Offset spatulas (see pic opposite) are a bit of an unsung hero for bakers. The wide surface area and raised handle mean you have less chance of sploodging cream or icing out of place, while the rounded edge prevents unprovoked jabs into batters and cakes. If you find yourself baking more than a few times a year, grab a baby one for the kitchen drawer; you'll use it far more than you think.

Longcuts: Crème pâtissière

Beloved of French pastry chefs, crème pâtissière is a stiffened custard used in sweet pastries and desserts where you want a custard that sets wobbly/firm, holds its shape and doesn't collapse everywhere.

To make your own crème pat from scratch, whisk 6 egg yolks with 100 g (3½ oz) caster (superfine) sugar using a hand whisk or electric mixer until bright yellow. Whisk in 50 g (1½ oz) cornflour (cornstarch) or plain (all-purpose) flour or custard powder (cornflour gives the lightest result). Meanwhile, heat 2 cups (500 ml) milk with the seeds and pod of a split vanilla bean to just before boiling. Pour half the milk into the eggy bowl through a sieve (to catch any milk skin and the bean pod). Whisk to combine. Pour the mixture back into the pan and bring back to a simmer, whisking until it starts to thicken. When thickening begins, whisk for another minute or two, then switch off the heat. Using a flexible spatula, stir in 50 g (1½ oz) butter. Pour onto a tin or flat tray with a lip to cool, covering with plastic wrap or baking paper to stop a skin forming. Give it a good whip before using, to make sure it's nice and smooth.

Recipe riffs

You could easily turn this Napoleon into a classic vanilla slice with crispy pastry and a thick topping of royal icing.

A French mille-feuille isn't far off, either — often lightened with fresh fruit such as strawberries or raspberries; mango would be another luscious option.

You could also create a flavoured version by subbing out the crème caramel for luscious lemon or passionfruit curd, sweetened chestnut purée, pandan essence, dulce de leche or a choc hazelnut spread.

Shortcuts

A simpler, old-fashioned version is The Matchstick, where the raw pastry is cut to about the width and length of an éclair and baked until very puffy (no need to layer the baking trays). Then, using only two pieces of pastry (a top and a bottom, like a sandwich or cream-filled biscuit), spread the pastry with jam, top with chantilly cream (thick/double cream whipped with vanilla bean paste), and finish by sieving a good dusting of icing (confectioners') sugar on top. A perfect easy bake for kids to make.

Lemon & poppy seed ant cake

125 g (4½ oz) butter, softened,
    plus extra for greasing
¾ cup (165 g) caster (superfine) sugar
2 eggs
zest and juice of 2–3 lemons, to yield
    at least ¼ cup (60 ml) juice
1¼ cups (225 g) self-raising flour
    (see Subs, page 273)
½ cup (80 g) poppy seeds
1 teaspoon salt flakes
½ cup (125 ml) buttermilk
    (see Subs, page 273)
1 teaspoon vanilla extract
    or vanilla bean paste

This started out as a classic 2–4–6–8 tea cake, which ladies of a certain generation would always have on hand for unexpected visitors (the handy sequence of numbers comes from the days when we used pounds and ounces). Nowadays, our measurement units have changed, and so have our tastes. This updated version has less sugar than the original for the modern palate (with a pinch of salt for balance), and because going heavy on the sugar is one way to sink a cake. A few more ways to avert disaster: use a preheated oven, make sure your ingredients are at room temperature (see Tips, page 273), and use a loaf (bar) tin — the less batter you're exposing to the heat, the less chance of a flat, dry cake.

Preheat the oven to 165°C (320°F). Grease a standard-sized (1 litre/35 fl oz capacity) loaf (bar) tin with butter; the heat from your fingertips is the best way to grease up the sides. Line the base of the tin with baking paper, lightly scrunching it into the corners if needed, to help mould it into place.

You can make the batter by hand or using a stand mixer — your choice! For the latter, using the paddle attachment, beat the butter on medium speed for 10–15 seconds, until paste-y, then, with the motor running, add the sugar in a steady stream. Keep beating for a minute, stop to scrape down the side of the bowl with a flexible spatula, then beat for another minute or two. You'll know it's ready when the mixture changes colour from yellow to ... well, cream. (For more on creaming butter and sugar, see Skills spotlight, page 273.)

Add one egg at a time, waiting until the egg fully mixes in before adding the next. Add the lemon zest and juice, then give the mixture another beat to evenly distribute.

In another bowl, mix together the flour, poppy seeds and salt.

Add half the dry ingredients to the batter and beat on low speed until everything is just incorporated — no overmixing! With the motor running, add half the buttermilk and the vanilla. Use your flexible spatula to scrape down the sides and turn the batter over a few times to incorporate any stowaways at the base of the bowl. Add the remaining dry ingredients and blend again, then add the remaining buttermilk and finish with one last turn of the batter with your spatula.

If you don't have a stand mixer, no biggie! You can use a wooden spoon and some elbow grease. It will take longer, but the process can be curiously satisfying. Just make sure your butter is super soft.

Put the butter in a large mixing bowl, add the sugar and use the back of a wooden spoon to incorporate them. First, squash the sugar into the softened butter, then, once the mixture starts to come together, hold onto the bowl and beat the mixture with your wooden spoon until the butter changes colour from yellow to a pale creamy colour. »

Lemon & poppy seed ant cake continued

Mix in one egg at a time, waiting until the egg is fully incorporated before mixing in the next.

Stir in the lemon juice and zest until combined. In another bowl, mix together the sifted flour, poppy seeds and salt. Add half the dry ingredients to the batter and mix until combined, then half the buttermilk and the vanilla and mix until combined. Repeat with the remaining dry ingredients and buttermilk.

Now you're ready to bake! Spoon the batter into the loaf tin and bake on the middle rack of the oven for 45–50 minutes, or until the cake is golden brown, bounces back when gently touched, and a skewer comes out mostly clean (a few crumbs are fine). If the top of the cake looks like it's browning too fast, drape a little foil over the top for the final 15 minutes.

Remove from the oven and leave to cool in the tin for 10 minutes, then turn out onto a cake rack, flipping it over to face the heavens to cool the rest of the way. This cake keeps surprisingly well for 4–5 days — just store it in an airtight container on the kitchen bench.

THE JOY OF BETTER COOKING

Bonus bits

Tips

Have all of your ingredients ready before you start. All the measuring is probably the hardest bit!

If you don't have a stand mixer — or the inclination to use a wooden spoon and some elbow grease — using the whisk attachment on a stick blender to cream the butter and sugar will do the job, too.

Subs

If you don't have buttermilk, use ½ cup (125 ml) milk with 1 teaspoon vinegar added. The milk will curdle, but don't worry — it will come together in the mix, and the acid will help the cake rise.

You can absolutely use gluten-free self-raising flour to make this cake. Adding 50 g (1½ oz) milk powder to help stabilise the proteins in the absence of gluten will help keep the cake nice and fluffy and high ... but consider the milk powder a nice-to-have, rather than a non-negotiable.

Shortcuts

Want cake in less than half the time? Bake the batter in a cupcake or muffin tin for 15–18 minutes.

Recipe riffs

This is one of those genius basic recipes that can morph into all sorts of other cakes. Ditch the poppy seeds, lemon juice and zest for one of the following combos:

- ½ cup (85 g) sultanas or raisins + orange zest and juice
- ½ cup (85 g) chocolate chips + mandarin zest and juice
- ½ cup (110 g) chopped crystallised ginger + any type of citrus zest and juice
- A mashed banana + ground cinnamon + chopped walnuts
- ½ cup (160 g) marmalade + ½ cup (50 g) almond meal for a grown-up tea cake
- For a cinnamon teacake, add 1 teaspoon vanilla extract to the batter. Brush the warm cooked cake with 2 tablespoons melted butter, then sprinkle with 2 tablespoons caster (superfine) sugar and 2 tablespoons ground cinnamon mixed together

- Bake the cake in a square or rectangular tin, then ice with chocolate glacé icing and sprinkle with desiccated coconut for the best lamington cake ever. Or, you can even cut the cake into squares and dip them all in chocolate icing, then dredge in desiccated or shredded coconut for your own lamington drive.

Extra extras

Mix 5 tablespoons icing (confectioners') sugar with 1 tablespoon lemon juice and 1 tablespoon lemon zest until smooth. Drizzle or pour all over the cooled cake, finishing with a sprinkle of extra lemon zest.

Skills spotlight: Creaming butter & sugar

Are you staring at the cold butter in your fridge, wondering if you could just skip the 'creaming' component of this recipe? Well, that depends on how attached you are to a fluffy cake. Creaming helps your cake to rise by cutting into the softened butter with the sugar crystals and forcing air into the mixture. As the cake bakes, the air expands and helps to lift the cake.

Even if a recipe doesn't say to cream, if butter and sugar are involved, a bit of creaming can't hurt. If using a stand mixer, 2–3 minutes of beating is plenty, but some bakers will continue to cream until they can't feel any sugar-crystal grit between their fingers.

Butter will take between 30–60 minutes to soften out of the fridge, but you can fast-track this by cutting it into small pieces, or even grating it on the coarsest teeth of your box grater. Melting the butter in a saucepan over low heat, or zapping it in the microwave in increments of 30 seconds, is an option too, but you won't get a genuine 'creaming' effect.

However, if the only thing standing between you and baking this cake is that your butter is too cold, melt the darn butter, or use the same amount of olive oil instead, which you can get away with in this one because the cake has other leavening devices as back-up, in the form of baking powder (in the self-raising flour) and the acid in the buttermilk/lemon juice.

Salt & pepper crème caramel flan

butter or cooking spray, for greasing
1 vanilla bean, split, seeds scraped
400 ml (14 fl oz) milk
⅛ teaspoon freshly ground black pepper
2 whole eggs, plus 3 egg yolks
⅓ cup (75 g) caster (superfine) sugar

Caramel
¾ cup (165 g) caster (superfine) sugar
heaped ⅓ cup (80 g) demerara
    or dark brown sugar
1 teaspoon salt flakes

Just like the hip-hop outfit Salt-N-Pepa, this dessert peaked in the late 1980s, and then disappeared almost entirely. Now there's a whole new generation ready to experience the wonder of wobbly velvety custard crowned with a complex-flavoured burnt caramel (salted, because it's not 1989, people!). This is not the time to 'Push It', though — you'll need a bit of patience to pull this one off, as 'wet' caramel takes its sweet time. This custard has a slightly different ingredient ratio to the one on page 262, and the addition of some eggstra yolks will really make you wanna shoop. (Sorry.)

Preheat the oven to 140°C (275°F). Grease a shallow 6 cup (1.5 litre) pie dish or baking dish.

Pop the vanilla seeds and pod into a small saucepan with the milk and pepper. Bring to just before the boil, then turn off the heat and leave to infuse.

To make the caramel, put the sugars in a heavy-based saucepan (preferably a stainless steel or enamel one, so you can see the colour change; see step-by-step pics on page 276). Pour over just enough cold water to cover, swirling around to combine (do not stir or the sugar will crystallise). Bring to the boil over medium–low heat and then, once the bubbles have started to get smaller, watch the sugar turn brown. The colour of rich mahogany is what you're after; it will also begin to smell a little toffee-like.

While you wait for the caramel to turn — which will take 15–20 minutes of bubbling — boil a full kettle. Place the salt flakes in a small heatproof bowl, pour over 2 tablespoons boiling water and stir until the salt dissolves.

When the caramel is ready, carefully pour the salty water into the pan (the caramel will spit and splutter, so watch those hands!) Swirl it around until combined and loosened, then pour into the base of the pie dish.

Spread a clean tea towel in the bottom of a roasting tin with tall sides, big enough to fit the pie dish in (the tea towel stops the dish sliding around later on). Place the dish in the tin, then pour enough boiling water into the tin to reach halfway up the side of the pie dish. Take the dish out, and pop the roasting tin into the oven.

Whisk the eggs, egg yolks and sugar in a bowl until creamy. Set a fine-meshed sieve over the bowl, then pour in the infused milk mixture. Whisk together until combined, being careful not to whisk too vigorously, to avoid air bubbles. Tap the sides of the bowl 5–10 times to get rid of any last bubbles.

Pour the custard through the sieve into the pie dish. Pop the dish into the roasting tin, and back into the oven. Poke a few holes in a sheet of foil and drape over the top of the dish. Bake for 45 minutes, or until the custard has just set; it will still have a decent wobble through the centre.

Turn the oven off and leave the door ajar. Once the moat water cools down to a safe temperature, carefully remove the pie dish from the roasting tin using tongs or silicon oven mitts. Allow to cool slightly, then refrigerate for 4–5 hours, or preferably overnight, to set. Serve straight from the dish at the table.

Try not to disturb the sugar too much, lest it crystallise

Bubbles are a good sign the liquid is evaporating, and caramelising will soon begin

This here is a good-lookin' caramel!

A little too far, my friend. Let it cool before disposing of, then start again

THE JOY OF BETTER COOKING

Salt & pepper crème caramel flan Bonus bits

Tips

Instead of making one large flan, you can use individual ramekins or dariole moulds (see page 245). To turn them out of the moulds, run a knife around the top of the moulds, as close to the edge as you can. Take a deep breath, pop a dessert plate on top of the mould and flip. Tap the top and lift off the mould. It should slurp out and sit proudly on the plate with a seriously sassy wobble.

Shortcuts

This 'wet' caramel takes at least 20–25 minutes of bubbling, so if you're in a hurry, you could try a 'dry' option instead. Add the sugars to the pan (preferably a stainless steel or enamel one, so you can see the colour change) and place over medium–low heat. Once the sugar starts to melt and change colour at the edges, gently flick these bits into the middle of the pan to help heat up the sugar evenly. To avoid crystallisation, don't start flicking until the whole circumference has melted, and even then, keep it to a minimum — and don't be tempted to stir! This will take 8–10 minutes if done patiently.

Recipe riffs

This custard mixture is also great as a crème brûlée. Bake in greased moulds, as per the recipe, then allow to cool. Rather than turning out to serve, sprinkle some granulated sugar across the top and either use a kitchen torch or place under a hot grill (broiler) to caramelise the sugar to a dark brown crust.

Play with different flavours in your crème caramel — instead of vanilla, try pandan, which can be bought either as a lurid-green extract, or as fresh, long thin leaves. (I also love popping pandan leaves into the rice cooker with my jasmine rice, for a fragrant bowl like no other.)

Ingredient spotlight: Salt in desserts

If there's one thing that can take your dessert from blah to BAM, it's adding a pinch of salt. How much really depends on your palate, but sensory testing experiments have shown that by adding salt to a recipe you can cut back on the sugar by up to 20 per cent, while still retaining the same sweet experience.

Salt is a flavour enhancer in general, whether making sweetness more rounded, or citrus zippier. It also helps to mitigate bitterness, rendering food creamier and more enjoyable, particularly when teamed with something acidic as well. Think dark chocolate and orange, with a sprinkle of sea salt flakes.

Even if a dessert recipe doesn't have salt in the ingredients, I'll add a teaspoon or so of salt flakes.

Side note: The salt level in different brands of butter will vary, which is why pastry recipes tend to include unsalted butter, plus an actual salt measurement, as the salt ratio is important for a successful outcome.

Queen Hera's honey cake

250 g (9 oz) unsalted butter, softened
1 cup (220 g) caster (superfine) sugar
¼ cup (90 g) honey
1 teaspoon lemon zest
4 eggs
1 cup (150 g) plain (all-purpose) flour
1½ cups (275 g) fine semolina
1½ cups (150 g) almond meal
5 teaspoons baking powder
2 teaspoons ground cinnamon
1 cup (250 g) Greek-style yoghurt

Saffron nut syrup
½ cup (110 g) caster (superfine) sugar
½ cup (175 g) honey
50 g (1½ oz) butter
3 strips of lemon zest,
    plus the juice of 1 lemon
3 strips of orange zest,
    plus the juice of 1 orange
1 teaspoon ground cinnamon
1 cup (125 g) slivered almonds
½ cup (75 g) shelled pistachio nuts
a good pinch of saffron threads
    (about 20 threads should do it)
a pinch of extra sugar

In Greek mythology, bees were the messengers of the gods, honey a source of wisdom and poetry, and saffron the blood of a fair and gentle youth. What this has to do with cake is dicey, but let's go with the convenient notion that the Greek gods were also very into feasting, and this slab bake is perfect for sharing with a crowd. The batter's robustness also means you can use even the strongest-flavoured honey — the kind that usually sits in the back of the cupboard after a few disappointed whiffs.

Preheat the oven to 175°C (340°F). Grease and line a baking tray measuring 25 x 33 cm (10 x 13 inches), and about 5 cm (2 inches) deep.

Use a stand mixer, or a wooden spoon and plenty of arm action, to cream the butter, sugar and honey for about 10 minutes, until light and fluffy. Add the lemon zest, and then the eggs, one at a time, beating well after each addition and scraping down the side of the bowl.

Sift the dry ingredients together twice, so they're well mixed and aerated.

Remove the bowl from the mixer. Dump in half the flour mixture and half the yoghurt and fold through with a flexible spatula. Add the remaining flour mixture and yoghurt and stir until well mixed. Mealy mixtures always yield a stiffer batter, so nothing to worry about here.

Spoon the batter into the tray and flatten down right to the edges, using an offset spatula (see Tips, page 268). Bake for 30 minutes, or until golden.

Meanwhile, make the syrup. Place the sugar, honey, butter, citrus zest and juice, cinnamon, nuts and ½ cup (125 ml) water in a saucepan. Bring to the boil, then leave to reduce by one-third. Meanwhile, grind the saffron with an extra pinch of sugar using a mortar and pestle, or the back of a teaspoon and a little bowl. Pour 2 tablespoons warm water over the top. Take the reduced syrup off the heat, stir the bloomed saffron through and set aside.

While the cake is still hot, use a sharp knife to cut it into diamonds or squares, à la baklava, to the size of your choice. Pour the saffron nut syrup over, spreading the nuts evenly and removing the citrus strips.

Return to the oven with the top element on to burnish the nuts; this should only take 5–10 minutes. Keep an eye on it, so those delicate nuts don't burn.

The cake will keep for 4–5 days in an airtight container at room temperature.

Bonus bits

Recipe riffs

- **Orange + almond:** Halve the yoghurt. Boil an orange until tender, then blitz and fold into the batter. Go heavier on the orange zest in the syrup.

- **Fennel + lemon:** Add 1 tablespoon fennel seeds to the batter. Swap the saffron with 1 teaspoon vanilla bean paste and the zest of 1 lemon.

- **Almond + coconut:** Stir ⅓ cup (30 g) desiccated coconut through the batter, along with ½ teaspoon almond extract. Heavenly!

THE JOY OF BETTER COOKING

Chocolate sour cream peanut butter cake

butter, for greasing
1 cup (250 ml) just-boiling water
1 cup (260 g) crunchy
   peanut butter

Wet mix
1 cup (250 g) sour cream
2 eggs
1 teaspoon vanilla extract
100 g (3½ oz) butter, melted and cooled

Dry mix
2 cups (300 g) plain (all-purpose) flour
1 cup (220 g) caster (superfine) sugar
¾ cup (80 g) unsweetened cocoa powder
2 teaspoons baking powder
½ teaspoon bicarbonate of soda
   (baking soda)

Ganache
200 g (7 oz) dark couverture chocolate
   (see Ingredient spotlight, page 282)
½ cup (125 g) sour cream
½ cup (125 ml) single (pure) cream

To decorate
plain pretzels (optional)
chocolate-dipped pretzels (optional)
chopped toasted peanuts (optional)

The weirdest thing happens to sour cream when you add it to sweets … it's like a cheat's salted caramel! I love how it elevates a simple chocolate cake to something far more interesting, and the way it cuts through the richness of chocolate and peanut butter to prevent them from becoming cloying. It's always handy having a go-to chocolate cake in your wheelhouse, and you'll find yourself wheeling this one out for birthdays and parties by request.

Preheat the oven to 170°C (325°F). Butter the sides of a 20 cm (8 inch) springform cake tin, lining the base with baking paper.

For the wet mix, whisk the sour cream in a bowl with the eggs and vanilla until smooth. Add the cooled melted butter and mix well.

Sift the dry mix ingredients together into a separate bowl, then add the wet ingredients, stirring with a flexible spatula while slowly adding the just-boiling water. Mix until smooth. Pour the batter into the cake tin and bake for 40–50 minutes, or until the top springs back.

Let the cake cool in the tin for 10 minutes, then turn out onto a cake rack and leave to cool completely. Trim the top using a serrated knife, or skip this step if you don't mind a mound.

Spread the peanut butter all over the top and sides of the cake, being generous with how you heap it on, so it's less likely to drag into the cake crumb. Place in the fridge to chill.

To make the ganache, chop the chocolate into small pieces and place in a heatproof bowl. Heat the sour cream and cream until just about boiling, then pour it over the chocolate and leave to sit for a minute. When the chocolate is melting, stir with a flexible spatula until glossy. Leave to cool a little.

Put a lined tray or board under the cake rack, to catch the ganache. Pour the ganache over the cake, smoothing with a flexible spatula. You can also wait until the ganache has firmed up, then spread it across the cake as more of a frosting, though this results in a thicker layer. If using pretzels and peanuts, press them into the ganache while still warm and leave to set. This cake will keep for 4–5 days in a cool spot in an airtight container.

Bonus bits

Shortcuts

For the quickest salted caramel flavoured topping, drizzle honey over sour cream and smoosh it together, then smear over the cooled cake.

Subs

My favourite peanut butter for toast — and for cake — is always crunchy … smooth just feels like something's missing. You're welcome to use straight-up crushed roasted peanuts, or any other nut or nut butter, for that matter.

Recipe riffs

Sprinkle freeze-dried raspberry powder across the top of the ganache, or dot with fresh or dried banana.

Bake the batter in cupcake pans and decorate with ganache and pretzels.

Chocolate peanut butter cake Bonus bits

Gadget spotlight: Springform cake tins

If you've ever had a sponge-splosion when turning out a cake, it might be time to invest in a springform tin — a real baker's gift. You don't need multiple tin sizes, either. My 20 cm (8 inch) springform tin serves me for all manner of cakes, cheesecakes and slices.

Aside from not actually needing to cut your baking paper into a circle first when lining the tin, the biggest benefit of one of these is that once the cake has had a chance to cool, you can unlock the external spring encircling the tin, remove the collar and you'll be guaranteed a clean dismount.

The only thing to note is that it's always worth indemnifying the tin against leaks, particularly with a thinner batter. Wrapping some heavy-duty foil around the base on the outside is usually enough (and very necessary when baking cheesecakes in a water bath). When baking a sponge cake, I prefer to pop a baking tray underneath the tin to catch any leakage.

Skills spotlight: Turning out a cake

To turn a cooked cake out of the tin without cracking, the first thing you need is patience ... don't go doing it as soon as the cake comes out of the oven. Allow the cake or loaf to cool for at least 10 minutes first, THEN use a palette knife or butter knife to cut all the way around, as close to the tin as possible, to release any baked-on bits. Line your cake cooling rack with a tea towel (to prevent rack marks on the cake, and stop it sweating underneath), THEN invert the cooled cake onto the lined rack.

If you're planning to serve the cake on a specific plate, you could even consider placing this flush on top of the cooled cake tin, then flipping the cake out with a flourish.

And remember, if all else fails, you can serve the cake as a 'skillet cake' straight from the tin.

Ingredient spotlight: Couverture chocolate

When chocolate is the hero, always splash out on the good stuff. Couverture chocolate has a higher cocoa butter content than the usual shop-bought stuff, and even 'cooking chocolate', and a finer texture. It melts easily and evenly, offers a smooth, glossy finish and tempers perfectly for the 'crack' you're looking for when making fancy chocolate desserts.

European couverture chocolate (usually Swiss, Belgian or French) is available as chips or blocks. I prefer the chips, because they're easier to work with for quick melting (and the odd pantry snack). You don't have to go Euro, though. There are some other decent-quality chocolates that will behave like couverture, so it pays to be a savvy shopper.

Check the label and look for a short ingredients list, as well as a higher proportion of cocoa butter, which you can tell by how high up the ingredients list it is. The cocoa percentage on the front refers to not just the cocoa mass, but the cocoa butter and liquor and the like — so if there's more of that, there's less room for other additives like milk or a plant-based equivalent (for milk chocolate), emulsifiers such as soy lecithin and, of course, sugar. White chocolate doesn't contain any cocoa solids — only the cocoa butter, which gives it that lovely melt-in-the-mouth texture, but also means it's far more sensitive to heat and much sweeter.

A higher cocoa percentage will likely mean less sweetness and often a crumblier finish, more bitterness and complexity — another thing to keep in mind when considering how to balance your desserts. Try to avoid compound chocolates that replace cocoa butter with other cheaper oils, which split far more easily under heat — let alone those that contain palm oil.

You can store any left-over choc in a cool, dark place (such as the pantry) in an airtight container. Couverture dark chocolate can last for at least 2 years, and milk chocolate for around 1 year. In tropical climates, it's worth storing yours in the fridge or even freezer, but remember to let the chocolate come to room temperature before using.

Turn the cake out onto a wire rack to cool

If you like a nice flat surface, carefully use a serrated knife to slice the top off

Add more peanut butter than you think you need, so the crumbs don't drag

Let the excess ganache drip onto the lined tray below

Coffee pecan babka scrolls

oil, for greasing

Tangzhong
2 tablespoons plain (all-purpose) flour
½ cup (125 ml) maple syrup
¼ cup (60 ml) strong espresso coffee

Scroll dough
2 eggs, at room temperature
4⅓ cups (650 g) plain (all-purpose)
    flour, plus extra for kneading and rolling
1 tablespoon dried yeast
1 teaspoon sea salt flakes
100 g (3½ oz) butter, cut into
    cubes and softened

Pecan & cinnamon sugar filling
½ cup (50 g) pecans, plus 12 halves
    for topping (see Subs, page 287)
¼ cup (55 g) raw sugar
2 teaspoons ground cinnamon
100 g (3½ oz) butter, cut into
    cubes and softened

Coffee glacé icing
1 cup (125 g) icing (confectioners') sugar
1 tablespoon hot strong espresso coffee

This is a gateway recipe to proper babka, in that you don't have to go to the trouble of twisting and twirling the dough into loaves (although you can — see Extra extras, page 287). Here, we just chop the dough into scrolls, which is a useful trick you can use for other doughs and pastries, folding the filling enough to protect it from burning, while scoring layered bits of flavour in shareable scroll form. The yeasted dough recipe is a gift from my favourite babka baker in Melbourne, Avi, lightened with the inclusion of a tangzhong step (a process that gives milk buns their fluffiness, and something I learnt from award-winning food-blogger Lorraine Elliott's excellent hot cross bun recipe; worth seeking out at Easter time). You can freeze any left-over baked scrolls, sliced in half, to pop into the toaster for easy refreshing.

Start by making the tangzhong. Add ½ cup (125 ml) water and the flour to a small saucepan. Stir vigorously with a wooden spoon over medium heat for 2 minutes; the mixture will start to thicken and become glossy at this point (65°C/150°F). Turn the heat off. Add the maple syrup, coffee and another ½ cup (125 ml) water and whisk well, cooling the temperature down to 45°C (115°F).

Next, make the scroll dough, which you can do by hand (gladiator, I salute you!) or using a stand mixer. If you're going with the second option, place the tangzhong and eggs in the mixer bowl. Using the paddle attachment, mix for a minute or so, until blended. Switch over to the dough hook and add the flour, yeast and salt. Give them a whir on low speed for 5 minutes, scraping down the side of the bowl now and then.

When the dough has stopped clinging to the bowl, up the speed a little to medium–low and, with the motor running, start adding the butter, a few cubes at a time. Wait for it to assimilate before adding more. Continue to do this for about 10–15 minutes, scraping down the bowl every now and then if need be, until the dough is lusciously soft and elastic and comes away from the side of the bowl with ease. If it is still sticking, add another tablespoon or two of flour — max! — and keep mixing until incorporated.

Slosh a teaspoon or so of greasing oil over a dinner plate or small tray, spreading it around with your palm. Pile the dough on top and shape into a 10 x 20 cm (4 x 8 inch) rectangle. Cover and leave to chill in the fridge for at least 12 hours, preferably overnight.

If you don't have a stand mixer, no biggie! Use a wooden spoon and some elbow grease to combine the tangzhong and eggs to a uniform custardy colour. Put the flour, yeast and salt in a large bowl, giving it a mix with your wooden spoon. Make a well in the centre and pour in the egg mixture, stirring until it comes together and is raggy and sticky.

Turn out onto a floured bench and start kneading. The mixture will be sticky and a bit hard to handle, but persevere, and keep some flour handy to dust the bench now and then — but not too much, as this is a loose dough. »

Coffee pecan babka scrolls continued

Start adding the butter, one cube at a time, and knead into an elastic dough; this will take about 10 minutes. The process will be messy, but it does work. Once done, transfer the dough to a clean bowl. Cover and leave in a warm spot for 2 hours, or until doubled in size.

Slosh a teaspoon or so of greasing oil over a dinner plate or small tray, spreading it around with your palm. Pile the dough on top and shape into a 10 x 20 cm (4 x 8 inch) rectangle. Cover and leave to chill in the fridge for at least 12 hours, preferably overnight.

To make the filling, spread the pecans on a baking tray and toast in a preheated 160°C (315°F) oven for 8–10 minutes, or until golden and aromatic. Place in a clean tea towel and give them a gentle whack with a rolling pin, remembering that you want the bits to still be chunky. Mix in a bowl with the sugar and cinnamon.

When the dough is ready to go, line a large baking tray with baking paper, and dust a clean bench and rolling pin with flour. Roll the dough out into a rectangle roughly 55 x 65 cm (22 x 25½ inches), keeping the dough well-floured by flipping it over every now and then. The dough is very pliable and forgiving, but will stick to the bench if there's no flour underneath to form a barrier. The dough should end up about 5 mm (¼ inch) thick.

Using an offset or flexible spatula, spread the softened butter across the whole surface to the very edges, in an even layer. Set some of the filling aside to sprinkle over the scrolls just after glazing. Sprinkle half the remaining filling over the dough. Fold the dough into thirds (like a business envelope). Roll out again and sprinkle with the remaining filling, folding until you have a neat rectangle about 2 cm (¾ inch) thick. Roll up tightly, starting at the long end. Cut into 12 even scrolls and place, swirl side up, on your baking tray. (To make these uniform in size, you can cut the log in half, then cut each of those halves in half, then each of those pieces into thirds.) Cover loosely and leave to prove in a warm spot for another 1 hour. Almost there!

Preheat the oven to 170°C (325°F). Bake the scrolls on the middle rack of the oven for 30–40 minutes, or until they're golden brown, and a skewer comes out clean of dough; a bit of filling is okay.

To make the icing, sift the icing sugar into a bowl, pour in the hot coffee and whisk until smooth. Spread or drizzle over the scrolls once they've cooled slightly. Sprinkle with the reserved filling and give yourself an artful pat on the back while you and yours dig in.

These scrolls are best eaten within the first 2–3 days, and can be brought back to life with a microwave zapping or a little time in the oven to reheat. Store in an airtight container in the fridge.

THE JOY OF BETTER COOKING

Bonus bits

Tips

When rolling out the dough, make sure your kitchen and hands are as cool as possible.

When proving the dough, you can create an optimum temperature microcosm by whacking your tray or dish into a cold oven on the middle rack, and popping a bowl of boiling water underneath it.

If you made the scroll dough the night before, let it come to room temperature before baking.

Subs

You can use any nut here, from walnuts to hazelnuts.

Extra extras

For a proper babka shape, split the filled log in half lengthways to expose the filling, and then wrap one side around the other to create a braid. Cut into two evenly-sized loaves and bake.

For a wreath, slice the filled log in half as above, braid the whole thing into a single long roll, then wrap it around into a circular shape. Pop a small ramekin or bowl in the centre to help it keep its shape. Glorious.

Recipe riffs

Weave some other magical flavours into the scrolls (for all of these riffs, omit the icing and replace the coffee in the tangzhong with water).

Choc hazelnut: Spread a few tablespoons of choc hazelnut spread over the dough, and use a handful or so of fresh hazelnuts instead of pecans.

Pistachio raspberry: Ditch the pecans. Spread a few tablespoons of pistachio paste and raspberry jam over the dough. Sprinkle a teaspoon or so of freeze-dried raspberry powder and crushed pistachios on top after glazing.

Choc orange: Add about 1 teaspoon orange zest and juice to the dough, and maybe throw in some chocolate chips for texture. Spread a few tablespoons of chocolate spread over the dough.

Boston buns: Divide the dough into 12 even balls and bake as described. Make an icing by whisking together 50 g (1½ oz) softened butter, 1½ cups (185 g) icing (confectioners') sugar and 2 teaspoons vanilla bean paste, then whisking in 1½ tablespoons milk as needed. Spread the icing over the cooled buns and dip face down in a plate of desiccated coconut to completely cover.

Pizza babka scrolls: Ditch the coffee, maple syrup and icing. Spread the dough with a few tablespoons of an excellent-quality tomato paste — and/or pesto! — and sprinkle with a handful of grated cheddar and chopped olives before rolling.

Ingredient spotlight: Cinnamon

You'll likely find yourself wondering if you need both ground cinnamon and cinnamon sticks. Well, if you're a poacher of fruit, sticks are your pal. For sprinkling on top of chai tea, or for adding warming spice to biscuits and cakes, ground cinnamon is the go.

Beware cinnamon sticks that seem too woody and cheap — these are most likely cassia bark, which is related to true cinnamon, but has a stronger flavour that is better reserved for savoury dishes. You can tell the difference by looking at the stick's shape — cassia sticks are looser and more hollow, and curl in on each side like a loosely rolled ancient scroll, while cinnamon is more tightly rolled, with multiple inner layers spiralling around in more of a whirlpool shape.

Cinnamon sticks lose their intensity over time, but if you're worried about a jar of ground stuff languishing on That Shelf, you'll still happily get a couple of years out of it. Feel free to incorporate it any time you make something sweet, from roast pears (see page 258), to a bowl of porridge (page 132), or even simply a bowl of yoghurt and honey to elevate.

Middle Eastern and North African dishes such as tagines will often have a cinnamon stick bobbing about in them, while sprinkling some ground cinnamon over orange root vegies when they're baking in the oven — such as for the one-tray soup on page 68 — can really take things to another level.

Beze (meringues)

4 egg whites (from large eggs; see Tips, page 291), at room temperature
1 cup (220 g) caster (superfine) sugar
1 teaspoon vanilla bean paste or extract

There is nothing more glorious than watching clear, snotty egg whites va-va-voom into a voluminous white gown of magnificent meringue. It is the ultimate culinary Cinderella story ... kitchen witchery at its finest. Meringues are also the perfect penultimate recipe to cap off this book, because they apply so many of the lessons we've learned together betwixt these purple-tinged pages. *Beze* is the Russian answer to meringues, and in typical stoic Eastern-bloc fashion, they are served unadorned.

Preheat the oven to 150°C (300°F) and line a baking tray with baking paper.

Before starting on the meringues, make sure your mixing bowl is scrupulously clean by swishing some white vinegar on a clean tea towel or paper towel and wiping out the bowl, to remove any traces of fat, which will stop the egg whites foaming properly. Also make sure your beaters are scrupulously clean.

Using a stand mixer with the balloon whisk attachment, or a hand-held beater and a large metal bowl, beat the egg whites on medium–high speed until the volume doubles and soft peaks form, which will take about 5–10 minutes (depending on your beaters).

Start whisking in the sugar, 1 tablespoon at a time, until it is all used up, whisking for another 5–10 minutes until the meringue is like glossy cumulus clouds, with no feeling of sugar-granule grittiness when rubbed between your fingertips, and tasting like marshmallow. Mix in the vanilla.

Put a few smears of meringue under the baking paper to make it stick to the baking tray. Use two big spoons to plop dollops of the meringue onto the tray, scooping with one spoon, then pushing off with the other; this will make six dessert-sized meringues. They'll puff up, so leave some space between each.

Turn the oven down to 100°C (200°F) and place the tray on the middle shelf. Cook the meringues for 1½ hours. They should look blonde (not brunette), be crisp on the outside and sound hollow when gently tapped on the bottom. Let them cool and dry out in the oven for several hours (overnight is good), with the door chocked ajar with a wooden spoon.

The meringues will keep in an airtight container in a cool place (not the fridge!) for up to 2 days.

Start adding sugar as soon as the egg whites are this foamy

Stiff peaks should sit proudly on the tip of your whisk or finger

Use a little meringue to stick down the baking paper

Turn off the oven when the meringues are still blonde

Glacé beetroot, blackberry & orange veringues

2 cups (500 g) unsweetened coconut
yoghurt, chilled whipped organic
coconut cream or your favourite
plant-based cream
a handful of pistachio nut kernels,
cut into slivers
baby red-vein sorrel leaves, to garnish

Glacé beetroot, blackberry & orange

½ cup (110 g) caster (superfine) sugar
2 slices of fresh ginger, about 2 mm
(1/16 inch) thick
1 medium-sized beetroot, washed, peeled
and cut into 1 cm (½ inch) cubes
250 g (9 oz) blackberries (frozen are fine)
1 blood orange, zested and segmented
(see Skills spotlight, page 41),
reserving any juice

Veringues

¾ cup (185 ml) aquafaba (the
drained liquid from a 400 g/14 oz
tin of unsalted organic chickpeas)
¾ cup (165 g) caster (superfine) sugar
or golden caster (superfine) sugar
1 teaspoon vanilla bean paste
or vanilla extract

A vegan meringue — a veringue! — tastes just like the real thing. Since the aquafaba that we're using instead of egg whites is already part of a cooked product, there's no need to actually cook these veringues, which is totally brilliant. You won't end up with crispy, crunchy meringues; they'll be more soft and marshmallowy, but still utterly delicious, with not a hint of chickpea flavour. Now they *all* lived happily ever after.

For the glacé beetroot, put the sugar, ginger and ½ cup (125 ml) water into a small saucepan. Stir until the sugar dissolves, then bring to the boil. Add the beetroot and boil for 30 minutes, or until only a few tablespoons of syrup are left in the pan. Gently toss the blackberries and orange segments through, squeeze in any juice from the orange membranes, then leave to cool. This will keep in an airtight container in the fridge for a day or two; remove the ginger before serving.

Before starting on the veringues, make sure your mixing bowl is scrupulously clean by swishing some white vinegar on a clean tea towel or paper towel and wiping out the bowl to remove any traces of fat, which will stop the aquafaba foaming properly. Also make sure your beaters are scrupulously clean.

Using a stand mixer with the balloon whisk attachment, or a hand-held beater and a large metal bowl, beat the aquafaba on medium–high speed until the volume doubles and soft peaks form, which will take about 5–10 minutes (depending on your beaters).

Start whisking in the sugar one tablespoon at a time until it is all used up, whisking for another 5–10 minutes until the veringue is like glossy cumulus clouds, with no feeling of sugar-granule grittiness when rubbed between your fingertips, and tasting like marshmallow. Mix in the vanilla.

If not using the veringue mixture immediately, detach the whisk and leave it in the mixing bowl with the whipped aquafaba, cover with plastic wrap and leave in the fridge for no more than a few hours. When ready to serve, reattach the whisk and whisk for another 5 minutes to reinvigorate the veringue. It'll fluff back up good as new.

To serve, spoon the veringue mixture onto plates. If you like, use a kitchen blowtorch to kiss the tips of the veringue and singe slightly. Spoon your chosen yoghurt or cream alongside and top with the glacé beetroot and blackberries; the syrup will delightfully stain the cream. Garnish with the pistachios and sorrel leaves and serve.

Meringue/veringue Bonus bits

Tips

You can scale the egg meringue quantity up or down. As a rule, for every egg white (each weighing about 30 g/ 1 oz), add ⅓ cup (60 g) caster sugar. So, as a rough guide:

- 2 egg whites + ½ cup (110 g) caster sugar
- 4 egg whites + 1 cup (220 g) caster sugar
- 6 egg whites + 1½ cups (330 g) caster sugar
- 8 egg whites + 2 cups (440 g) caster sugar (the upper limit for a stand mixer).

If you feel like turning egg meringue into a pavlova, for every 2 egg whites, add 1 teaspoon cornflour (cornstarch) and ½ teaspoon white vinegar when you add the vanilla. This will help stabilise the bigger form and give your pav a lovely marshmallowy middle. You will need to vary the cooking time to suit; it may take a few attempts to learn what works best for your oven.

Waste knot

Keep the egg yolks to use in a mayo, quiche, frittata or even a custard (like the one on page 274).

You can use the chickpeas from the veringues to make some hubba-babaghanoush (page 200), or bag them up and freeze them, ready to add a quick protein hit to soups and stews.

Extra extras

If you want pink meringues or veringues, beat in about 1–2 teaspoons beetroot and berry powder (from the health food section in shops). Go crazy with decorations, if you like — rose petals, gold leaf, pearl sugar ... whatever you can get your hands on — to create a show-stopper worthy of your fairy-tale ending.

If you have a kitchen blowtorch handy, you can kiss the tips of the meringues or veringues for a bit of a singed s'mores situation before piling on the toppings.

Gadget spotlight: Fancy stand mixers

If you find yourself staring wistfully at shiny stand mixers on sparkly kitchen benchtops, wondering if it's time for you to fork out the coin, then let's weigh up the return on investment. Like a Burberry coat, stand mixers are infinitely covetable. But there's no use forking out for a bougie coat if you live in the tropics.

Firstly, be honest with yourself ... how in knead are you, really? Stand mixers become a spare pair of hands if you're regularly mixing batters, kneading dough and creaming butter and sugar, but many of the jobs you end up delegating to stand mixers can be done sans SM. If you're the kind of person who'd prefer to whip some cream and serve up a big ol' bowlful of strawberries alongside instead, then you might just be better off with a stick blender with a whisk attachment (more about these on page 151) or some old-school hand-held beaters.

If you're reading this thinking 'come on Alice, I just need a little enabling over here', then sure, I can do that too. With accessories aplenty, modern-day stand mixers can also be transformed into pasta machines (knead dough, then roll dough!) or spiralisers, or even mincers (grinders) and sausage makers.

But let's not get ahead of ourselves. Beyond the bells and whistles, things I look for in a quality machine are a stainless steel bowl (which will last you a lifetime and is easiest to clean), a single tool attachment (twin attachments like on hand-mixers are fine, but you'll still need to knead dough by hand if you go down this track), and sturdy craftsmanship that can withstand high speeds without my needing to stand next it and hold it down .... who's the stand mixer here, anyway?

**Glacé beetroot,
blackberry
& orange veringues**
Page 290

Cheerio cherry yule log

,

Dark chocolate roulade

200 g (7 oz) excellent-quality dark
    chocolate (above 50% cocoa solids)
6 eggs, at room temperature
a splash of vinegar
¾ cup (165 g) caster (superfine) sugar
½ teaspoon sea salt flakes
¼ cup (30 g) unsweetened cocoa powder
    (optional, but excellent)

Chantilly cherry filling

1 cup (200 g) pitted sour morello cherries
    (from a jar or tin), plus 1 cup (250 ml)
    of the sour cherry juice
300 ml (10½ fl oz) whipping cream
2 teaspoons vanilla bean paste

To finish

icing (confectioners') sugar, for dusting
foraged (unsprayed) foliage,
    for decorating
250 g (9 oz) fresh cherries (optional)

There are so many things to love about the festive cheer of this retro celebration yule log. For me, it marks the culmination of my cooking journey to date, so it feels fitting to leave the conversation here for now. It reflects the flavours that I love to share — something familiar and decadent like dark chocolate, with something a little bit Eastern Euro and exotic in the sour cherries. It's gluten-free, which makes it infinitely inclusive. It leans on a bunch of techniques we've trekked through together, from melting chocolate to whipping egg whites. It's also extremely forgiving – the cracks in the log aren't just welcome, they're encouraged: dust with icing sugar and they go from faulty to fancy. It's also my chance to say 'cheerio' to you, with a sweetie that I hope you'll challenge yourself to make and share with the ones you love. Go forth, cook, create — and remember, if things don't go to plan, there's nothing a bit of icing sugar can't fix.

Preheat the oven to 175°C (340°F). Grease a 25 x 35 cm (10 x 14 inch) Swiss roll (jelly roll) or brownie tin and line with baking paper.

For the roulade, put the chocolate in a heatproof bowl placed over a pan of simmering water, ensuring the base of the bowl isn't touching the water. Stir occasionally to melt the chocolate, then leave to cool a little.

Separate the eggs into two small, clean bowls.

Splash some vinegar on a clean tea towel and wipe the mixing bowl of a stand mixer until scrupulously clean and dry. Place the egg whites into the bowl and, using the balloon whisk attachment, whisk on high speed for 5 minutes, until they form stiff peaks — you should be able to hold the bowl over your head without an egg hat appearing. Use a flexible spatula to carefully transfer the whisked whites into a new bowl. Set aside.

Add the egg yolks and sugar to the stand mixer bowl — no need to clean out any stray egg white. Whisk for 3–4 minutes, until thick and creamy. Pour in the melted chocolate, folding it through with a flexible spatula until incorporated. Sprinkle in the salt, with some firm encouragement from your fingertips to help with even distribution. Sift in the cocoa powder, if using.

Pull the bowl out of the mixer. Add a big spoonful of the beaten egg whites to lighten up the mixture, then add the rest, folding it through in a figure-eight motion, being careful not to knock the air out.

Transfer the batter to your lined tin and bake for 10–15 minutes, or until the top springs back when gently touched. Take out of the oven and leave to cool, covered with a tea towel.

Meanwhile, to make the filling, place the sour cherry juice in a small saucepan, bring to the boil over high heat, then allow to cook for a few minutes, until reduced by half. Pour over the sour cherries and pop into the fridge to chill. »

Gently fold the melted chocolate into the egg yolk mixture with a spatula

No need to mix the sour cherries into the cream too uniformly

Schmear on as you might cream cheese on a bagel

Use the baking paper to help you roll the cake into a log

THE JOY OF BETTER COOKING

Cheerio cherry yule log continued

Clean the stand mixer bowl and place in the fridge, ready for whipping the cream (this is much quicker when the cream and utensils are cold). Using the balloon whisk attachment, whip the cream with the vanilla bean paste until billowy but still soft, then briefly fold through the cooled cherries and juice to form a ripple.

Line a cooling rack with a fresh sheet of baking paper. When the sponge cake has cooled, lift off the tea towel. Place the cooling rack over the sponge, baking paper face-side down, and invert the cake onto the rack, so it's sitting face down on the fresh baking paper. Slide the baking paper and the cake onto your workbench and peel off the old paper that was used to line the tin.

Spoon and schmear the whipped cream over the sponge, leaving a 2 cm (¾ inch) edge all around. Then, using the fresh baking paper underneath to help you, very gently roll your log from the long side, making allowance for the cream to spread. There will be a few cracks and graceful wrinkles in the sponge, but these are part of the festive charm. If you like, trim one of the log ends off on an angle, then add it to the side of the log (see photo on page 295), to make it look more loggy. Transfer to a serving platter or board.

Sift icing sugar all over and into the cracks. If there are any particularly gnarly cracks, sprinkle a little cocoa powder into them, then more icing sugar, and no-one will ever know. Garnish with foliage and serve with fresh cherries.

This log is best served on the day it is made, but you can make the filling the day before and assemble the rest of it on the day.

Bonus bits

Tips

You can use a fine sieve as a sifter for icing sugar and cocoa (and flour for other recipes, I should add). If you don't have a sifter, you can use a balloon whisk to help aerate and incorporate the dry ingredients before adding them to the wet mixture.

Skills spotlight: Melting chocolate

Chocolate burns easily, so it's not just a case of bunging it on the stove to melt. Instead a 'double-boiler' method is used to melt chocolate gently over simmering water. To do this, grab a small-ish saucepan that a heatproof bowl can rest in without sitting too close to the bottom of the pan. Pour about ½ cup of water into the pan and bring to a simmer. Pop the bowl of chopped chocolate on top (ensuring the water doesn't touch the bottom of the bowl) and stir frequently until melted.

An easier way is to use the microwave. Pop chocolate in a heatproof bowl (preferably not glass), then zap in the microwave in 30-second bursts, stirring to help distribute the heat evenly.

Some for 'Ron

The more I cook, the more bits and pieces end up in my freezer than ever before. But they're not for me. They're for 'Ron.

'Ron is, of course, 'later on', when you're scratching around for the makings of a meal, and then suddenly, as if by magic, something twinkly tumbles out of the freezer: a parmesan rind, a lime leaf, some forgotten sprigs of thyme, frozen in time. When the contents of your fridge and pantry are looking a little wiped, there's nothing more gratifying than finding that little extra something to whip your meals into shape.

In Western countries, roughly every fifth shopping bag of food per household goes in the bin. Most of that is super avoidable — it really comes down to knowing how to store fresh and cooked ingredients for maximum shelf-life.

If you're cooking as a single or couple, or for a family, there's always value in making more for 'Ron — he's a great mate to have around, especially when you're hungry and in a hurry. Leftovers are like the gift you leave yourself without even realising. Learning to love them is learning to love food on a whole new level.

FREEZER SAVOIR FAIRE

Although 'fresh' and 'frozen' are often viewed as mutually exclusive, the nutritional value — and taste — of some fresh produce is actually higher when snap-frozen on site than sitting around at room temperature in a shop for weeks. This is especially true for veg such as peas and corn, which begin losing their natural sweetness as soon as they're picked, and is why I'll often opt for frozen peas in winter, even if they're available fresh.

Rather than let leafy greens like spinach and silverbeet (Swiss chard) wilt into a puddle in the crisper, freezing them is a good way to extend their shelf-life for up to a year.

With freezing, the key is to do it quickly and decisively, to help prevent the dreaded ice-crystal crunch; the slower the temperature drops, the bigger the ice crystals.

As soon as cooked foods have cooled to the point where they've stopped steaming, pop them into freezer-friendly containers and straight into the freezer. Smaller items freeze faster, so divide your sauces, soups and stews into 1–2 portion packs, and shape things like pastry and minced meat as flat as possible.

To save space and minimise air pockets, you can create your own 'vacuum seal' by portioning your food into a snap-lock bag and, before sealing the bag, carefully immersing the bag in a bowl of water to 5 mm (¼ inch) below the opening — the pressure helps push all the air out of the bag — then snapping it shut. Some people even suck the very last vestiges of air out of the bag with a straw!

Although you won't be able to replicate the glacial temperatures of a commercial processing plant, most vegetables can be 'snap-frozen' at home, and most benefit from a quick blanching first, to help deactivate the enzymes that accelerate the deterioration of colour and flavour.

THE JOY OF BETTER COOKING

A couple of minutes in boiling water should do it for most green leafies, as well as brassicas like broccoli and cauli. Drain, then plunge straight into iced water to quickly chill them. Squeeze out the moisture, chop into fistful-sized clumps, lay out on a tray and freeze overnight, then portion, label and vac-seal using the water-pressure method described earlier. This all helps prevent big clumps and watery ice crystals, and lets you pick out a few pieces of veg at a time if you don't need the whole lot.

Hard herbs like rosemary and thyme freeze really well, as do lime leaves and curry leaves, in their packet. Pandan leaves really make steamed rice sing, so to extend their life, I'll rinse them well, pat dry, cut into rice cooker-friendly lengths, then bag and freeze.

Root vegies are also best frozen after being cooked, which is why those frozen potato chips in the shops have already been parboiled and fried before hitting the deep-freeze. However, veg with a high water content — lettuce, tomatoes, celery, radishes, cabbage — shouldn't be frozen as they'll turn to mush, unless they're blitzed first, bound for a sauce. (Luckily, most of these are also easy to grow at home, and require only a small pot on the balcony for leaves, radishes and the sweetest cherry tomatoes on a summer's morning.)

Ice-cube trays are your new best friends, so consider stocking up on those novelty oversized silicon ones available for cheap. Fresh herbs can be blitzed with olive oil and frozen in ice-cube trays for popping straight into sauces and soups. Add some parmesan and pine nuts to that oil and you've suddenly got yourself a pesto for pasta. Make your very own stock cubes by straining stocks and reducing them right down. Wait until they've stopped steaming, then pour into your ice-cube trays, freeze, then seal in snap-lock bags. (Especially impressive if you've used frozen vegie scraps like leek tops and onion peelings to make the stock in the first place!)

You can freeze a whole bunch of stuff from fresh to extend shelf life, and make a little last a lot longer. Nuts and seeds, particularly oilier ones like pine nuts and macadamias, can last in the freezer for up to two years, and you can always toast them a little to bring them back to life. Once opened, I usually store packs of almond meal or other ground nuts in the fridge, but for longer storage, I'll pat the nut meal into a muffin tin and freeze overnight, then pop the portions into labelled freezer bags or containers. Before using, let whole nuts and nut meals come to room temperature, to stop them clumping or sweating.

Anything baked — loaves, bread rolls, cakes — can definitely be frozen. Slice loaves and halve rolls before freezing. Pizza dough thaws quickly at room

temperature, especially if frozen as a flattish disc. Flatbreads can be baked from frozen, with the extra moisture giving a delightful interplay between crispy outside and doughy middle. I like to freeze souvlaki-shop pitta breads in individual bags, ready for easy home-souvas and pitta-pizzas (something kids are especially fond of decorating with chopped veg and cheese).

Leftover cooked *al dente* pasta can be frozen. Toss some olive oil through to avoid clumping, cool, swirl into greased muffin tin holes and freeze overnight, then bag up, ready to add to a hot sauce or plunge into boiling water to refresh later. Cooked gnocchi is especially easy to freeze and then reuse. If you've been practising your pasta rolling, clump portions of fresh pasta on a tray and freeze overnight, then bag up, label and store.

Cooked leftover rice needs to be used within a day if kept in the fridge, but can be portioned and frozen for up to 1 month. Pull out what you're not going to use as soon as it's cooked and wrap tightly, then label with the date and whack straight into the freezer. Magically, trapping in the steam and moisture actually means you'll have fluffy, moist rice at the other end! Thaw overnight in the fridge as needed.

MAKE A DATE OF IT

Always remember to clearly label and scrawl the date on whatever you're freezing, even if you're just wrapping small parcels such as surplus bacon rashers and hard herbs like thyme and rosemary in a layer of baking paper, then foil. It's amazing what clarity labelling brings three months down the track.

Giving the freezer a quick once-over monthly, to rearrange older stuff to the front and newer to the back, is also a good way of making sure you get through everything in time.

OUT FROM THE DEEP-FREEZE

Thawing larger frozen foods is always best done overnight in the fridge. You can thaw vegetables quickly by popping the sealed package in a bowl of cold water, or popping smaller frozen items in a colander under running water. I like to toss smaller frozen veg, such as corn and peas, straight into a bubbling soup or stew, or into a boiling pan of pasta water for the last few minutes of cooking, then strain with the pasta.

To defrost meat, put it on a high-sided plate or tray (so melting icy liquid doesn't leak everywhere), and thaw on the bottom shelf of your fridge, where there's less danger of any bacterial cross-contamination with cooked foods above. Frozen meat and poultry — particularly the bone-in variety — can take more than 24 hours to fully defrost, so plan ahead if you've a hankering for a roast.

If you *must* cook meat from frozen, simmer or bake it, rather than grilling or sautéing, and cook it for longer than you would from fresh, making sure to bring it to the boil at least once to zap any latent potentially harmful bacteria.

CHILLIN' IN THE FRIDGE

The fridge is where you should be storing most 'perishable' items. The airtight environment and colder temperature inhibits the growth of bacteria, and helps to protect fresh stuff from exposure to oxygen — the two major contributors to spoilage.

The fridge does suck moisture out of fresh produce, though, so it's something to be mindful of for fruits and vegetables that live and die by their juiciness — such as cucumbers, soft herbs, watermelon and celery. Wrap anything leafy in damp kitchen paper, or pop it in the fridge door in a jar with a little water. For herbs that prefer sunnier skies, I'll even whack a plastic bag over the top, to create a kind of 'hot house' effect to eke out way more life from these notorious wilters.

The crisper compartment is designed to counteract moisture loss, with a higher level of humidity, helping to extend the freshness of leafy stuff that's prone to wilting or sagging. If you have two crisper drawers, it's best to keep fruit in one, and veg in the other, as most fruits — particularly bananas, apples and melons — emit a gas called ethylene, which accelerates ripening, and is also the reason why brassicas go yellow and asparagus droops.

Aside from ol' mate basil, a good rule of thumb for fruit and veg is if they grow best in warmer conditions, then they'll do better out of the fridge, so consider storing bananas outside of the fridge entirely.

If you have a ripe avocado, keep it in the fridge, but if it's still coming around, store it in your pantry or even on top of your fruit bowl. Tomatoes are a no-no in the fridge, as their delicate flesh sucks up fridge smells, and they lose their sunny disposition.

Potatoes don't need refrigeration (unless you're in tropical climes) but they do need darkness, so store them in a cool, dark place — BUT away from any onions, as the two have a terrible influence on each other. If you only have one cool, dark place, potatoes take precedence. Onions are fine on the pantry shelf. Half-onions belong in the fridge door, wrapped in beeswax or the like to prevent shrivelling.

Eggs have always proven a bone of contention. Even though many fridges come with an egg-storage insert, they're actually counterproductive for good eggs! The shells are porous, so you might be infusing them with some confusing fridge aromas and flavours. The easiest thing is just to keep them in their carton, which is designed to both cushion them and protect them from pongs. If you're a burgeoning baker, room-temperature eggs are a top tip for failsafe cakes. If you buy them at room temperature, you don't have to store them in the fridge.

For condiments, even if the label doesn't say so, most will do better in the fridge. I have a condiment shelf towards the top, and circulate them every now and then to remember to use them.

Unless you live in a really hot climate, butter can be left out in a butter-bell or dish at room temperature — particularly in winter.

Bread and baked goods should be kept out of the fridge — particularly sweets, unless you're worried about an ant infestation. Cakes and breads dry out and cookies become bendy. Much better to pop them under a cloche or some foil and off to the side of the kitchen bench.

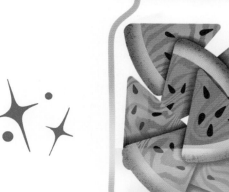

Acknowledgements

Having popped a couple of books out already, this is the bit I always love flipping to in other people's, because although there's but one name on a cover, it covers only the very tip of the iceberg of ingenuity that goes into the wonder that is book publishing.

To my husband Nick, whose calm, considered, detail-oriented Virgo-ness is what gives me the space to be the constructively chaotic Gemini that I am. It's also Nick's heavy lifting on The Nut front that makes our family the toight little triangle that it is. Hazel, thank you for being a delight in every way, and for taste-testing every recipe in this book, if not helping cook most of them too. Talk about joy!

Speaking of family, to my parents, Frada and Arkady, for continuing to be amused by me, and for instilling in my brother and I a love of food and of knowledge. To my in-laws, Jackie and Razmo, thank you for cultivating a farm full of produce to inspire, and to give Nick and Hazel somewhere to go when I'm holed up in my culinary cave. My brother Stan didn't cop a mention in the last list of acks, which is something that I regret, because it was Stan who helped to reheat the borsch every day after school, and who bought me a ticket to Tony Robbins' Unleash the Power Within when I was 18. I walked on hot coals, I learnt about limiting beliefs, and I'm probably still unleashing said power too, come to think of it. Thanks also to his family, for the regular updates and photos of meals my nieces have recreated.

Now, to my Murdoch Books family. I mean, HONESTLY, I started thinking about what book to write next as we were wrapping up the shoot on *In Praise of Veg*, partly because I knew I'd miss having you all in my life too much if I didn't get right onto it. You have become a steady source of inspiration, support and encouragement, and I am in constant awe of your talents.

To Jane Morrow, my publisher. You are the ballast that I can return to when my course needs steadying, and the wind when I need a little extra puff in my wings. I know I'm on the right track when I see the trademark twinkle in your eye, and it's striving for that twinkle that makes the books you publish sparkle so.

Speaking of SPARKLE! Does art direction get any better than Megan Pigott!? How marvellously you manage to whisk words into wondrous visual language before our very eyes. You have a rare gift, and winding up and letting you go is one of my favourite elements of this process. Lynn Bremner, the illustrator behind these trippy dippy designs — Megan pushed you to the limit, and you met and exceeded every expectation. I've scarcely seen magical realism deployed in this way across a food book, and it's made it truly transcendent. Designer Jacqui Porter at Northwood Green has once again managed to take all the bits and bobs and make them feel so cohesive and such a sight to behold.

Equally so, Lucy Tweed and Ben Dearnley, I am awestruck by the way you serve up the dishes in their styled photographic form, bouncing natural light and fluoro flourishes into the sublime imagery contained within these pages. To photo-chefs Lucy Busuttil, Jaimee Curdie and Vikki Moursellas — thank you to this divine kitchen team for fiddling with the food and asking the questions, to ensure that readers don't have to as they cook the food at home! And to my food editor, Jane Grylls ... Grylltown ... the salt to my pepper, my fellow teacher forever. Here's to continuing to teach each other every darn day. Red dirt to red carpet all the way.

Keeping the string wound tight on the kite of creativity (oh wow, they're both going to cringe so much at all of these metaphors) are editorial manager Virginia Birch and editor Katri Hilden, who've again managed to whip these words into shape and shine. VB, thank you for going above and beyond, for the bleary-eyed proofreads and bright-eyed belief in this book. Thank you, especially, for spinning my streams of consciousness into coherence where need be, and for letting my freak flag fly every now and then too. And Helena Holmgren, your indexing ingenuity is on show once more — hundreds of pages, rendered infinitely more accessible thanks to you.

To my Murdoch publicity team, Sarah Hatton in Australia, and Jemma Crocker in the UK. I'm thanking you in advance, because your bit is but beginning, though thanking you also for laying so much of the groundwork already. You are some of the hardest-working spruikers in the biz, and I'm grateful to have you both on speed-dial. Thanks in advance to the many hard-working publicists and advocates, like Kaz and SW and Jam and Bowley and DV and MJ and MB, for doing the work in their spheres of influence. And more broadly, to Britta Martins-Simon for being our books' champion, and spreading the Praise and The Joy across the world.

And to you, my champions at home (or 'champignons', as my pal Nat's What I Reckon might say). If this is our first foray, I'm so thankful that you've picked up what I put down — there's plenty more to come, and plenty to catch up on. If you've been a long-time follower of my journey, or met me midstream, thank you for sticking around, for being my pen-pals, and for amplifying my work by telling your friends about The One with The Glasses, and/or gifting them the fruits of my labour. I hope this brings you as much joy in reading it and cooking from it, as it has to me in writing it and... cooking from it!

With light and lovage always,

alice.

Index

Entries in italics indicate Subs/Recipe riffs.

THE JOY OF BETTER COOKING

Published in 2022 by Murdoch Books, an imprint of Allen & Unwin

Murdoch Books Australia
83 Alexander Street
Crows Nest NSW 2065
Phone: +61 (0)2 8425 0100
murdochbooks.com.au
info@murdochbooks.com.au

Murdoch Books UK
Ormond House
26–27 Boswell Street
London WC1N 3JZ
Phone: +44 (0) 20 8785 5995
murdochbooks.co.uk
info@murdochbooks.co.uk

For corporate orders and custom publishing,
contact our business development team at
salesenquiries@murdochbooks.com.au

Publisher: Jane Morrow
Creative Direction: Megan Pigott
Editorial Manager: Virginia Birch
Designer: Northwood Green
Editor: Katri Hilden
Food Editor: Jane Grylls
Illustrator: Lynn Bremner
Photographer: Ben Dearnley
Stylist: Lucy Tweed
Home Economist: Lucy Busuttil
Assistant Home Economists:
Jaimee Curdie, Vikki Moursellas
Production Director: Lou Playfair

Text © 2022 Alice Zaslavsky
The moral right of the author has been asserted.
Design © Murdoch Books 2022
Photography © Ben Dearnley 2022

*Murdoch Books acknowledges the traditional owners
of the lands on which we live and work. We pay our
respects to all Aboriginal and Torres Strait Islander
elders, past and present.*

ISBN 978 1 92261 604 3 Australia
ISBN 978 1 91166 855 8 UK

 A catalogue record for this
book is available from the
National Library of Australia

A catalogue record for this book is available from
the British Library

Colour reproduction by Splitting Image Colour Studio
Pty Ltd, Clayton, Victoria
Printed by C&C Offset Printing Co. Ltd., China

OVEN GUIDE: All these recipes were tested in a
fan-forced oven. You may find cooking times vary
depending on the oven you are using. For conventional
ovens, as a general rule, set the oven temperature to
20°C (35°F) higher than indicated in the recipe.

TABLESPOON MEASURES: We have used 20 ml
(4 teaspoon) tablespoon measures. If you are using
a 15 ml (3 teaspoon) tablespoon add an extra teaspoon
of the ingredient for each tablespoon specified.

10 9 8 7 6 5 4 3 2 1

For more **Joy**,
scan the camera
on your smart device
over this QR code.